The Politics of Rite:
Jesuit, Uniate, and Romanian Ethnicity in 18th Century Transylvania

William O. Oldson

EAST EUROPEAN MONOGRAPHS, BOULDER, CO
DISTRIBUTED BY COLUMBIA UNIVERSITY PRESS, NEW YORK
2005

EAST EUROPEAN MONOGRAPHS, NO. DCLXVI

ISBN: 0-88033-564-5

Library of Congress Control Number: 2005924344

Printed in the United States of America

for
My Family

Table of Contents

Preface

Besides being an extraordinarily interesting occupation, obtaining the varied research materials for this study required the staff cooperation of several outstanding archival facilities. Special thanks, then, are due to the insightful individuals who helped me at the British Museum, the Academia România Biblioteca Filialei Cluj, and the Babeş-Bolyai University. Their untiring assistance and concern for my research difficulties were greatly appreciated. Likewise the Florida State University and the International Research and Exchanges Board were openhanded in their financial support and provisions for released time. Without such imaginative initiative this project could not have been undertaken.

As the reader will notice immediately in the endnotes and bibliography, the orthography of the Romanian language has changed considerable since the inception of the Uniate movement and Jesuit influence in Transylvania. Trying to impose uniformity on references ranging from the second half of the seventeenth century to the present day would be tedious and would possibly mislead those attempting to find the materials used. I have, therefore, retained the original spellings and diacritical mark usages. In the text, obviously I have employed the conventional and contemporary standards.

Finally, I would like to express my deepest gratitude and love for my wife, Judy, whose courage and endurance were truly remarkable. Those with children will recognize immediately how necessary and exceptional these qualities were in a daunting expedition to Eastern Europe with a year old child. She not only handled the many demands of this adventure in motherhood with aplomb, but brought to our sightseeing outings her usual high spirits and good humor.

William O. Oldson
Tallahassee, September 2004

I
Introduction: Politics and Religion

At the close of the eighth decade of the seventeenth century Transylvania once again passed to the flag of the Habsburgs. This "Transylvania regained," however, did not come without problems or with the surety of a confidently and safely possessed province. Given the resistance, even hostility of the native princes, the Habsburgs faced considerable odds in profiting from the retreat of the Muslim Ottomans. With Leopold I on the Habsburg throne since 1658 the Viennese government confronted during the 1680s not only renewed pressure from the Ottoman forces to the East but also the threat of French continental interests as well. In the early part of the decade the dangers of a two front war did not seem exaggerated, when the subject of conjecture in the Central European capital.[1] The East, though, did offer Leopold and his successors the luxury, not possessed in the West, of indulging their absolutist tendencies without necessarily paying attention to the desires of other Great Powers. Moreover, this area of receding Ottoman influence and power proffered Vienna the opportunity to obtain amends for the consequence it had lost in the West. The Habsburgs' definitive victory over the Ottomans in the 1690s, then, provided improved status along with a vastly enhanced defensive frontier.[2] What he and all other Habsburgs would disregard at some great risk was the nature of the resistance to their return. For by the 1660s the Emperor was already receiving warnings that the Magyars of Transylvania hated all things German and those who showed themselves friendly to Germans. Indeed, even among an ethnically similar group such as the Saxons, the Habsburg reentry into Transylvania in the 1680s brought with it fears of the burdens to be imposed by a modern state as well as a well justified anticipation of efforts to reduced the extent of local autonomies.[3]

Of the greatest concern to Leopold's government and posing one of the severest tests for the reimposition of imperial control was the virtual extinction of Roman Catholicism in Transylvania. The Reformation in that province had been a death blow to the institutional structure of the Roman Church causing both the secularization of its property and a precipitous diminution in its adherents. For approximately one and a half centuries after Luther's protest the Catholic bishopric in Alba-Iulia remained vacant.[4] Conducting themselves not only as men of their times, but also as politically oriented individuals as well, the sixteenth century Protestants masters of Transylvania fully exploited to the benefit of their state and sect the contemporary adage "*Cujus est regio, illius est etiam religio.*" In the place of the former Catholic bishop there was now to be found a Calvinist superintendent. With such a considerable portion of the formerly Roman Catholic population changing its sectarian allegiance and with the governors of the province looking now to Istanbul for political support, Rome's influence and the decisive impact of its hierarchy suffered seemingly irreparable damage.[5] Of foremost import for both the returning Habsburg forces and the indigenous majority of Romanian Orthodox believers was the dominant position attained by the seventeenth century by the Calvinists. By far the greater portion of the non-Romanian inhabitants of Transylvania had, by the time of the Habsburgs' re-emergence as a determinative force in the province's fortunes, gone over to the gospel according to John Calvin. Reinforcing, indeed magnifying the numerical advantage enjoyed by the Calvinists at the end of the seventeenth century, was the fact that the political leadership and aristocracy of the province likewise embraced the Genevan creed. When the Viennese dynasty reasserted its hereditary and political rights over Transylvania in May of 1688, then, it encountered deeply entrenched opposition. This recalcitrance could only be assuaged by pledging to respected the existing institutions, and thus in large part the political-religious status quo, to be found there. Whether sincerely meant or not, the price demanded by the Calvinist princes of Transylvania for acquiescing in the transition of authority from Muslim Ottoman to Roman Catholic Habsburg was the guarantee of their privileged position. This irreducible demand Leopold I met with his Diploma of December 4, 1691. Here he confirmed in an unmistakable fashion that the traditional entitlements enjoyed by the province were continued as the basic law of the land. Having gained entrée into this strategically important area in Central Europe through negotiation with its native leadership, the Habsburgs now proceeded with similar craft to avoid a too obvious a clash with those interests.[6] As they reentered Transylvania, then, the Habsburgs and their advisors had the dual intent of regaining political control of the province and also of expediently dealing with the Protestant political opposition. To enhance their position it would be necessary to augment that of the Roman Catholic Church, both in terms of number of adherents and the institutional significance of the hierarchy. Only after the battle of Zenta (1697) and the successful conclusion of the most recent Ottoman conflict could a more vigorous and elaborate effort in this direction be afforded. Now seeking the factional supremacy commensurate with an absolutist state they could move more robustly, if still circumspectly, against the privileged interests of the entrenched ethnic and religious groups of Transylvania. Loath to encountering once more the necessity of using force in the area, the imperial government concentrated on more bureaucratic even not always diplomatic means to ensure the tranquil possession of Transylvania.[7]

To understand the Habsburg political tactics in Transylvania one must keep foremost in mind that religious concerns enjoyed, along side the more mundane ones of military and fiscal anxieties, considerable play. The Emperor and his principal advisors had every intention from the very beginning of rendering all possible assistance to the reconsolidation of institutionalized Roman Catholicism in Transylvania. Though deferring both to Protestant sensibilities and to the legal traditions of the province to obviate the most obvious occasions of defiance, their goals remained other than their surface manifestations proclaimed. The Habsburgs would pursue throughout the eighteenth century a policy that projected a clearly centralizing and absolutist bias. Moreover, in stalking these objectives Vienna at the same time followed a calculated course of Catholic entitlement. Even for an age in which religious sympathies brooked little discrepancy, Leopold as well as the court around him carried Catholicism as canon to be ultimately safeguarded whatever the twists and turns of expediency might occasionally require. Thus, his religious antipathies and strategic aspirations brought him to a point where he faced the irreducible opposition of Protestant traditionalists in the province. These forces would cling with fierce determination not only to their faiths, but likewise to the constitution and privileges they had guarded so adamantly since medieval times.[8] In this context, therefore, the Transylvanian observation that for them "the eighteenth century started with 1691" rings true indeed. The imperial diploma of that year did, of course, ostensibly concede to provincial and sectarian feeling the preservation of the extant legal and social order. However, at the same juncture, Leopold gained for his dynasty the administrative and mandated ability to interfere in local trusts. Vienna could now quite licitly function as a principal factor channeling, if not always resolving, the path of Transylvanian phenomena. What perhaps appeared to the privileged estates of the province as a document stabilizing their situation in fact guaranteed to the Habsburgs ample scope to seek their covert ambitions.[9]

For the next one hundred and fifty years, then, Leopold I's diploma of December 4, 1691 delimited the arena for the contest over if and how the Transylvanian status quo might be altered. Three years prior to this, in the spring of 1688, representatives of the province's estates had pledged "sincerely and in good faith" to forswear Ottoman dominion for that of the Habsburg. They demanded in return imperial confirmation of their freedoms and endowments as well as of the religious liberty they so dearly treasured. Precisely the same points they would want reiterated in 1691. On neither occasion did the province's agents wish to provide improved entrée for Habsburg ambitions, political or religious. Bowing to the exigencies of Roman Catholic weakness in the province and Protestant persistence in refusing to relinquish any of their traditional rights, Leopold conceded them the 1691 edict. But he did so to forestall an open break rather than any abdication on his part of the intent of rebuilding Transylvania's Catholic structure.[10] In this epochal diploma Emperor Leopold first of all guaranteed the status of the four "received" religions; namely, that of the Calvinists, Lutherans, Roman Catholics, and Unitarians. These sects received legal assurance that their established constitutional rights to their beliefs and religious foundations would not be modified or adulterated. Their affairs as customarily conducted would suffer no change under the Habsburgs including any that might result from the interjection new religious elements. The diploma of 1691 explicitly and with no reservations established the assured acceptability under Habsburg law of all the existing provincial legal codes, municipal rights, and constitutions. This sweeping authorization included arrangements peculiar to select ethnic groups such as the Transylvanian Saxons.[11]

In entering into this compact with the prevailing orders in Transylvania, Leopold's government endorsed the possession of certain cherished privileges. Just as importantly for the history of the province over the next century and a half, the exclusive retention of such entitlements would remain the birthright of Calvinists, Latin Rite Roman Catholics, Lutherans, and Unitarians. Only these denominations could rightfully claim full religious liberty and their own governing bodies independent of the state. The Habsburg state acquiesced in the jurisdictional and administrative autonomy of the ruling councils of all the "received" religions, but only of these four persuasions. Others they might treat differently. On a less elevated plane, these four faiths had a seemingly ironclad provision assuring them of the untouchable status of their real property and all other worldly goods. They even possessed the right of "arithmetically" equal representation in all the important offices in Transylvania. Their clerics enjoyed the benefits of aristocratic standing as did all their ecclesiastical benefices. Finally, the four "received" religions could a expect a legally enforceable, exact, and formally equal status in all "mixed" transactions. No one of the four could henceforth maintain a superior position under the laws now recognized by the Emperor in this diploma.[12]

The patent purpose of the diploma of 1691, then, was to placate the three Protestant interests groups (i.e., Calvinists, Lutherans, and Unitarians). Making up as they did consistent majorities in the legislative body and all the councils of the principality of Transylvania, the Habsburgs had to meet their most pressing demands or face the possibility of an armed uprising. However the Protestants might differ among themselves on occasion where matters of religion and the politics flowing therefrom came into action they remained united. The Habsburgs and Catholics constituted the primary enemy. Besides forming the majority of political opposition, these three sects along with the province's magnates had also profited from the confiscation of Roman Catholic ecclesiastical properties in the previous century. The tenuous, even alarming, state of things Catholic could clearly be seen in the lack of clergy to staff the newly reacquired province. In an effort to stabilize and then improve on this distressing situation, the Imperial government began importing scores of Roman Catholic religious into Transylvania both to bolster the clergy's numbers and to meet on a more equal basis the qualitative challenge of the Protestant preachers. At this convergence of sectarian and factional aspirations the Society of Jesus entered the province and the fray. Given the suspicion, even hostility, that this militant religious order invariably generated, the Jesuits initially came not only openly but also as ordinary clerics or perhaps as civilians.[13]

The appearance in Transylvania of a religious force like the Jesuits, one with such a long and controversial history as educators and missionaries during the Counter-Reformation, had to give the Protestant pause. The diploma of 1691 in laying the foundation for the province's annexation by the Habsburgs, supposedly mandated no modification of the existing religious order. The Jesuits promised otherwise, at least in the Protestant view. Though moving cautiously in the beginning Vienna intended to designate whenever possible the course of events in Transylvania. The Jesuits and the use to which they might be put fell into this rationale.[14] From the point of view of the privileged Protestants the interpretation to be put on the diploma of 1691 was that it froze conditions as they were and in the favor of the *selecti quidem*. This elite status received definition not only from participation in one of the "received" religions, but also by being born into one of the constitutionalized recognized three "nations" (i.e., Germans, Magyars, and Szeklers). Leopold's promises in the 1691 diploma were meant to dispel the "nations'" anxieties not only regarding religious matters, but also concerning the territorial and administrative integrity of the districts they inhabited. Without a doubt the diploma confirmed that no other ethnic group qualified for the essential legal distinction, and hence all the benefits derived therefrom, of being a "nation." This left the Romanians, overwhelmingly peasant with a distinctive cultural and ethnic character, outside the constitutional pale, just as they fell beyond the borders of religious recognition. Although there has been since the opening of the eighteenth century an interminable dispute over statistical verification of matters Romanian, Romanians did constitute at this point a certain majority of the Transylvanian population. The 1691 pledges to the Protestant and established orders of the province also, then, guaranteed their continued lack of representation and subordinate status. In that crucial year and in that pivotal document more than simply the positive claim to traditional rights, religious and secular, of the three Protestant churches and the Roman Catholics had been resolved upon. Everyone else, most especially the Romanian majority, felt the onerous categorization of being labeled in constitutional terms an outsider. The entitlements and scope for religious expression endorsed in 1691 focused all too narrowly in demographic terms.[15]

If the letter of law as defined in the diploma of 1691 ran so obviously counter to the interests of the Romanian majority of Transylvania, the political and sectarian implications loomed as no less inimical to those of the Habsburgs. Though a calculatedly prudent gesture in the face of the numbers and nature of Protestant requirements for ancestral perquisites, what the Habsburgs promised in 1691 hardly conformed to the permanence and consolidation of their position in Transylvania. Unless they wished the process of encroaching on the Transylvanian status quo to become an armed conflict, they would have to find more subtle, if slower, methods. Just as they had with the Ottoman Sultan the Transylvanian leadership now compromised with the Habsburgs to achieve a state of limited autonomy. Whatever mental reservations Leopold may have had in mind when issuing this decisive diploma, his pretense of forbearance encountered a countervailing recalcitrance in the province's political establishment. They intended to avoid, where possible, the increasingly direct and pervasive control from Vienna. A cunning circumspection on the part of Leopold ran counter to the adamant finesse with which the aristocracy of the province fought its diplomatic battle to ensure their ensconced advantages.[16]

The year 1691, even if a slightly precipitous start to the eighteenth century, certainly represented a major legal concession to the "*unio trium nationum*" (a union encompassing Magyar and Szekler as well as Saxon). It made more permanent the seemingly good auspices of the Habsburg reentry in Transylvania in 1688. And it perpetuated a social order in which the Romanian Orthodox majority not only economically disadvantaged, but politically leaderless as well. Their ethnic nobility had either found a more comfortable home among the Magyars or, if it had not assimilated, then sunk to the level of the mass of the Romanian peasant population. The Orthodox Church, though not among the four "received" faiths, offered the Romanians their sole framework for corporate life.[17] In this manner the single greatest apprehension of the three nations had been assuaged. For domestic purposes their feudal autonomy now had Habsburg acquiescence if not support, while the provincial religious structure continued to have its customary tolerant cast despite the wraith of Jesuit and Counter-Reformation influence. The Romanians in 1691 found themselves in the condition of being an exploited majority and had every likelihood of remaining so. The Habsburgs, having foresworn any direct assault on Transylvanian mores, did begin the drawn out process of impinging on the province's administration. Vienna now erected a Transylvanian office in an effort to extend its control over local affairs. Though this political intervention would grow over the course of the next two generations, immediate impact occurred through the financial exactions of the imperial treasury and the military which was controlled from the Court's Council of War. Through its power of confirmation the Habsburg central power would gradually converted the provincial governor into an efficient instrument for fostering its administrative apparatus. The *quid pro quo* in 1691, therefore, extended the Imperial Court the possibility of extensive though cautious implementation of its absolutist designs, while leaving the elaborate seigneurial structure of the *unio trium natium* and four "received" religions sacrosanct. This bargain on imperial privilege and territorial prerogative, however, had a adamantine exclusivity which for the moment ignored the Orthodox Romanians as not integral to the governing equation.[18] This quarantining of the Romanians signified far more than their not belonging to the ruling strata of Transylvania. Completely disregarded despite being the bulk of the population and the most ubiquitous religious component in the domain, the Romanian Orthodox lived in a Calvinist dominated environment. This milieu did not allow for either a separate Romanian "*natio*" or a permanently separate Romanian spirituality with a unique cultural expression.[19]

As definitive as the Habsburg concessions of 1691 seemed on paper, Leopold discovered almost immediately the need to replicate these commitments. In an additional diploma dated the spring of 1693 he once more endeavored to undercut the most inveterate Protestant opposition. He repeated the pledge to the four "received" religions that they would continue to enjoy all their religious and property rights without "any interference whatsoever." Such guarantees and the bureaucracy introduced into the province by the Habsburgs did at least as much to enhance imperial sovereignty as they did to uphold provincial integrity. Implicit behind the administrative and fiscal reins now reaching into Transylvania remained the paramount plan of the Viennese court for an authority that was not commensurate with either Protestant claims or the seeming intent of these documents. Though Leopold, as a facade, even sustained the provision of the Transylvanian constitution banning the Society of Jesus. This he did despite his close association with the Jesuits and the use he would make of them throughout his reign for encroaching on the preserve of the three nations. The extent of the Habsburgs' problem in Transylvania clearly reveals itself in the physical resistance offered between 1691 and 1696 despite all these concessions to regional testiness. By this latter year, though Leopold's realm was still threatened from the south by Ottoman threats of invasion, he had induced the last Hungarian claimant (Mihail II Apafi) to the Transylvanian crown to renounce this legacy in his favor.[20] This repetition in 1693 of the earlier denial of any aggressive intent reflected more the need to temporize momentarily on the religious issue due to the Moslem menace than an authentic moderate attitude. Only the successful outcome of the battle of Zenta in 1697 with the subsequent Treaty of Karlowitz (1699) would finally allow fuller scope for the oblique objectives of Vienna. Meanwhile, an interim truce fully acceptable or underwritten by neither side abided for the moment. With the last native prince off the scene and the Ottoman Turks shoved south of the Carpathians for good, the Catholic Habsburgs vs. Protestants duel for mastery in Transylvania could begin in earnest. For the inevitable if surreptitious strategy had always been to promoted Roman Catholicism along side Habsburg imperial interests. Only the staging and most apt devise remained to be agreed upon.[21]

Art. 1 of the Treaty of Karlowitz gave the House of Habsburg diplomatic possession of Transylvania, the Ottoman Empire retiring from the scene in what proved to be a definitive fashion. Besides changing the nature of the "Eastern Question" with its centuries long struggle between Habsburgs and Ottomans, this climatic compact likewise permitted an alteration in the Habsburg mode of intervention in Transylvania, one that would present clearly the value of the diplomas issued in the 1690s.[22] At this point, then, through the means of an expanded and reoriented religious policy Leopold I declared his intent to undermine the political base of the Transylvanian Calvinists. In this endeavor he would have the enterprising support of those members of the Society of Jesus who were already returning to the area despite their legal proscription. The emperor and the Jesuits set their sights on a reinvigorated and, more importantly perhaps, vastly extended Roman Catholic presence in Transylvania. An increase in the number of Catholics would have a beneficent effect in not only spreading the faith, but at the same time accomplishing the long term goal of lessening Calvinist power in the province. The means selected consisted in removing the Romanian Orthodox inhabitants from under the influence of the Calvinist church and converting them into a major political prop for the Habsburg regime. The urgency surrounding this endeavor found expression in Leopold's realization that, even after Zenta and Karlowitz, the Protestant ruling elements of Transylvania assuredly preferred the Moslem Ottomans to Catholic Habsburgs.[23]

Peculiar to the province and distinguishing it from most other areas of Europe was a method of registering inhabitants not only by legal and social traits, but also by ethnicity and confessional affiliation. This scheme of things gave enormous weight to the numerically predominant Magyar Calvinists. For when the Habsburgs entered Transylvania as rulers again in the 1680s the Catholic contingent in the province had almost entirely magyarized, greatly reducing its numbers and the support Vienna could subsequently expect. The concessions contained in the diploma of 1691 simply led to a jockeying for position, if not outright hostility, between the faiths of Transylvania. These sectarian tensions Leopold had to discover a method of controlling and, hopefully, of directing. For unless such could be achieved neither the political aspirations of the court nor its intention of accomplishing a "*restitutio in intregum*" for the Roman Catholic Church could be hope for. This sweeping "restitutio" was to encompass all rights and properties antedating the Reformation. Moreover, it called for the free access of all categories of Roman Catholic clerics into the province. This, of course, would bring to the fore the highly charged issue of the Society of Jesus, the indispensable factotum of the Habsburgs as well as the *bête noire* of all Protestants.[24] This impasse did not, however, seem insuperable. For outside of the existing constitutional and power structures stood groups distinguished by ethnic and pietistic lineaments, factions that could be manipulated to serve the Habsburg-Catholic cause, if not necessarily their own.

As early as 1664 the Jesuits had been discussing the possibility of reuniting the Orthodox Romanians with Rome. The Order's reports of that year mentioned this long cherished aspiration of undoing the break of 1054 as a "glimmering prospect." From the early 1690s Leopold had viewed the schism between Rome and the Orthodox East as not only a religious affair, but also as "the fount and origin of many misfortunes" in the area. To succeed in abolishing this schism, then, would be to reap both a sectarian and dynastic advantage.[25] The Emperor, primed on both the secular and doctrinal levels, proved readily susceptible to practical suggestions as to how best move on this point. In the wake of Mihail II Apafi's relinquishing all claims to the province in 1696, Count Stefan Apor devised a stratagem for instantaneous growth, and hence partisan advantage, of the Catholic party. A Romanian Roman Catholic serving in the Transylvania treasury, in his correspondence with Leopold Apor mapped out a blueprint under which the Romanians of the province would divorce themselves from Eastern Orthodoxy. In return for the enjoyment of all the privileges currently possessed by the "received" religions, the Romanians would unite with the Roman Catholics. Apor went on to point out that "The Romanians are not separated by very much from...the Catholics of the Latin Law [i.e., Rite]...."[26]

In this inaugural statement of the motivations and rationale for the Union with Rome of the Transylvania Romanians a number of the confusions and misunderstanding which would plague it throughout its course were summarized. Leopold and his ecclesiastical retinue believed from the start that relatively little separated the Orthodox from Roman Catholicism, certainly not the chasm that divided them from the Calvinist. Since the Romanians had more in common religiously with the Habsburg interests than with the Calvinists, Union could be expected. Indeed the religious leaders of the time, both the hierarchically prominent and the Jesuits working in the field, minimized the differences between Roman Catholic and Orthodox doctrine. At the same time they stressed that it would be less difficult to "convert" the Romanians than the Calvinists and Lutherans. This initiative went to the extent of claiming a general similarity between Catholic and Orthodox doctrine, a near identity that was promulgated through a Jesuit edited catechism that was now distributed among Romanians, the young especially.[27] This optimism found expression in the work of a Jesuit active in this movement to reunite Romanians and Rome. For political as well as dogmatic purposes the intent remained as much to accent the differences, and hence the lack of any likelihood of convergence, between the Orthodox and Calvinists as to illuminate the distinctions between Rome and the Eastern Christian world. The fact that the authors of such works also dedicated them to or obtain publication funds from the Cardinal Primate of Hungary, the major church voice for the Union, renders their auspicious prognosis somewhat suspect in terms of its pragmatic analysis of the situation.[28]

Also the overview presented initially labored under a misapprehension that was not always or with complete candor acknowledged; namely, that Apor's original proposal to the Emperor Leopold did not say simply reunion with Rome, but rather with "Catholics...of the Latin Law." The "law" (i.e., "*lege*") for the Romanians encompassed rite, liturgy, and the whole amalgam of traditional and folkloric practices making up Romanian peasant devotion. Neither the Romanian rank and file nor the leadership as a group ever contemplate exchanging their service, garb, and customs for the Tridentine Mass and the mores of Latin Rite Christianity. Unfortunately the processes of Union with Rome and the acquiring of political advantages by both sides became fused with a fear of, and occasionally an attempt, to "Latinize" the cult of the Romanians.[29] However great the "general similarity" of the two forms of Christianity might have been in doctrinal terms, the physical expression and stages of cultivation contained marked dissimilarities. The depth of understanding of these disparities would only emerge over time and with considerable variations of appreciation by Latin and Greek Rite adherents. These vastly different sets of background perceptions would also profoundly affect the two sides' interpretation as to what "union" entailed. Each would attentively poise its stewards to discover bad faith and deficient execution of a religious compromise only partially fathomed.

In the mid-1690s, however, as the Viennese Catholics and Transylvania Orthodox tentatively felt their respective ways towards union, Leopold's court at least seemed to have every reason to presume success. Besides having the Union of Brest (1596) as a propitious precedent, the Habsburgs' re-Catholicizing efforts had more recently enjoyed "great success" with the 1648 Union of the Ruthenes of Hungary. As would the Romanians later, the Ruthenes expected to receive the same privileges, most especially the financial ones, that the Latin Rite clergy did. When they finally took their oath to Rome in 1652 they manifested the same mix of motivations and concerns that would be the Romanians' about a generation afterward. The Ruthenes proclaimed that

> We believe everything and each particular that our Holy Mother, the Roman Church, commands, and recognize the Holy Father Innocent X as our and the entire Church of Christ's Supreme Shepherd, upon whom we and our followers wish to depend.

Indicative not only of their mentality at this juncture, but also of that which would characterize the Romanians as well, was the fact that the Ruthenes continued on to specify that they committed themselves in this fashion "on the condition" that certain guarantees were forthcoming. These included the practical privileges already mentioned plus the integrity of the Greek Rite and the certainty that one amongst them would be chosen by the Pope to be the Uniate Bishop.[30] As the Habsburg church leaders and the Emperor surveyed this "great success" with the Ruthenes, then, they had to be aware of the very human incentives moving such "converts" as well as the extraordinarily developed sensitivities on the issue of "the Law" or "*legea*." The fact that the Romanians would partake of comparable dreams and sympathies should neither have come as a surprise nor occasioned any serious chagrin. If, that is, the Empire's authorities had in mind to require no more of the Romanians than they, or their religious formulae employed, had of the Ruthenes.

The other factor promising success in dealing with the Romanian Orthodox of Transylvania revolved around the existing institutional structure in Rome for handling such unions. In January of 1622 Pope Gregory XV had founded the *Congregatio de Propaganda Fide* with the status of a "Cardinal congregation." In doing so the Pope gave that body jurisdiction in all areas and matters that served the goal of spreading the Catholic religion. The following June Gregory XV issued the Papal Bull *Inscrutabili* through which he gave the *Congregatio de Propaganda Fide* its unique cast and the singular boon of budgetary autonomy. In 1627 his successor Urban VIII, in the Bull *Immortalis Dei*, founded the international educational establishment destined to provide missionaries equipped to deal with different cultures and religious backgrounds such as those found in Eastern Europe. *The Congregatio de Propaganda Fide* took control of this college on the eve of the union of the Ruthene Orthodox with Rome (i.e., in 1646).[31] Well over a generation before the Romanian Orthodox committed themselves to the Union with Rome, then, the bureaucratic and educational support systems for such an enterprise were already in existence. Furthermore, both the local authorities and those in Rome had had the experience of successfully (at least, in their view) negotiating this type of pact with the Ruthenes. Seemingly, with this major exploit as a guide they could accomplish the same goal again in Transylvania.

In addition, of course, the doctrinal schematic specifying what had to be asked of the Orthodox had been in existence since the Council of Florence. In the summer of 1439 Pope Eugenius IV promulgated in the *Bulla Unionis Ecclesiae Graecae et Latinae* the preceptual norms to be followed in merging once more the Greek and Latin churches. Rome rejoiced, then, as "the Mother Church sees her formerly dissident sons returning one by one in peace and unity," asking only that these prodigals accept what came to be known as the "Four Points." Reunification of Orthodox and Roman Catholic worlds would be considered consummated, once the Eastern Christians embraced the administrative and doctrinal Supremacy of the Roman Pontiff, the binding character of the "*filioque*" clause in defining the Trinity, the existence of Purgatory as an intermediary locale between Heaven and Hell for temporary punishments, and the use in the Eucharistic service of unleavened bread.[32] As daunting as these required beliefs had been, and would continue to be, for many Greek Orthodox Christians, they constituted a discrete and easily cataloged list to arbitrate and perhaps adopt. Acquiesce in these few articles and you can define yourselves as Rome's "returning, formerly dissident" children once again was supposedly the message and total reckoning for the Orthodox. As a limited litmus test for devoutness and future fidelity it told Catholic and Orthodox alike where to find the minimum of theological rectitude as well as the magnitude of outside intrusion into ancestral church practices. In comparison with what the Ruthenes promised in 1648 the Florentine "Four Points" stood out as far more specific and encompassing. The Ruthene Uniates simply had to state that "We believe everything and each particular that our Holy Mother, the Roman Church commands…."[33] But for the Romanians even this enhanced formula of commitment would not serve to silence the critics of their *bona fides*.

Also to be observed here is the discrepancy between the first three highly technical theological points required by the formula of Florence (i.e., Papal Supremacy, the "*filioque*" clause, and Purgatory) and the demand for the utilization of unleavened bread in the Communion liturgy. A portent of the difficulties to be encountered in the career of the Romanian Union, this cultural standard obviously stood on an entirely different level than the first three. It also augured quite accurately the incomprehension and intolerance that Latin Rite Roman Catholics in Transylvania would evidence towards the Greek Rite Catholics with their ethnically oriented ecclesiastical heritage. Perhaps, the Florentine Bull on the reunion of Greek and Latin churches, if carefully read, should have warned the Romanians. For, after the required accent on primacy of place for the Bishop of Rome, that document goes on to list the pecking order of all other patriarchs in punctilious detail.[34] As a matter of protocol and diplomatic gesture, one might expect this. Unfortunately, it also appears to have presaged the condescension endured throughout the entire period of combined Jesuit-Habsburg patronage of the Greek Catholic Romanians. With whatever degree of earnestness the Orthodox might have espoused the "Four Points" of Florence, the cultural ambiance of their liturgy still led the eighteenth century Latin Rite Catholic to the verdict that "...they [the Uniates] are not true Catholics."[35]

Roman Catholicism, then, or more specifically its Latin Rite version offered Vienna a invaluable foundation for the unity of the monarchy and the chosen mechanism by which to augment loyalty to the Habsburgs' *Hausmacht.* Along side the military and imperial administrative agencies, the common faith was seen as instilling a cohesiveness unobtainable otherwise. Though a particular enthusiasm of Leopold I's, spreading Roman Catholicism also represented an established *modus operandi* through which absolutist control might be expanded. Catholicism offered a uniquely effective factor, therefore, for the accomplishment of the dual aspirations of "domination and unification" in Transylvania.[36] Although primarily motivated by the necessity of increasing the number of Catholics in the region, Leopold now approached the Union with the Romanians from the viewpoint of securing a more profound influence over them and thus over their political environment. In the terms of twentieth century Romanian historians, the Emperor sought an "ideological" fulcrum with which to dislodge the power of the Protestants especially the Calvinists. In less melodramatic and more humanly pertinent terms, the Viennese court urgently needed "partisans" to support their cause in Transylvania. These "partisans" could be procured by motivating the Romanian Orthodox to become Greek Rite Catholics through financial incentives. Or to paraphrase for the Transylvanian case an earlier dictum applying to the lands of the crown of St. Stephen, a somber political quip by the leading ecclesiastic sponsoring the Union, "Take them hostage, then make them hungry, and finally turn them into Catholics" ("*Faciam Hungariam captivam, deinde mendicam, postea catholicam*").[37] Blunt, indeed, but this aphorism constituted an intriguingly precise synopsis of the government's projection of the role envisaged for the Romanian Orthodox.

Though the Habsburgs erected a central office in Vienna for the processing of Transylvanian affairs (the *Cancellaria Caesareo-Regia Transilvanio-Aulica*), their primary impact on the scene consisted in the power exercised through two other agencies. The first of these was a governor chosen by the Transylvanian Diet and confirmed by the Emperor. This individual presided over the provincial administration with the assistance of the second of these agencies; namely, an imperial governing council (i.e., the *Consilium Regium Guberniale*). The possible constraints on imperial policy, especially where the extension of Romana Catholic influence was involved, were immediately obvious in the composition of the *Consilium Regium Guberniale.* Only three of the twelve counselors had to be Catholic, the rest being drawn from the ranks of the Calvinist Magyars and Unitarian Szeklers as well as the Lutheran Saxons. Thus, the interplay of everyday practical politics with only a minority of Catholics on this important council reinforced the concern over their percentage in the population and the desire to isolate the Transylvanian Romanians from their fellows in the Danubian Principalities.[38] Habsburg dominion in the province would, then, never be completely consolidated or as extensive as they envisioned until they possessed a counterweight to the sway of the "political nations." Without this offsetting force they felt that imperial reliance upon the Protestant strata of the population could all too easily miscalculate the margin of their constancy.

While the Imperial Council comprised the most prominent supervisory mode to be contested for, Leopold also had to contend with entrenched Protestant resistance in the Transylvanian Diet and social order. With the close identification between sect and ethnicity as well as the insistence upon proportional representation, the Diet's configuration of 161 Magyars, 114 Szeklers, and 35 Saxons heralded unrelenting resistance to Habsburg political plans. The scheme of using Romanian Orthodox converts to change the proportion of the Catholic population would also clash with this ingrained configuration of the Diet on another level. For while the Romanians to be transformed into Greek Rite Roman Catholics were overwhelmingly of peasant origin, all but five of the 310 members of the "political nations" in the Diet were either nobles or bourgeoisie. In this complex of competing interests, the social status of the Romanians became an integral part of the struggle between a assertive Habsburg Catholicism intent on centralizing its control over Transylvania and a Protestant recalcitrance bound up with issues of local autonomy.[39] If the Union of the Romanian Orthodox with Rome could be effectuated, the Habsburgs would be in a position to cripple their Protestant adversaries through the increase in numbers involved. This gain in political leverage would then permit Vienna to break the well anchored power of their primary opponents, the Magyar Calvinists. The combination of religion and ethnic discontent was perceived as the most likely vehicle both to curtail Magyar influence and secure the foundations of Habsburg imperial rule in Transylvania.[40]

Catholicism was, thus, once again to be the overreaching sectarian presence in the province. And through this means the Habsburg would attain not only the primordial "Catholic state," but would at the same time attempt the more modern centralized one as well. Capitalizing on the Romanian aggregate in Transylvania, the Habsburg forces could acquire an instant majority. For the addition of the Orthodox would make the Catholics not only the largest single cult, but would in fact make their population total greater than that of the Calvinist-Lutheran-Unitarian alliance. No matter how loud or prolonged the later protestations regarding the legitimacy of the Union by either the privileged estates or the Orthodox in Transylvania, the Habsburg party line adamantly would insist that Catholicism was now the primary denomination. Not only was it the faith of the Emperor, but with the addition of the thousands of Romanians it now had obtained the position of predominance among the representatives of the provincial government. By means of the Romanian peasantry, then, the imperial party could begin the skirmish by which it hoped to configure to its specifications the statutory topography of Transylvania. Led by the interests of their priests, the Union of Romanian Orthodox and Imperial Catholic interests would provide the political handle needed to accomplish all the Habsburgs' intentions.[41]

The Magyars, with their factional dissatisfactions and confessional discontents, had an impact however not simply on Habsburg blueprints for the area, but also on that majority of the population composed of the Romanians. To begin with, their nobility especially took an exceptionally disgruntled stance due to the separation of Transylvania from

Hungary proper. Then they obviously returned the intolerance of the Catholic Habsburgs with some considerable verve. As would be true throughout the seventeenth and eighteenth centuries on the part of all the sectarian players, the Calvinists used compulsion of various types and intensities in order to compel the adoption of their views and/or practices. Foremost among the beneficiaries of such regard by the Reformed Church were the Orthodox Romanians. As soon as Leopold led the Habsburg forces back into Transylvania his government manifested acute anxiety over Calvinist control of the Romanians and their church. So marked was this concern with its corollary of danger for Habsburg *Hausmacht* that the Viennese court preferred to see the Romanians more committed to their ancestral faith, more nearly like the Orthodox of the Balkans, than under the aegis of the Magyars. Well before the opening phrases of the negotiations leading to the Romanian Union with Rome, the Habsburgs were settled on separating this group from the Calvinists for reasons of bettering their position in Transylvania. But to all apparent intents and purposes, the Emperor had confirmed this situation in his diploma of 1691.[42]

While the Protestant Reformation in Transylvania had secularized the Catholic Church's property and exiled its clergy, it had not had quite the same devastating effect upon the Orthodox. However, the religious transformations of the sixteenth century did convulse the Romanian Church and instigate a systematic program of doctrinal-administrative intrusion. Despite the occasional reprieve either due to regional conflicts or the interests of the few remaining Catholic magnates, the framework of the Romanian Orthodox Church was subjected to repeated attempts to generate a Calvinist edifice within its confines. Much as would be the mundane portion of the Roman Catholic intention at the end of the seventeenth century, the Magyar Calvinists of the sixteenth century and later tried to parlay their dominance into a Romanian church that would be their "political creature." Such a creation was to serve their partisan goals, subordinate as it was to the direct instructions of the secular princes.[43] In contrast to the Lutherans who had labored in vain for sway if not conversions among the Orthodox Romanians, the Calvinists impress would stretch across the century and a half from Luther's death. For more than five generations, even after the advent of the Habsburgs and of the Union with Rome, Romanian religious establishments and beliefs labored under the Calvinist influences that had been insinuated into their midst.[44]

Both Calvinists and Lutherans endeavored to reach the Orthodox hierarchy and the small literate portion of the priesthood through the active engagement of their printing presses. For the Calvinists who ended up with preeminent political presence in Transylvania as well as position of dominance in the affairs of the Romanian Church, this evangelistic effort also entailed an undeclared but ever present process of assimilation. As it had likewise transpired for Lutheranism among the Saxons, Calvinism took on for the Magyars of the domain a distinctly "national character." Though not fruitful amongst the mass of the Romanian peasantry this pressure for immersion within the Magyar "nation" through the agency of canonical metamorphosis did engulf many of the aristocracy.[45] Despite the "passive resistance," then, of the bulk of the Orthodox of Transylvania, the dual jolt of evangelization and assimilation stood out as omnipresent facts of life until the coming of the Habsburgs. Part of that reality entailed the disappearance of the talented and ambitious element from within the Romanian aristocracy. A significant number of the prominent dispensers of power among the Magyars in the time of Leopold I had, according to Romanian lights, roots among the Orthodox.[46] Whatever the Calvinist triumph in fact among the rank and file of Romanian Orthodox, their official stance promulgated the opinion that total absorption had occurred. Regarding church functions they appropriated for themselves the prerogative of determining all matters for the Romanians. In the late 1680s this was so much the case that contemporaries felt compelled to comment that the Calvinists "...considered the Romanian nation and church definitively incorporated within their sect and nationality." This would figure as a major complaint of the Romanian leadership well into the eighteenth century, indeed until such time as the Uniates possessed in their own denominational schools a means by which to avoid the loss of the talented. Interestingly, given the criticism it would receive from all quarters (Orthodox, Protestant, and Uniate), the Society of Jesus was credited by contemporaries as constructing through its education of Uniate youth the first impediment to this denationalization.[47]

For the Magyar Calvinists of the sixteenth and seventeenth centuries as for the Catholic Habsburgs on the eve of the eighteenth the efforts to impinge doctrinally on the Orthodox faith sprang from several stimuli.

And in both instances the secular and religious determinants flowed together making their demarcation extremely difficult and tentative. Each spiritual mentor maintained that no official mandate existed to employ the device of evangelization to the end of "denationalization" of the Romanians. Though the Transylvanian diet did ordain in 1566 that "The Romanians will convert to Calvinism, or in the case of resistance will be exiled from the province." Whether so formulated or not Romanians from Luther's time to the suppression of the Jesuits in 1773 would see such "tentative endeavors" to mold their ecclesiastical conventions to Occidental norms as aggressive proselytizing. It would make them yet more obdurately attentive to and possessive of their traditions.[48] The few Romanians who could be reached by the Protestant ploy of using the printing press to spread Calvinist literature viewed this as a tactic designed to prevent their becoming a "political nation." Perhaps as much as the posited furtive blueprint on the part of the Magyars, the Orthodox of Transylvania simply lacked any semblance of a piety comparable enough to support the Calvinist effort among them. They shared with the Protestants a profound animosity to the papacy and all that Rome stood for in their view. A more encompassing alliance, certainly any attempt to foster a common spirituality, the Magyar Calvinists found to be not only a failure but a "perfect illusion" on their part. The Romanian Orthodox, then and now, perceived the Protestants to embody simply another species of the Western devotional protocols and doctrinism which so sharply separated them from Rome. The bald fact of a coincidental and shared veneer of anti-papalism did not suffice obscure the chasm dividing them.[49]

Romanian Orthodox sensitivity to the impact of Calvinism galvanized, as it later would with the Roman Union, around the physical expression of their belief. The Magyars interfered with the liturgy so greatly treasured by the Orthodox reducing the number of traditional feast days through the liberal admixture of the Calvinist notions of religious services. Though the purpose here, as it would be with Catholic contractions of the customary Greek Rite holidays, centered on obtaining more work days from the peasantry.[50] The similarity between the Calvinists before 1688 and the Habsburgs afterwards in their approaches to influencing the Orthodox also emerged in the focal point of their conversion attempts; namely, the village priests. Throughout the period of Magyar overlordship the Romanian priests endured the same conditions of serfdom and poverty as did the Orthodox peasantry. Standing out as the leaders in all communal matters, they could both shape the perceptions of their congregations and were vulnerable to blandishments that might better their lot. Though some of these allurements amounted in the view of the later Romanians to outright "bribes," the priests were offered enticements that would enhance the level of village culture in general (i.e., on the secular as well as spiritual plane). Thus along side the possibility of escaping the robot and other feudal dues came the prospect of books and schools specifically for the Romanians. "The question for them then, as they were under the assault of these seductive proposals, was to arrange to obtain the most on the material level and to sacrifice the least on the spiritual."[51] To improve their status, to escape from the grinding burdens of the feudal system they had but to accept Calvinism. Hopefully their example would serve to bring the peasantry along in their wake. Thus, in January of 1608 Sigismund Rakoczy decreed that "every Romanian priest who converted to Calvinism would enjoy the same privileges as did the Magyar priests." Propositions like that of Rakoczy would occur some five other times in the course of the seventeenth century (i.e., in 1643, 1669, 1673, and 1680).[52]

A pattern of offering material recompense, and perhaps by implication even some access to the political status of the "Three Nations," had been long on the ground before Leopold's use of it. And there were those among the clergy, as there had been in the aristocracy, who made this transnational trek taking with them their villages and even whole districts. But the bulk of the priests, along with their parishioners, clung to Orthodoxy despite the pressures and lures.[53] The Roman Catholics who both initiated and then serviced the Romanian Union with Rome later encountered the same wide spread resistance. The fact that under each Western denomination the feudal magnates refused cooperation and, indeed, failed to recognize the new rights of the Romanian priests helped fuel Orthodox tenacity. The fact both brands of Western Christianity also attempted to build a replica of themselves among the Romanians, perhaps, had a even greater role in the antagonism encountered. The Magyars Calvinist in the seventeenth century saw themselves presented with a uncommon chance to undo the schism of the eleventh century. The road to reunification, in their view, led through a Romanian Reformed Church with its own hierarchy to eventual incorporation within the body of the Calvinist community. Unfortunately for their enterprise, such alteration or loss of the traditional Romanian rite ("*lege*") was equated with forfeiture of the most essential of spiritual heirlooms.[54]

However credible the Calvinist claim to spiritual hegemony over the Orthodox of Transylvania, the Reformed Church did leave a notable legacy in matters of observance, ecclesiastic organization, and even dogma. In affairs of substance, a template for the eighteenth century Union with Rome persisted. For the doctrinal forays of Calvinism, as later with Latin Rite Catholicism, often remained confined to the clergy and bore witness more to ecclesiastical ambition than to creedal conviction.[55] In terms of a profound and lasting impact on the Orthodox Romanians of Transylvania the role of the Superintendent of the Magyar Reformed Church overshadowed all others in the institutional realm. By the eve of the Habsburg return to Transylvania the Orthodox bishop was constrained to seek the Superintendent's approval for even the most minor of administrative decisions or reassignments. This subordination went far beyond the bureaucratic extending to an obligation to accept Protestant approval of doctrine and certification in office. The Superintendent even possessed the authority to revise canonical verdicts and decide jurisdictional matters for the Orthodox. But far more indicative of this individual's true role in the life of the Romanian Church was the title he arrogated to himself. The Calvinist Superintendent by the time of the battle of Zenta also signed his official documents as "Bishop of the Romanians" ("*Episcopus Valachorum*"). Calvinist control of Romanian ecclesiastical affairs was all pervasive, while the only element of Orthodox autonomy remaining was to be found in the passive resistance of the peasant.[56]

Whatever the visible structure of the Romanian Orthodox Church after the beginning of the Reformation in Transylvania, the true administrative head was the Calvinist Superintendent. Besides signing himself as such, he did in fact exercise conclusive jurisdiction over both the Romanian bishop as well as the Orthodox General Synod. Just as subsequently in the Union with Rome the Jesuit Theologian would oversee the Romanian Church, so too in the earlier period the Magyar Superintendent played the role of examiner. As a prelude to the Romanian Orthodox experience under Leopold and the Jesuits, in the preceding century and a half the Calvinists had theoretically abstained from any theological or ritual modifications. However, again presaging later events, the Superintendent did interfere in Orthodox responsibilities by serving as the medium by which candidates were recommended to the secular authorities for confirmation as bishop. He likewise took for himself what the Romanians would judge the rather heavy handed right to remove from office all those who did not pay him proper deference. Although not defined as formally and legalistically as would be that under the Habsburgs, for all intents and purposes the Calvinists had achieved a "union" with the Romanian Orthodox. In this instance rather than having the theme of "reunion" as would the Catholics, the resulting connection the Calvinists christened "protection." The fact that Romanian burdens and discontents mushroomed apparently left their Protestant "protectors" indifferent. They should not have, since they fed directly into the missionary efforts of the Jesuits and Habsburg Catholic hierarchy of the late seventeenth century.[57]

The Superintendent's unrivaled charge extended into the very center of Orthodox life in Transylvania; namely, the profile and function of the Great Synod ("*Sobor mare*"). This institution possessed ultimate authority for the Romanian Church, both deciding those issues subject to legislative resolution as well as being the final channel of administrative governance for the Transylvanian Orthodox. The Great Synod constituted the court having irreversible say not only in all matters ecclesiastical, but also in the personal life of its adherents. For it composed the decision making body determining the finality of marriage and the permissibility of divorce in individual cases. As far as day to day affairs were concerned, the Synod also regulated the financial life of the Church as well. This council, then, possessed definitive jurisdiction over clergy, laity, and the bishop (bearing the honorific of Metropolitan) who traditionally presided. By the time of the Habsburgs, however, the Calvinist Superintendent did far more than merely sign himself as "Bishop of the Romanians." By presiding over the Great Synod, he (and through him the Magyar princes of Transylvania) took to himself absolute dominion over the Orthodox Church of the province. In this manner, the Metropolitan was reduced to a creature of the Superintendent, one chosen from among candidates he elected to have presented to the Great Synod for approbation. Once culled and placed in this impotent position, the Romanian Metropolitan of Transylvania could affect nothing without the prior cognizance and sanction of the Superintendent. A humiliation analogous to what the Orthodox would experience through Jesuit tutelage after the Union with Rome flowed naturally from the preening ascendancy enjoyed by the Superintendent.[58]

Both the Calvinist Superintendent and through him the General Synod of the Reformed Church in Transylvania became, then, avenues of Western influence into the Romanian Orthodox world. By these means, doctrinal as well as institutional values made themselves felt. Though perhaps not as obviously as it would be in the eighteenth century, the preconceptions of Latin Christianity still had begun to shape Transylvanian Orthodox long before the departure of the Ottomans. The configuration of the Great Synod under the Superintendent's sovereignty during the last half of the sixteenth and the entirety of the seventeenth century foreshadowed the even greater impact of Latin conventions once the Roman Union under Jesuit auspices was concluded.[59] Whereas in his own Reformed Church the Superintendent stood out simply as a "*primus inter pares*," his stature as "Bishop of the Romanians" not only gave him an eminence obscuring that of the Romanian Metropolitan, but also a comprehensive scope for his ecclesiastical power not enjoyed in his doctrinal home. This was especially the case once it became apparent to the Magyar lords of Transylvania that the effort to convert the Romanian Orthodox *en masse* would fail and that their doctrinal impact would be peripheral. With an ethnic bishop (thought not always and necessarily a Romanian) as a facade in the post of Metropolitan, the Calvinist Superintendent exercised whatever powers of governance remained to the Orthodox. Nothing was much different in this instance than would be the case with the status of the Romanians under Leopold once they united with Rome, accepting not only the "Four Points" but perforce Latin exemplars of management as well.[60]

With a view to insinuating as much Calvinist influence as possible into the life of the Romanian Orthodox, the leaders of the Reformed Church had to face the same dilemma as would their Catholic successors. The Orthodox of Transylvania, priests and laity, neither understood nor displayed any conspicuous interest in the theoretical side of religion. The liturgy and other palpable manifestations of rite captured their attention. A scholastic debate on the fine distinctions between sectarian tenets aroused no enthusiasm nor indeed was commensurate with the educational background enjoyed by most Romanians. In their perception, then, manipulating and molding the religious institutions of the Orthodox became the most effective method of accomplishing their purposes. Fashioning the Romanian Great Synod ever more in the image of the Calvinist General Synod seemed the most apt route to the desired end. If the outward forms, especially the singular organs of institutional religious life such as the synods, could be rendered basically similar in form and function, then hopefully the Romanians would begin to see an "identity" between themselves and the Calvinists. In time they would come to "believe" as Calvinists just as their highest church council would act in a manner increasingly reflecting the structure of the Reformed Church. Through this imitation of the Calvinist assembly, the position of the Romanian Metropolitan was reduced from being head of his church to occupying the position of an agency head charged with the supervision of ecclesiastical administrative details. The Metropolitan did not even enjoy the status of being "*primus inter pares*" as did the Calvinist Superintendent. Final authority in Transylvanian Orthodoxy now became located in the assembly of priests sitting as the Grand Synod. This church official with so many centuries of tradition ingrained in his status and powers no longer in any real sense possessed the prerogatives or station dictated by his Orthodox legacy. He was not a true archbishop by any standard of the Latin or Eastern churches.[61]

The most visible indication of the growth of Calvinist penetration into the Orthodox Church of Transylvania could be found in the suppression of the suffragan bishops of the province. This elimination of all auxiliary hierarchs accomplished the dual goals of isolating the weakened Metropolitan and creating an Orthodox Church analogous structurally to the Reformed. At this point the Romanian Metropolitan endured a situation in which he was subordinate to both the Calvinist Superintendent and his own Great Synod. The formerly most distinguished ruling body in his church, the Metropolitan Synod composed of himself and his suffragans, no longer existed. Like the Reformed Church, the Transylvanian Orthodox community now had a single hierarchical representative. Its constitutional framework subsequently mimicked, in a trite and contrived form, that of its mentors.[62] The trend here was, however, one that envisioned more than the simple diminution of the Metropolitan's authority and stature. Though those aims were certainly incorporated within the overall intent of rooting Calvinism in the minds and hearts of the Orthodox faithful. More was intended than merely rendering this ecclesiastical distinction an empty title. In diminishing the role of the Metropolitan the Superintendent had arrived by the end of the seventeenth century at the point that the very rank was no longer conveyed upon the installation of a new Romanian bishop. By the time of Leopold the occupants of the Romanian episcopal dignity would not be called a "metropolitan" but rather listed as being designated to "take care of the metropolitanate."[63] The Calvinist Superintendent, having fashioned an organizational simulacrum of his sect, could move on to more substantive efforts designed to turn Orthodox into Reformed adherents.

Again the status of the Metropolitan serves as a meter by which to gauge the extent of the Superintendent's authority and of Calvinist success vis-à-vis the Romanians. In 1628 and once again in 1669 the general theme of the Metropolitan's subservience took frank form in the Superintendent's dictate of obligations to be assume upon accepting that office. Growing from a single requirement in 1628 to some nineteen just over a generation later, these pledges encompassed everything from obedience to the Superintendent and payments in kind to acquiescing in Calvinist paradigms for church offices and customs. These most unsubtle expectations for qualifying as Metropolitan foreshadowed the extent of Calvinist control and demonstrably reminded the candidates of the Superintendent's veto. The Metropolitan as a symbol of his church and people had, at best, the character of an appendage of the Calvinist official who approved his elevation.[64]

Most significantly, of course, the Metropolitan though titular head of Romanian Orthodoxy in Transylvania became clearly subordinate to the Calvinist model of presbyterian church governance. Besides being an innovation for the Romanian Church, this factor would help explain the prominence of the assembly of priests in the execution of the Union with Rome at the end of the seventeenth century. The annual assembly of archpriests ("*protopopi*"), with the Calvinist Superintendent at their head, assumed an unprecedented and uncommon jurisdiction eclipsing that of the erstwhile Metropolitan.[65] From this juncture on the Romanian Metropolitan could not initiate any actions without first obtaining the consent of the Superintendent, whose sanction was likewise required before the discharge of any decisions by the synod. The conditions for enthronement as the supposed leader of Romanian Orthodoxy eventuated not only in the somewhat vague burden of proselytizing for the Reformed congregation, but also far-reaching cultural changes such as the eradication of Old Church Slavonic from all church services. The introduction of Romanian as the mandatory language for all ecclesiastical endeavors amounted to a fundamental alteration that would affect the Orthodox community far longer than the evangelization campaign of the Calvinist. In following the lead of Luther in this regard and in attempting to open the Romanian church to a more profound Calvinist imprint, the ecclesiastical and secular leaders of Transylvania laid yet another portion of the foundation that would serve to open the Orthodox community to the influence of Rome and the West. This language conversion would fail as a measure to sink Calvinism deep into the Romanian soil. But it did begin a process that would go on for generations of an ever burgeoning realization of ethnic-cultural differentiation and of a heritage that gave hope, if not immediate support, for Romanian political aspirations. The Metropolitan, however, could not foresee any of this and, more to the point, was treated in such a cavalier, disrespectful fashion as not to have any say at all. In any resolution of moment, whether issuing directly from the Superintendent or tendered through the more circuitous mechanism of a synod, he either accepted the prescription or faced peremptory dismissal.[66]

Whatever the facade of Calvinist control the result remained the same. The Superintendent constituted the real, indeed only significant, power in the Transylvanian Orthodox Church, since his political appointment as its head in 1567. True, the Romanians did regain the right to choose their own bishop in 1579, but only with the fetters already mentioned. Even the beneficial aspects of this monitoring, the modernization of church culture and the vain attempt to eradicate superstition, met with prolonged recalcitrance. This derived both from the uneducated nature of the peasantry and the sternness with which the Calvinist approached the project.[67] The Romanian Metropolitan's acceptance of the conditions imposed by the Superintendent went beyond his personal commitment to either his superior or a personal espousal of Reformed Church practices. He took a vow which committed him to the Calvinization of his flock in the same way he had accepted the Superintendent's surveillance of his every canonical action (including even his ordination of future Orthodox priests). This paramount plight confirmed in the minds of later observers that the Metropolitan served as the door through which "heresy" entered the Orthodox world.[68]

Given the Romanian prelate's "absolute dependence" on the Calvinist Superintendent, he could neither fulfill the traditional functions of his post nor protect his clergy from the badgering that ensued from their resistance. Stripped of institutional defenses with the loss of the Metropolitan Synod and the domination of the Great Synod by the Superintendent, the Romanian bishop was without political resources.[69] In this context the Calvinist resolve to employ the Romanian hierarch's accommodation to the end of evangelization assumed a contentious focus. The Superintendent's charge, and the use to which he put this submissive ecclesiastical figurehead, was to so administer the Romanian Church that he "corrected its mistakes and shortcomings." The disappearance of the Metropolitan Synod and the loss of autonomy by the Great Synod served as a precondition for the systematic promulgation of Calvinist dogma among the Orthodox rank and file. For besides being constrained to appear before the Calvinist General Synod to obtain its approbation for all decisions made at the Romanian Great Synod, the Metropolitan had pledged his support for the Reformed Church's official credence. One of the obligations assumed in order to become Metropolitan specified that the Romanian notable "would accept for himself and for all the Orthodox faithful the Calvinist catechism." The sweeping nature of this onus as well as the repercussions it opened the Romanian bishop to are best appreciated if one remembers that the promise was made not simply to the Reformed Church but through him to the Calvinist princes of Transylvania.[70]

Acting under the Superintendent's guidance and goad, in 1640 Prince Gyorgy Rakoczi I financed the printing of a Calvinist catechism specifically directed at the Romanian Orthodox population. An indication of the zeal with which this project was launched is the fact that the catechism was distributed not merely in the Prince's own realm, but also in the Romanian inhabited Danubian Principalities which were still under Ottoman suzerainty. This Romanian language guide to the Calvinist articles of faith the Superintendent compelled the Metropolitan to accept and use in his ministries. As the cutting edge of the Protestant evangelistic movement in Transylvania the Romanian bishop was to have the catechism read in all his churches and popularized amongst Orthodox congregations.[71] The employment of this catechism merged with the broader effort at influencing the religious frame of mind of the Orthodox. It accompanied not only the unsuccessful effort to attract adherents through material rewards (seldom forthcoming due to the reluctance of the landowners), but also the insinuation of Calvinist doctrines and usages into the Orthodox service. In this fashion Reformed Church interpretations replaced those of the Eastern Christian world regarding the sacraments, while Calvinist prayers and other ceremonies were inserted in the place of the Orthodox legacy. The promulgation of the Calvinist catechism went hand in hand, then, with the more visible exertions (and much more alarming to the uneducated peasantry) to alter such important rituals as the baptismal observance and the announced nature of the communion service. Not being literate, and perhaps not comprehending the theological nuances read to them from the catechism, the Orthodox peasants could not miss the impact of that volume's contents in their religious life. Not to venerate saints, not to honor the cross, not to have icons in the home or church, and not to follow the hallowed liturgies for the start of a marriage or the end of a life entailed enormous cultural (if not always profound spiritual) shock.[72]

Looking back on this effort at catechesis and sectarian metamorphosis Romanian historians would, of course, comment severely on the pressures applied by the Calvinists. Somewhat anachronistically they have implied that the duress suffered by the Orthodox was meant to "denationalize" as much as to Calvinize the Transylvanian Romanians. More accurately and of greater interest in understanding the Habsburg/ Roman Catholic impact beginning at the end of the seventeenth century is the judgment by such historians that Calvinist and Catholic efforts had many similarities. In particular, the Reformed Church's lack of regard for Orthodox sensibilities regarding ceremonial proprieties caused alienation from their evangelistic essays helping to prepare the way for Leopold's Union in both negative and affirmative manners. Also the "theoretical" character of publications like the Calvinist catechism precluded comprehension much less fervent endorsement by a backward peasantry and a clergy drawn from it.[73] To try to obviate this barrier the Calvinists had founded a school for Romanian religious instructors at Făgăraş in 1657. These same historians who concentrate on the "national" impact of the Calvinists' efforts have also conceded that these adjustments had many beneficial effects. Besides the school at Făgăraş others were established a Lugoş, Caransebeş, and Alba-Iulia. The change of the language of the Transylvanian Orthodox service from Slavonic to Romanian resulted in not only new liturgical books from the Reformed Church's presses, but a literary catalyst that spread across the Carpathians into the Danubian Principalities and assisted in initiating a refurbished ethnic consciousness.[74] A well established Catholic viewpoint echoes this evaluation even going so far as to say that this Protestant proselytizing background amounted to a "providential" factor supporting the eventual Union with Rome. The insertion of Romanian into the Orthodox liturgy for reasons of Protestant evangelism is seen as not only affecting the culture and access to the Gospels, but also "emancipating them [the Romanians] from the guardianship of their Orthodox clergy…." These refinements as well as the deliverance from "a centuries long stupor" resulted in a situation where the Romanians were ripe for the Habsburgs' and Jesuits' efforts. Though this was not always for the reasons the Roman Catholics would have preferred.[75]

With the advent of the Habsburgs in Transylvania in the last quarter of the seventeenth century, then, they discovered a Romanian Orthodox Church clearly subordinated to Reformed Protestantism and which had accepted an extremely powerful Calvinist impress in its organization and prescribed tenets. The exceptional ignorance of people and ordinary clergy (all peasants) amounted to such an obstacle, however, that the Calvinist catechism could have only the most marginal of impacts. In an environment where the parish priest often could not recite the "Our Father" or identify the Trinity, the fine points of Reformed Church Christianity eluded the grasp of all but a few.[76] Rite, the one item of the Romanian pietistic legacy which the Calvinists largely left alone, endured. In doing so the traditional ritual guaranteed the preservation of a sense of Orthodoxy and of ethnic community. From the Calvinist perspective the heedless zeal of the early Reformation had been replaced in the seventeenth century by a more patient approach emphasizing the already mentioned cultural improvements. This gradual amelioration of the Romanians' educational and spiritual conditions would, supposedly, eventuate in a truly Calvinist church for them. Replacement of superstition by a better informed clergy and a service in Romanian was to lead to "a love for reading the Bible and a taste for Protestant ideas." Unfortunately, both contemporary and later Romanian observers did not share this opinion. Despite the schools, the vernacular, and the catechism, the Romanian Orthodox resisted. Calvinism presented itself in their vision as "arbitrary and aggressive." What they remembered of its proselytism revolved primarily around its militant, not its magnanimous, mannerisms.[77]

The Calvinist appreciation varied considerably from this. Though extremely conscious of strong ties between the Romanians of Transylvania and those of the Danubian Principalities, the Calvinist perspective has continued to stress that the authorities in Transylvania concerned themselves fundamentally with the Romanian "religious mandate, and consequently with the ecclesiastical and cultural." Despite noting the "sentiment of racial solidarity" among Romanians on both sides of the Carpathians and indeed that conversion of the Orthodox "offered an opportunity to pursue political purposes," the Calvinist conceit employed a rationale portraying political gain as secondary. The self-examination and rather gentle consequent assessment of their actions towards the Orthodox left the Calvinists, as would be the case of the Catholics later, feeling that their impositions had been less harsh and complete than claimed. But even from the Reformed Church standpoint the Romanians "saturated as they were in the spirit of their Orthodox Church, Greek and Oriental, never ceased to offer an instinctive resistance to that Protestantism grown in the West."[78] Part of the traditional procedures helping to maintain that "instinctive resistance" had been the practice in the seventeenth century, permitted by the Calvinists, of having the Orthodox Metropolitan of Transylvania consecrated in the Danubian Principalities. The forging of a generations long hierarchical link with the Romanians of the Ottoman Empire bolstered the very sense of ethnic individuality the Magyar princes of Transylvania wished to see diminished. The undeniably favorable impact of those rulers' adjustments in the areas of Romanian publications, admittance to education, and use of the vernacular for secular as well as religious functions all amounted to a vast expenditure of resources to little avail.[79]

On the eve of the Union with Rome, then, Romanian Church remained Orthodox "only in rite, having been Calvinized in belief and institutions." Socially and organizationally, if not in profundity of faith and commitment, Transylvanian Orthodoxy had suffered a major dislocation in the course of the seventeenth century. Even with all the exertions the Calvinists had put into evangelization and education, their bequest to the Orthodox remained not so much one of theological inroads, but rather a more opportunistic impact revolving around the condition of the clergy. Instead of schism in a technical sense (one generated on the basis of dogmatic innovations taken seriously to heart), the Romanians emerged from Calvinist tutelage "demoralized and unstable." Certainly their clergy and hierarchy had a significantly shaken regard for customary formulae and ceremonials, especially when temporizing over their exact nature might result in an appreciable gain in entitlements.[80] The mentality involved here saw alleviation of a century and a half of Magyar ecclesiastical exploitation and oppression to be obtained only in the form of "de-Calvinization," or more exactly in the eventual Union with Rome as a counterweight. Just before the turn of the eighteenth century, therefore, the most the Calvinists could and did aver entailed "an administrative union" between the Orthodox and Reformed Churches of Transylvania. One Romanian historian, admittedly anti-Calvinist as he was, has described the feeling on the part of the Orthodox as being one of revulsion for a proselytizing mode that sank into "acts of coarse brutality."[81]

When the Habsburg regained Transylvania, then, the Orthodox Church there was reluctantly but thoroughly the bailiwick of Genevan Protestantism. With a puppet Metropolitan and a clergy partially coerced into the new spirituality, it served the convenience of its ecclesiastical and temporal overlords boasting of no sovereignty of its own. But the penetration of Calvinist concepts was limited, as far as most of the Romanian populace was concerned, to "the official legal actions and instruments of church authorities." There existed a predisposition to change and even acceptance of Catholicism as a shield to the harassment of the last five generations.[82] Although the Superintendent had long possessed the power to dominate the decisions of the Great Synod and to advance priests to a higher ecclesiastical rank on his own initiative, this did not translate into a lasting impress. At best it meant a tangential approximation of Reformed Church mannerisms. As the Roman Catholics would learn, and at least partially though not completely manage to incorporate into their dealings with the Romanians, the Calvinists foundered on the visible elements of religion. Not the catechism but what he was accustomed to hearing and seeing in the Orthodox service mattered supremely to the Transylvanian Romanian.[83] At the terminus of the seventeenth century organized Calvinism made a final effort to retain Orthodoxy as its private preserve. The fortuitous combination of Romanian passive resistance, support from their ethnic relations in the Principalities, and the incursion of the Habsburg doomed that venture. The resentment, the political and social unrest, guaranteed a amenable audience once the Jesuit advocates of the Union with Rome appeared on the scene. Though within a generation the Romanians of Transylvania, both Uniate and Orthodox, would be voicing against the Jesuits complaints similar to those directed against Calvinist administrative control during the sixteenth and seventeenth centuries. The touch would, perhaps, be more discreet and the insight into Romanian attachment to the visible elements of their religious tradition more shrewd. But to the Romanian analyst Calvinist control over the Transylvanian Orthodox during the one hundred and fifty years before Leopold's armies appeared in the province all too well foreshadowed a similar loss of self-government to the Jesuits in the eighteenth century. "In both cases church autonomy became...a word in the wind." Reaction to the Society of Jesus' pains to make Catholics of the Romanians would likewise suffer from that group's perceived disdain for the visible aspects of Eastern Christian worship.[84] Finally, the Reformed Church failed with the Romanians because by the time the Habsburgs reappeared in Transylvania the material lot of the majority of the province's population had still not improved. This failure grew out of the fact that such betterment was the basis upon which Calvinist preaching had been founded. Leopold and the Jesuits understood this fundamental convention; namely, that for a complex of religious, ethnic, and just as importantly acquisitive reasons the Orthodox were primed for the appeal for Union with Rome.[85]

To understand the Romanian agitation at the end of the seventeenth century and the opening given to the Habsburgs and Jesuits, one must recognize that in the Transylvania of that time legal taxonomy determined the foundation of one's life. More to the point of Romanian complaints and difficulties, privilege derived organically from personal status. Thus the Romanians found themselves excluded on both the religious and secular levels. The established constitutional order in Transylvania, one reaffirmed by Leopold's diploma of 1691, simply set the Romanian majority to one side. Neither as an ethnic group nor as members of the Orthodox Church could they depend on anything more substantial than the goodwill of the prince as manifested until the current moment.[86] In the realm of sectarian rights, the provincial diet had decreed in 1595 that "In what concerns religious matters...we have determined in the course of law that the four received religious, namely the Roman Catholic, the Lutheran, the Calvinist, and the Unitarian, shall at all times be treated as free." This legal charter left the Transylvanian Romanians with no recognized corporate rights or with an unimpeded claim to be able to worship as they chose. Constitutionally, their church did not exist and possessed no prerogatives enforceable under statute. It did not participate in the "*lex patriae*" in the fashion that the four "received" faiths did. By the time of Leopold the common law of the province likewise considered this condition to have been reinforced by innumerable other political documents. The Romanian Orthodox and their lot had been frozen into a juridically stable environment.[87]

On the temporal plane as on the spiritual, the Transylvania Romanians found themselves relegated to a seemingly permanent state of inferiority. Again, according to the strictures of the "law of the land" they had been lumped together with everyone else who did not belong to the select ethnic groups; namely, the Magyars, Saxons, and Szeklers. In this predicament, rather than isolation, the Romanians enjoyed the company of "Armenians, Greeks, Jews, Moravians, Poles, Russians, Bulgars, Serbs, Slavs, and Gypsies" as being legally branded as "tolerated." Bearing the mark of "tolerated" meant the Romanians had no admittance to either the judicial system or public offices and honoraria monopolized by the three "received" nations. They did not enjoy the classification of citizen nor did they have any right to permanent tenancy in the province. They served as serfs and as inhabitants of Transylvania only so long as it suited their feudal masters.[88] Perhaps, most indicative of their perceived and possibly actual station was the fashion in which they were classified with the small and scorned Jewish community. To be on the same list of "tolerated" civil groups as the Jews and Gypsies constituted one species of disrespect. However, to have Orthodoxy and Judaism equated as "tolerated religions," to be ostracized from the communion of other Christians assemblies, would rankle for generations. Under Transylvanian law both sets of communicants could claim the "free exercise of their opinions." But the very fact that the majority of the population that belonged to the "Oriental Greek Church" found itself in a category so distanced from the acceptable and habitually abused for centuries speaks volumes for the disdain and constraint the Romanians felt themselves to have endured for too long.[89]

Categorized in this manner, the vast bulk of the Orthodox population of Transylvania had no legal protection whatsoever. Even Magyar and Saxon writers acknowledged that the Romanians were bound to the estates of the landowners in a condition approximating that of helots. The results produced by this juristic vulnerability and economic exploitation were a depressed cultural level among the Romanians and virtually no opening for social enhancement. As one observer commented, the Orthodox of Transylvania displayed "an uncommon roughness of manners and morals" due to this constitutional dispensation. Despite all the promises of privileges and the evangelistic efforts during the Calvinist period the Romanians, laity and clergy, were bound to the soil as serfs. The village priests had to fulfill all the feudal obligations of the population to which they ministered. The desperation and physical plight is, perhaps, most graphically highlighted by a law of 1667, at a time where approximately one hundred years of Calvinist solicitude and glimmerings of alleviated circumstances had elapsed. The repute and standing of the Romanians under the provincial charter were such that this innovative statute could impute guilt based on ethnic origins. Thus, "...wherever the butchered carcass of stolen livestock happens to be found, the nearest Romanian inhabitant shall pay the damages for the loss on the grounds that that people is well know for this type of theft."[90] The three privileged nations of the Magyars, Saxons, and Szeklers had long since determined to keep the Orthodox in this state. Their mutually agreed upon constitutional understanding provided not only that their respective religions would be protected and free, but also that "each nation had an obligation to the others to defend their rights." Their oaths of fealty to this scheme of things likewise bound them to do their best to influence the rulers and government of Transylvania, whoever those might be, to maintain this privileged order. Not to act in this fashion was to be considered and punished as "high treason." By implication continuing the Romanians in their role as serfs and economic foundation of the feudal system constituted an integral part of the rights of the privileged nations.[91]

Obviously, with the return of the Habsburgs to Transylvania, some adjustments however informal had to be made to this constitutional framework. That this was possible and that the resistance of the privileged nations and religions would not on all occasions and in every instance be dogged can be seen in the case of the Society of Jesus. The Transylvanian constitution clearly precluded the reentry of that Roman Catholic religious order into the province. It stated that "...the eternally banished and proscribed Order of the Jesuits...shall at no time be summoned, led, or suffered back into this fatherland by any man no matter what his rank."[92] Yet the Jesuits did indeed accompany the Habsburg armies and administration in their trek to the East. By the beginning of the eighteenth century, "a critical time of spiritual rebirth for the history" of the Habsburg Monarchy, the Society of Jesus was supplying not only advisors to the Catholic hierarchy, but also to the central government. They were present in force and as the cutting edge of a renewed Counter-Reformation. And as far as the stability of the constitutional status quo in Transylvania was concerned, the Jesuits helped initiate and then direct the movement to reunite the province's Romanian majority with Rome. But their mere presence in the region, no matter how objectionable and illicit, did not of itself change the established order for the three political nations and four received religions. They could, if they found the pressure from Vienna sufficient and to placate Leopold, look the other way where this militant Roman Catholic religious order was concerned.[93] Such could never be the case, though, with the definitively stipulated economic and legal station of the Orthodox Romanians. To maintain their privileged state and to observe their pledge to guard each other's rights the three political nations could never permit the Romanians to become a fourth Transylvanian "nation." Such a alteration in their capacity as serfs and merely "tolerated" inhabitants would signify a true "revolution." The only conceivable avenue out of this predicament was the one presented by the resurgent Habsburgs who returned to Transylvania with more in mind than just filling in for the former Ottoman rulers. With their intent of combating "heresy" in all its forms (Calvinist, Lutheran, and Unitarian) as well as to impose a "German" governance structure on the area, the Habsburgs stood out as the sole hope of the Romanians. For Vienna could satisfy the basic desire of increasing the compass of Catholicism and at the same time suppress the "superstition" of the Orthodox. The constitutional blockade to Romanian aspirations for an improved lot in life and the indigenous hostility to things "German" and/or Catholic might be circumvented by maneuvering through religion towards a "national" status for the Romanians. Affiliation with institutionalized Roman Catholicism might offer the Romanians the otherwise unattainable rewards of citizenship. In turn it could also guarantee the Viennese court a "religious alliance" that would allow it to achieve "a complete and enduring conquest" of Transylvania that was probably not within its grasp otherwise.[94]

Lurking always in the background, then, even in the minds of the sincerest of converts and most zealous of missionaries were somewhat tenuous ambitions to correct this state of affairs. Both Romanian Orthodox and Catholic clergy respectively mused about "cultural renaissance," "political liberty," and "propaganda" as a governmental as well as educational instrument. As numerous observers, of all sectarian persuasions, have remarked in their varying manners the rapprochement that would eventuate in the Union with Rome owed as much to a "political calculus" as it did to religious conviction.[95] For the Orthodox Romanians, almost universally peasants, the cardinal constant in that calculus was the description of their social and economic status found in the Transylvanian constitution (i.e., the *Approbatae et Compilatae Constitutiones*). Those collections, in spelling out the fundamental rights and obligations of the province's inhabitants, stamped the Romanians with the burdens of serfdom. Under this onus they could never hope to achieve ownership of real property, since that right of citizenship was reserved to their rulers. They had no right whatsoever to the land or its wealth other than what they might earn as hired cultivators. The landed proprietor, having sole power over his estate, could manage it as he chose. He had the prerogative, then, of imposing on the peasantry any regime he cared to inflict. Since only the aristocracy could establish a legal title to the land, the peasantry could be displaced at whim and without any compensation being required. With no standing as a "legal person" the Romanian peasant could not will his goods to another in an unfettered fashion and all too often might have them confiscated by the estate's owner upon his death. Given the economic regime as well as the fact that the individual peasant was subject to denunciation and arrest in an arbitrary fashion, the constitutional order of Transylvania was for the Romanian a series of laws "written with human blood."[96]

The premier Romanian historian of the twentieth century, in attempting to capture this sentiment of desperation, noted that

> the character and situation of the Romanians of Transylvania at the end of the seventeenth century...consisted solely of a mass of serfs who lacked a leadership class, cultivated strata, privileges, rights, or any role above that of simple unfree agricultural laborers.[97]

The "mass of serfs" did not present itself, however, as an undifferentiated conglomeration. Part of the group consisted of serfs proper (*iobagi*), the progeny of those who had originally provided fighting men to the castle and then had been fixed to the soil surrounding it. A second segment of the serf population (*jeleri*), mostly the descendants of more recent immigrants into the area, received land to till as a concession from the lord in return either for cash payment or a specified amount of manual labor. A third division of the rural populace went by the epithet of "neighbors" (*vecini*), enduring a lot very similar to that of the archetypal serf. A final element, the *libertini*, filled niche slightly superior to that of the bulk of the Transylvanian *hoi polloi*. Through the portions of the seventeenth and eighteenth century under study, the type of serfdom experienced by the Romanians differed somewhat from that of the medieval period in the forms of exactions suffered, but certainly not in the discontent generated. One allowance to a more modern, even if not yet nationalistic, world was the use on all Magyar estates of an ethnic Romanian to deal with the servile population. This individual, the "lordling" ("*petit seigneu*r" or "*domnisor*"), represented the lord's economic interests and could pass judgment on the peasant subject to his jurisdiction. In some instances his charge approached that of a counselor ("*span*" in the vernacular of the time) permitting him even to sway the election of the local Orthodox priest.[98]

Otherwise merchants made up the only non-peasant element to be found among the Orthodox of Transylvania. This small bourgeoisie, formed in the course of the seventeenth century, resided in the towns of the province most significantly in Braşov (Hermannstadt) and the Şchei district of Sibiu (Kronstadt) along the southern border. As indicated by the name of the guild located in Braşov, the "Greek Company," a considerable proportion of these middle class merchants came from non-Romanian stock. Being Orthodox they had had no difficulty in assimilating with the local community. Besides their extensive economic activity in the locality (usually as grocers), this exceptional fragment of the Orthodox of Transylvania had commerce with Central Europe and across the Carpathians with the Danubian Principalities. Forming "an aristocracy of wealth, education, and prestige," this modest commercial stratum gave their ethnic cohorts a rudimentary but seminal pattern for a corporate life transcending that of serfs. In addition to their stores and foreign accounts, the merchants of Braşov and Sibiu managed their own courts and administration. They served as legal advisers and in general exercised a substantial autonomy in their personal, religious, and business affairs. Though the mercantile group as a whole would present a common defense of Orthodoxy against all outsiders, the community of Şchei in Kronstadt would achieve particular celebrity in speaking out against Western sectarian pressures. Its contacts with the Eastern

Christians in the Ottoman held Danubian Principalities both paralleled and augmented those of the Transylvanian Orthodox Church.[99]

By the mid-seventeenth century all of these adverse circumstances had become even worse in the Romanians' view. Whether measured on an economic, a political, or religious scale in the 1660s they felt themselves falling into worsening, ultimately unendurable, circumstances. With the final series of armed encounters that first brought the Habsburgs to Transylvania and then resulted in the Peace of Karlowitz's (1699) final eradication of Ottoman sovereignty in the area, the increased hardships compelled them to investigate any and all avenues of escape.[100] Leading that process of discovery by virtue of its position in the village and the increased exactions directed at it especially stood the Romanian priestly caste. These men drawn from and subjected to the same physical deprivations as the peasantry also suffered severe humiliation in comparison with the political and social deportment of their corresponding numbers among the "received" religions. Accompanying the already discussed growing pressure to Calvinize their ritual and flocks, the Romanian priests underwent an intensification of their own dire circumstances. As the Habsburg were forcing their way back into the area in the third quarter of the seventeenth century, Transylvania's Magyar princes imposed on the Romanian priestly families the obligation of inordinately escalated subsidies. Poor to start with, the village priests watched impotently as the additional contributions required by provincial law, their feudal lords, and the Calvinist Superintendent worsened their cultural and material predicaments.[101] Lacking any of the distinctions of nobility, culture, or economic status enjoyed by the priests and ministers of the four "received" faiths, the clergy of the Orthodox Church worked right alongside the peasants in the field. The contrast of sect or of rite, then, translated also into startling dissimilarities in social level. These were all the more resented for their renewed relentlessness and the total absence of adequate spokesmen to address Orthodox complaints. The ill-tutored Romanian priest went from his labor as a farm hand to officiate in the estate's church. Whereas other ethnic groups had a clergy drawn from an aristocratic element, the Transylvanian Orthodox had lost theirs to absorption by the Magyars and the Latin Rite Church of Rome. Again the province's constitution spoke quite eloquently to the rationale behind the deteriorating plight of the Romanian village priests and their aggravated sense of deprivation at the end of the Calvinist period. The three political nations promulgating their own vested interests through the diet declared that

> although the Romanian nation does not belong to either the Estates nor one of the received religions in the fatherland, their presence has only been tolerated here and their church retained for the utility these bring to the state.[102]

Bereft of a noble leadership, obstinately adhering to a non-"received" church, and counted only as guests possessing some utility for the province, the Romanian Orthodox faced a continuation of their unacceptable lot for the foreseeable future.

In reviewing the long list of complaints and aspirations one must keep in mind how restricted a world all of this took place in. For the century and a half that Protestants, primarily Calvinists, monitored the Orthodox Transylvanians, the orbit of these Romanians was limited to family and church. Whatever chance for a public political posture they might have had, and there was all too little likelihood of this without total loss of ethnic identity, they choose rather to cling to the spiritual inheritance of their denomination. This represented the larger, still traditional ancestral order that was cherished above all else.[103] In this context, the Romanian peasantry and its clerical leadership voiced a strenuous opposition to not simply their lack of rights and status, but also more pointedly to the fact that this suppression was engineered by "a different people and a different law" (i.e., "*lege*" or rite). This difference of rite meant that the Orthodox clergy had to bear the increased tax burdens required to finance the rejuvenated Habsburg presence in Transylvania on top of all their other obligations, while the clerics of the four "received" churches were excused precisely because of this constitutional difference. This *cri de coeur* on the part of the Orthodox clergy became, then, a complex amalgam of determination to preserve the outward forms of their spiritual sanctuary in Eastern Christendom and an all too mundane yearning for the perquisites paraded before them by the pastorates of the "received" religions.[104]

The arrival in Transylvania of the troops and administration of Leopold I, then, opened the way for new possibilities for the Romanians and their Orthodox religious culture. Somewhat melodramatically, later Romanian historians have seen the Habsburg acquisition of this strategic outpost against Ottoman Islam as the intervention of "fate." Destiny intervened in the form of a determined Habsburg judiciousness that the recently gained advantage in Transylvania should be translated into more than a tenuous military foothold. The dynasty wanted considerably more purchase than a superficial re-conquest and endemic local antagonism would abide. This the Orthodox Romanians saw a chance finally to escape along a new path, one that would lead away from the insufferable Calvinist influence that had reduced their church to impotency. Protestant pressure and the loss of additional autonomy or dignity might finally be evaded, even if the final destination of the new direction remained nebulous.[105] Approximately a generation, then, after first being broached in the internal memoranda of the Society of Jesus (i.e., in 1664), influential figures in the Habsburg supervision of Transylvania began the process of "converting the schismatics" among the Romanians. The fulfillment of this "cherished idea of the Roman Church" found a forceful and decisively placed advocate in the person of Stefan Apor. In 1696 he became treasurer of the Habsburg administration in Transylvania in which guise he employed the bureaucratic power at his disposal above all to consolidate Leopold's hold over the area. Furthermore, as a Catholic and an inveterate enemy of the Reformed Church he stood out as one of the premier patrons of the Jesuits and their mission. For want of a better weapon with which to attack the Magyars, Apor employed the Romanians and the prospect of their union with Roman Catholicism. Along with the Jesuit missionaries already active in Transylvania by this time, he became a principal player in pursuing this goal of religious amalgamation.[106] In the words of his nephew and secretary, Michailu Cserei, Stephen Apor supported the Jesuits and sought the finalization of the Union with Rome because of keen hatred of the Calvinists, a rancor which in his mind justified the use of "all means and ways." Apor represented, therefore, the leading faction of the "Catholic party" in the province. This religious-political partisanship entailed a direct challenge to the foremost goals of the Calvinist in the sectarian and secular arenas. Most importantly, the Magyar led Calvinist element wanted above else to obtain for Transylvania an independent standing vis-à-vis the new Habsburg regime, one where Leopold would simply be their "protector." Apor and the Roman Catholics who were so sensitive on their minority position in Transylvania were perfectly willing to renounce the region's sovereignty and to opt for a "total union with Hungary." In this fashion they and their realm would be immediately bound to the Catholic majority in Hungary proper.[107] Stephan Apor's interest in the Romanian Orthodox Union with Rome would continue after its beginnings and on more than the political plane. He also stood out as a generous financial supporter, contributing to both the Uniate Church and the apostolate of the Jesuits. One of the more obvious and important examples of his largesse was his underwriting of the Jesuit academy in Cluj (Klausenburg). Despite his being accused by later Orthodox historians of being a "fanatical patron of the Jesuits," this backing of education for the Transylvanians in the end served the interests of all blocs as well as helping to lay the foundation for a modern national-minded intelligentsia. Along with the Emperor, the Cardinal Primate of Hungary, and the chief Jesuit missionary in Transylvania, (i.e., Stephan Baranyi), Stephan Apor, then, emerged as one of the principal policy makers who helped to establish both the fact and character of the link the Orthodox Romanians were about to forge with Rome.[108]

Another significant contributor to the momentum towards the Union with Rome by the Orthodox Transylvanians was the Greek Rite Bishop of Munkacevo (Munkacs), Johann de Camillis. As background to the movement to the south of his diocese he had held in 1690 a synod in Sathmar (Satu-Mare) at which some sixty Romanian Orthodox priests were in attendance. These having declared themselves to be "ready for Union with the Catholic Church," he passed this message and his endorsement upwards through the ecclesiastical hierarchy. At this synod it was also determined that for those priests who did unite with Roman Catholicism their status as serfs was incompatible with their dignity as priests and should not be endured in the future. This tone of "social-political" purpose arose at the earliest possible moment, then, and would persist as both a interminable and determinative characteristic of those Romanians approaching Rome for purposes of integration.[109] In 1696 De Camillis visited Transylvania for with the intent of gauging the receptiveness of the Orthodox there to the appeal of "union" with Rome. Particularly important for understanding how the Romanians decided to become Roman Catholic and how many influential members (secular and religious leaders) later viewed such Uniates are De Camillis' comments on their quality. Although very much dedicated to the reduction of the schism and the creation of a Uniate Church in Transylvania, the bishop pointed out the large number of clerics of unlawful ("*illegitimos*") status or questionable ordination. He further wrote of the abuses he observed on their part, infractions of both church rules and "the law of God." Due to the poverty and lack of schools, he thought it most unlikely that these clerical misdemeanors could be corrected. Since in the eighteenth century Roman Catholic and Protestant alike would criticize the Union with Rome as well as the Romanians' intentions and ability to effect it, De Camillis' notes on the level of priestly education are extremely insightful: "...Romanian priests have no other instruction in matters of faith or in the customs of the church other than they can pick up from each other when visiting nearby homes or churches." Yet, despite this apparently gross ineptitude in the area of faith and morals, the bishop advised his superiors of the desirability of the union and worked for it himself.[110]

Along with the Society of Jesus as an institution, perhaps, the most significant influence on the execution of the Romanian Union and the character it would imprint on the Orthodox consciousness was Leopold Cardinal von Kollonich (1631-1707), Archbishop of Esztergom (Gran) and Roman Catholic Primate of Hungary. As one of the most important men in Leopold I's court at the end of the seventeenth century, he shared the Emperor's appreciation of the Orthodox clergy's vulnerability and susceptibility to material enticements to reunion with Rome. His approach to that clergy, then, was a blend of religion with socio-political inducements. Kollonich came to share a widespread contemporary opinion that, due to the virtually total lack of educational and religious formation among the Romanians, a conversion of conscience could not be looked for. Lacking this theological background necessary for informed judgment, the way to approach the Orthodox of Transylvania and eventually lead them to a more mature moral responsibility was by improving the economic and social level of their priests. Such utilitarianism would be effective and to the point. But disingenuously Kollonich and other Roman Catholics would later severely criticize the depth of priestly culture and quality of commitment of the Uniates, using this acceptance of practical incentives as an excuse for extensive control over the Romanian hierarchy. The author of the first of Leopold's diplomas effecting the Union with Rome for the Transylvanian Orthodox (1699), Kollonich not only sketched out the basis for reunion and the general focus it would have, but also sent a very clear signal of political intent to the Protestant establishment. In accounting for the ensuing bitter resistance and criticisms we should keep in mind that "...the Transylvanian

Estates were convinced that sooner or later the Union of the Romanians would revolutionize the province's constitution."[111]

In his role since 1694 as Prince Primate of Hungary Cardinal Kollonich exercised a degree of control that many saw as autocratic. A pronounced adversary of everything Protestant he and those following his lead would in very short order also be seen by the Romanians as the nemesis of the Eastern Rite (whether Roman Catholic or Orthodox). For eventually his perceived intention would one to strengthen his church by "converting" the Greek Rite Romanians to the Latin Rite. However great their material hardships under Calvinist "protection" and regardless of how ardent the clergy's desire for the privileged position to be garnered by the Union, there is no contemporary demonstration of an "authentic" inclination towards adopting the mores of the Latin Rite. Due to Cardinal Kollonich's attitude towards "schismatics" in general and towards the motivations of the Transylvanian Romanians in particular, many Uniates and Orthodox would during the course of the eighteenth century see the original route laid out by him to be one entailing the ultimate "Catholicization" of their rite. If the Protestant Estates saw the outcome of the Union with Rome as the revolutionary undoing of their elite constitutional status, the Romanians feared the loss of the cultural expression of their Christianity, something quite distinct from any half-understood doctrines they might have to subscribe to.[112]

As a former Knight of Malta Kollonich brought a late seventeenth century crusading spirit not only to the enterprise of undermining the Protestant position in Transylvania, but also to what he wanted in terms of the final expression of the Romanians' Union with Rome. As would gradually appear in more detail, both parities obviously saw this reunion as a "compromise." Indeed they viewed it as a rather prosaic "transaction" through which the Roman Catholics would eventually obtain all that they desired, while the Orthodox could hopefully hide behind the "camouflage of the traditional forms of the Eastern Rite."[113] The Orthodox belief that they "would loose nothing" through this compromise did not assess the Cardinal's zeal correctly, especially where the highly visible matters of their "errors" and rite came into play. Having brought an additional two hundred Orthodox priests into the fold of Eastern Rite Roman Catholicism through the Union of Munkacs (1692), Cardinal Kollonich planned to accomplish this much and more in Transylvania. The educational process begun under his leadership would admit

Romanians youths and priests to what had previously been an exclusively Latin Rite school system. The point of view taken, though, was that Latin and Greek Rite beliefs, and by implication other more culturally determined practices, were (should be) identical.[114] The difference in mentality and sensitivities was perhaps best illustrated by a Jesuit authored tract published under the auspices of the Cardinal. In explaining why and how the Orthodox could return easily to Roman Catholicism, the author stated that the causes of the schism of 1054 "were not sufficient for separation from the Roman Church." Whatever the soundness theologically of this pronouncement it certainly overlooked the Orthodox intellectual position and, more to the point for the uncultured Romanian priests, their apprehensions over form rather than substance. This rather cavalier dismissal of the peasant's adherence to – above all else – what he could see and hear would also be demonstrated in what that Romanian Uniate (as well as his still Orthodox compatriot) would later view as attacks on his cultural core, the Eastern Rite with its unique liturgy. The fact that the same Jesuit pamphlet, dedicated to and approved by Cardinal Kollonich, likewise maintained that "through this Sacred Union, the Greek [Catholic] Church retains all its rites and ceremonies...and liturgy" did not impress him. In fact, the day to day administration of that Union would, in his view, often belie the theoretical assertion of his Rite's supposedly sacrosanct status.[115] Kollonich's views and goals, including Latin Rite dominance and the gradual infiltration of Western church practices into the Uniate ecclesiastical scheme of things, would be as dominant as his overpowering presence in Leopold's territorial administration. Certainly from the very beginning of his impact on the Romanians, their hierarchy, the Metropolitan included, came cap in hand to him. By the fall of 1698 the Romanian bishop, Atanase Anghel, would write Kollonich making his verbal obeisance and acknowledging the Cardinal's intent to engineer a "catholicized" Romanian church. If "In the last twenty-five years of Leopold's reign" there was virtually no matter touching on Hungary or Transylvania not influenced by the Cardinal, then too his structuring of the Romanian Union with Rome gave that church a definitive cast. The reaction to his granting of primacy of place to Latin cultural and liturgical biases would endure for the entire eighteenth century, certainly through the suppression of the Society of Jesus, and in some regards down to the current sensitivities of a newly non-Communist dominated Romanian Orthodox Church to the reconstruction of a Greek Rite hierarchy.[116]

The key to the process of reunion was, obviously, in all sides' views the village priests. From Kollonich's time through the demise of the Jesuits in 1773 and well into the nineteenth century, "For the majority of peasants' sons the priesthood also represented, as it had for centuries, the first step in intellectual and social advancement." In the personality of Cardinal Kollonich and in Leopold's vigorous prosecution of dynastic and religious advantage, the pressures on the Orthodox Transylvanians were intense. With the Lutherans indifferent to the struggle and the Calvinists opposed, the Catholics both offered the greatest apparent prize and appeared the most pressing.[117] Primed by the feudal structure of Transylvania, an edifice which set the Romanian Orthodox off by reason of class and religion as well as economics, the peasant clergy responded in some desperation to Kollonich and the Jesuits. Caught in this embroilment and with decades of oppression by their Protestant "protectors" the Romanians prepared to trade a known problem for one they hoped might be more manageable. They would adjust their faith, though perhaps not in the fashion or to the degree a Kollonich might prefer, to become reunited with Rome. Whether or not this was a "conversion" was probably not clear even to them. But then the view from Vienna and Rome remained equally muddled and hurried.[118]

In the last few years of the seventeenth century Vienna and Cardinal Kollonich surveyed the Transylvanian situation with the design of incorporating the Orthodox Romanians into a larger strategy of ecclesiastical and dynastic augmentation. The Romanians stood ready to receive such approaches. Their priests, almost to a man, lived and worked as bondsmen. By the late 1690s pastors and parishioners in the village could see no way out other than some realignment regarding the "question of [their] religious conscience." Though a pivotal matter, it had to be set off against "the questions of physical emancipation, of personal liberty, and material subsistence for the Church, priests, and people."[119] Caught between the Roman Catholic Habsburgs, newly installed and innovating rulers of the province, and the Protestant proponents of a prejudicial status quo, the Romanian Orthodox felt they had no choice but the Union with Rome. If this made their commitment initially political and only on a secondary level religious, it still encompassed both rationales. Everyone involved recognized the dual lines of preoccupation. True, the Union owed as much "to the politics of Vienna and the utilitarianism of the Romanian clergy" as to pious idealism. But the miserable conditions of the Orthodox in Transylvania, especially those resulting from the increased impositions stemming from the exactions required to fight the Turks once more in 1688, left little time or capacity for the latter.[120] Romanian historians have pointed out in no uncertain terms that the impact of a century and a half of Calvinist "protection" was not simply to produce an Orthodox clergy that was unschooled, but also one "lacking in ideals...and without noble ambitions." Very importantly this was no longer a clergy that had a capacity to resist the incursions of the Reformed Church. Romanian culture, ecclesiastical and secular, had reached a stage of infirmity that left no option but to seek the aid of the Habsburgs on such terms as were offered by that dynasty. With instruction for the clergy at an absolute minimum and nonexistent for the laity, the Romanians could not match the trained and skillful sectarian rhetoricians of any of the Western churches.[121]

In gauging the progress of what some chauvinistic historians have labeled the "catastrophe" of the late seventeenth century, the almost total lack of trained leadership among the Orthodox of Transylvania has to assume a primary focus. If such had been available, this disadvantaged ethnic group would still have had its leaders pitted against men of the stature of Leopold Cardinal von Kollonich and the institution of the Calvinist Superintendent. This would not have been a equal match even for most ecclesiastics receiving considerable more instruction than was the Romanian experience in these conditions. On a slightly more estimable scale the Romanians' Union with Rome can also be viewed as a last urgent attempt "to regain their church and national rights." With five generations experience with the Calvinists and nothing good or new to be expected from that quarter, the Catholic Habsburgs at least proffered an alternative. That that other road was hedged in by religious restrictions and hazards for the liturgy represented nothing novel. After all the Superintendent maintained that a *de facto* (i.e., "administrative union") already existed between his church and that of the Romanians. Whatever the Catholic connection might portend, it at least presented the possibility of acquiring those privileges pertaining to class and "received" religions which the Calvinists had already reneged on.[122]

"Just as the Romanian people are not received in Transylvania, so too they are everywhere to be tolerated only as long as it pleases the princes and the state." This segment of the province's constitution forever segregated the Orthodox from the rest of the population. But to understand fully their dilemma the implication of the Latin phrase used to indicate their dependence on the goodwill of others has to be grasped also. They were to be tolerated to the extent of the forbearance ("*ad beneplacitum*") of the ruling personages and estates. Beyond mere inferiority and contempt, however, was the second meaning; namely, that they can remain in what they considered their homeland "only as long as…decided upon." "Tolerated" not "received" carried the connotation of possible eviction, since they had no birthright or citizenship to guarantee their tenure in Transylvania.[123] Beckoning to the Romanian clergy and its hierarchy, then, was the extraordinary prospect of obtaining the status and privileges of the Roman Catholic priesthood. Every village priest would thereby become a member of the nobility with all the perquisites that flowed therefrom. For their part, the bishops and abbots would be counted among the province's leading element having an impact on politics and the passage of legislation through the diet. And, of course, this advance to the aristocracy would elevate the social and material conditions of the clergy "to an uncommon degree."[124] In addition to what such *ennoblissement* might do for the individual, it would also reverse a centuries old process by which the Romanians had lost all participation in the "Corporation of the Nobility" ("*Universitas nobilium*"). For in the course of the fifteenth century, antedating by more than a century the inception of Calvinist preponderance over the Orthodox, the Romanians lost both their nobility to a gradual Magyarization and the status of equality that they had attained by 1400. By the mid-point of that century the remaining Romanians found themselves lumped together with all other peasants and stigmatized as nothing more than a "tolerated" people. Periodic and massive jacqueries, beginning with that of the "Brotherly Alliance" in 1437 and extending to one at the end of the century in 1784, helped cement the opposition of the nobility and freeze the Romanian peasantry in its disadvantaged state.[125]

This state of mind helping to predispose the Orthodox Romanians towards the Union with Rome also aided in the generation of the most persistent of the allegations against their bona fides; namely, that they "converted" only for the material benefits accorded them. As was quite plain by this juncture, and even allowing for devout motivations as well, the sharp edge of Romanian desire focused on the here and now, on the "utilitarian." Freedom from feudal dues and the chance for a higher culture through education blurred the edges of any theological doubts that the few among them might have had.[126] To be fair as well as accurate in one's evaluations, the intellectual state of these men must likewise be remembered. For the vast majority the doctrinal judgments behind some of what they were asked to accept to become Uniates simply did not impinge on their concrete world of religion or life. The "*filioque*" clause and other recondite references remained for them merely a matter of words which they did not necessarily perceive as having any bearing whatsoever on their traditional worship. To accuse them, then, of not being careful theologians or of complex intent has been the urbane thing to do from the very beginning of the Union continuing through the Jesuit period and into the modern world. One eighteenth century opponent of the Union aspired to have it both ways, beginning his condemnation with an aside about "a rustic folk" and then excoriating the priests for profiteering from that ecclesiastical alliance.[127] Even if they had appreciated the nature and vehemence of this criticism, it would certainly have left them cold not being particular germane to the decision to be made. Had they and their predecessors not spent the past several generations being influence by outside (e.g., Magyar) sources? They had for a long period been under the sway of factors more foreign to their "Latin ethnic" heritage than the Roman Union might turn out to be. For many becoming Uniate meant "liberation," indeed as a "providential" salvation, from the Calvinist pressures described earlier.[128]

In tracing the historical course of Habsburg and Jesuit influence on the Romanians of Transylvania, the state of mind of those conducting the negotiations and about to becoming Uniates assumed paramount importance. For many of these men the Union with Rome was accepted as the least of many possible perils, as "an inevitable evil, but one delivering them from yet another evil." If considerable debate would eventuate over whether the Roman Catholics honored their commitment to a more privileged rank for the Romanians than had the Calvinists, even the staunchest of modern nationalistic historians conceded that this Union opened up to the Uniates the Western world of education and the Enlightenment. From a modern perspective it led to a "revolutionary...reaffirmation of [the Romanians'] Latinity."[129] Though obviously anxious to obtain the better treatment accorded the clergy of the Latin Rite Roman Catholic Church, the future Uniates likewise fell prey to:

> an appeal...in the first place made to national feeling, which had been stirred by the language questions. ...Should the descendants of the Roman legions of Trajan, who alone preserved their Roman language and had it as their Church language in spite of all Slav and Greek influences – should they alone not belong to the Roman Church, which was using their Latin sister language in the Liturgy?[130]

Caught as they were, then, in the transition from "Protestant Constitutionalism" to "Catholic Absolutism" the Union with Rome seemed to offer many of the material benefits that had eluded them under the Calvinist dispensation. At the same time it purportedly embraced the position "that the rite should be maintained" and that their Church "should be free of the direct influence of Latin church dignitaries."[131] These last two would hardly have been base incentives and would have solved major problems stemming from the Reformed Church's impact, if they had been proven to be true in the course of the eighteenth century. From the very start of the Union in 1697 there were misunderstandings on both sides. From the Uniate point of view the position of their Rite and the autonomy of their hierarchy were challenged despite all the initial promises and disclaimers.

II
Rome and Ethnic Schism

Twenty-seven years after the first Jesuit report on the prospects for establishing a Greek Rite Roman Catholic Church among the Transylvanian Romanians the Society's *Annual Letters* for 1691 returned even more optimistically to the same topic. In the words of a later editor, the Jesuit intelligence summary for that year forecast a "massive return to doctrinal unity." The Jesuit missionary resident in Alba-Iulia, Paul Ladislaus Baranyi, described for his Order and superiors what he evaluated as a Romanian predisposition to reunion with Rome.[1] The preparatory setting for such a Union with Rome had already been sketched out by the Greek Rite Bishop of Munkacs, Johann de Camillis. This prelate, who had been brought to the scene by the personal intervention of Cardinal Kollonich, arrived in northern Transylvania in 1689 and in 1690 met in synod (at Satu Mare) with Romanian Orthodox priests wishing to discuss reunion. In this environment the "social-political" tone of the rapprochement, or perhaps more exactly the negotiations, between Kollonich's representatives and those of the Orthodox was set. This note of religion *cum* personal advantage would continue through the formative phase of the Union. It would also help determine the mutual appreciation and relationship between the Uniates once they took their oath to Rome and the Latin Rite officials who oversaw that crucial event in Romanian history. By 1697, then, Cardinal Kollonich found himself in the position to begin the serious work of "re-Catholicizing" the lands regained from the Moslem Ottomans. His twofold intent was to lay a better foundation in the region for the exercise of the Emperor's power as well as for the reestablishment of a fully formed and functioning Roman Catholic hierarchy. The essential prerequisite for this goals, the weakening of the Protestant political position in Transylvania, could be attained only by securing the largest possible number of Romanian Orthodox adherents to a Union with Rome.[2]

The chosen instrument for Kollonich's project of simultaneously multiplying the Catholic presence in Transylvania and assuring the Emperor's will there was the Society of Jesus. His choice was dictated not only by the evident quality and training of the members of that Order, but also by the pattern already set for its use by Leopold himself.[3] In the persons of two of its most capable members, Paul Ladislaus Baranyi and Gabriel Hevenesi, the Jesuit Order provided the Primate with a cadre of missionaries whose enduring impact on the Romanians would be second only to his own. While Hevenesi's impact was mainly felt in his role as a Jesuit superior and as a major factor at court in facilitating the diplomatic aspects of the Union, Baranyi in his role as pastor in Alba-Iulia interacted in an immediate and direct fashion with the Orthodox clergy.[4] Between 1692 and 1697, acting in the context of Cardinal Kollonich's and the Papal Nuncio's (Cardinal Buonvisi) request that the Emperor encourage this predisposition to Union, Baranyi spent his time in private, often secret, conversations with the Orthodox bishop and the protopopes under his jurisdiction. These archpriests, supervising as they did several Romanian parishes, would represent the views and wishes of their clergy and parishioners at any future synod. The Jesuits and the Catholic hierarchy they served saw the impact of Baranyi as one that "deepened a climate conducive to reunion and one that made the approach [of the Romanians] to Catholicism easier." Certainly in the Catholic view, contemporary and later, Paul Baranyi stood out as the "moral author of the union [with Rome]."[5]

Baranyi's religious influence as well as the more political leverage of Kollonich and Leopold, began to manifest themselves in events in 1697. Between that year and the early years of the eighteenth century a sizable portion of the Orthodox Romanians of Transylvania would accept the leadership of Rome. Unfortunately, for the goals of all the factions involved and as the genesis of a rather distressing historiographical dispute over highly disputed statistics, the "conversion" of the Orthodox was only partial. Equally perturbing would be the questioning by Catholic, Orthodox, Protestant, and even some among the Uniates themselves of the sincerity and legal proprieties relating to the Union with Rome. By the year in question the attractiveness of the promises of improved status for the Orthodox priests, hints that were hardly concealed or presented as anything other than incentives to action, bore fruit. As pressing as the political and economic disparities seemed, though, the "confessional" character of the disabilities the Romanians lived under had by then assumed the greatest urgency.[6]

On the Metropolitan throne of the Transylvanian Orthodox at that time was Teofil (born Toma Szeremi of Teius and taking his clerical name at the name of his vows as a monk of the Order of St. Basil), the sixteenth individual to hold that distinction. Confirmed by the Calvinist Superintendent and secular authorities in the same year (1692) that Baranyi began his apostolate of private evangelizations among the Romanian hierarchy, the new bishop came to his see at a most inauspicious time for the fortunes of his church and people. Calling these hard times would be both too trite and to belittle the adverse factors facing the Romanian church leader. At this point it appeared that the only road to "de-Calvinization," indeed to "de-Magyarization," lead through Rome.[7] Perhaps, nothing brings this predicament of both the Orthodox Metropolitan and of the Romanian population in general home more forcefully than the circumstances under which Teofil received his position as hierarch. As was the custom at the time, he was consecrated in Bucharest on September 13, 1693. Besides the historic and cultural reasons for this relationship with the Danubian Principalities, the lone remaining Orthodox hierarch in Transylvania had since 1680 been subject to the Metropolitan in Bucharest as a dependent suffragan bishop. Though variously termed a "metropolitan" or an "archbishop," by this date the post Teofil was filling in Alba-Iulia (Belgrad) was "canonically" only a episcopate. Whatever the extent of his authority, that of bishop or something more elevated, the titles remained important and would serve as the focus for considerable discord once the Union with Rome was finalized. The fact that he made that journey and for that purpose, however, the Calvinist decided. Despite being reassured by his noble ancestry, rather than the peasant lineage to be found in most Romanian families, the Calvinist authorities still insisted on guarantees as to his future conduct.[8]

The Magyar representative of the Viennese government, acting in a time honored fashion, required of the candidate for the metropolitan office that he agree to a long list of stipulations. In his capacity as Governor of Transylvania, George Banffi of Losoncz, demanded an oath of office of Teofil that would have rendered the Orthodox Church even more like the Reformed. After one hundred and fifty years of Calvinist encroachments, the privileged orders decided to interfere to a greater extent and on a more remorseless basis than ever before. If nothing before had had the effect of bringing home the ultimate aims of the those who spoke through the Superintendent, this charge of Banffi's did so in unequivocal terms. Teofil and the Romanians after this could only turn to the Emperor, whatever demands he and the Roman Catholics might make, as an escape. What amounted to "administrative persecutions" executed by the Romanians' religious and ethnic adversaries led in the view of many, both contemporaries and later commentators, to a sense "of great desperation" on the part of Teofil and others.[9] For a man like the candidate for the metropolitan's office, the provisos under which he assumed his post emphasized as nothing else could the lack of power in the bishop's hands by the 1690s. Even before experiencing the perhaps overstated "administrative persecutions" Teofil and his predecessors had to committed blindly to preemptive restrictions. And they were well aware of the competing nature of not only the Calvinists but also of other Orthodox of different ethnic extractions. They seem to stand alone and undefended before a host of enmities.[10]

Banffi, in his confirmation decree of 1692, obliged Teofil to subscribe to nineteen separate items in the oath constraining him as Metropolitan of the Romanians. This list of conditions for Teofil's installation seemingly aimed at leaving as little as possible to the Romanian churchman's discretion, regulating his administration to the minutest conceivable degree. In addition to addressing such major and expected issues as the necessity to teach the Reformed Catechism and how the annual synod of the Orthodox Church was to be run, Banffi's regulations covered a multitude of lesser agenda. Teofil was instructed to, and had to pledge his word to, such diverse requirements as the use of the vernacular in services, how an Orthodox baptism should be conducted, the norms for excommunication, and the filling of church offices. If this degree of management of Orthodox affairs were not sufficient, the prescriptions for the new Metropolitan went on to include details of church decoration (e.g., use of statues and crucifixes), the proclamation of marriage bands, the intricacies of divorce, the status of converts, and the exclusion of Magyars in all but the most unusual of cases from Orthodox ceremonies. In this all encompassing effort at control, the Magyar Governor of Transylvania also mandated the use of Latin should any Romanian youths receive an education, the printing of books in the native language, the proper approach to veneration of the saints, and the eradication of all superstitions associated with burial services. All of these injunctions were issued to insure the maintenance of "correct doctrine" might be insured. And above all else, these conditions which

Teofil now committed himself and the Romanian Orthodox Church to would guarantee that "the obligation to conserve the tranquility" of Transylvania might be met.[11] Whatever they might do, keep the peace included, they certainly reiterated the cramping Calvinist control over the Romanian hierarchy and left Teofil as Metropolitan more dependent than ever on the Superintendent. For interestingly enough given the dependence of Transylvania on the Habsburgs, Banffi promulgated these traditional requirements not in Leopold's name, but in his own as a prince and as "a principle member of the Reformed Calvinist Church."

Teofil's and the Orthodox Church's place in the province's political as well as religious pecking order received confirmation through his having to take the oath to the Calvinist Superintendent. Having watched the Roman Catholic approach to his predecessor, Metropolitan Varlaam, Teofil was all the more primed by this list of strictures to listen to Baranyi and the other Jesuits now entering Transylvania. Despite being severely criticized for following up on the tentatives regarding union with Rome begun under Varlaam, Teofil had far more substantial reasons than simply the imputed and perhaps factual desire for the "transitory goods of this life." Even if he ended up acting to bring his church into the orbit of Rome for "personal reasons," the terms of his installment clearly demonstrate the continuing and burgeoning character of Calvinist pressures. If the Union would allow the Habsburg to subvert the political position of an entrenched Calvinist aristocracy, it would likewise permit Teofil to escape from the type of dominance illuminated by Banffi's prescriptions and from the power of "an intolerant, Calvinist Magyar nobility."[12] Transcending the Metropolitan's "personal reasons" and also the widespread desire of the Orthodox clergy for equality with the ministers of the "four received" religions stood the logic behind Banffi's nineteen points. The politics of religion in Transylvania at the end of the seventeenth century obliged him to include in the conditions imposed on Teofil the largest possible measure of freedom for the conversion of individual Romanians to Calvinism. At the same time, he as a representative of the privileged estates intended that there should be no alteration in the their corporate identity as merely "tolerated"; namely, permanent exclusion from the ranks of the constitutionally sanctioned. The other patent objective of these customary Calvinist impositions on a candidate for the Romanian Metropolitanate resided in a reinvigorated "tendency…to transmute Romanian Orthodoxy...into a satellite church...."[13] The continuing process of canonical, ceremonial, and structural scrutiny which would be furthered by the specifications forced upon Teofil promised a yet greater approximation of the Reformed Church norms among the Romanian Orthodox. "Fear of Protestantism and need of protection caused the Orthodox to contemplate union": whatever supplementary motivations, base or noble, Teofil and the other Orthodox clerics may have entertained built on this pivotal and seasoned foundation. His personal problems and ambitions obviously played a role, but his approach to the Catholic mien could be fully justified on purely ecclesiastical and ethnic grounds.[14]

With the persuasion and assistance of Paul Ladislaus Baranyi of the Society of Jesus, then, Metropolitan Teofil began in 1696 the move towards Rome that would result in a process of Union in the next year. Baranyi's cultivation of the Romanian clergy, especially their bishop, resulted in the orchestrated petition for Union with the Papal See. An application which, of course, the Emperor and his Primate had been anxiously awaiting.[15] An eighteenth century Calvinist gloss on Teofil's "personal reasons" for embracing Rome detailed a series of charges against the Metropolitan from which the Jesuit Baranyi supposedly promised to protect him. Among these accusations the Protestant minister leveled at the Romanian were that he had compromised himself by "drunkenness, ... violation of fast days, ... infractions against the laws and canons of the Greek Church, ... and fornication." The Reformed Church's analysis, then, centered on the charge that the Orthodox under Teofil "had been drawn away...by various contrivances." The Metropolitan, being "desperate, ... sought refugee" among the Roman Catholics. Interestingly, given the later charges of disingenuousness that the Protestants would direct against the Union with Rome, this Enlightenment Calvinist conceded Teofil the honesty of having dealt forthrightly with his Jesuit contacts. According to this version, the Metropolitan informed them that Baranyi's proposal of a *quid pro quo* (i.e., "protection, ... if the whole Romanian nation joined the Union with the Roman Catholic Church...") was "impossible." This critical, if not hostile source, also substantiated the subsequent Uniate stance that they agreed only to something approximating the Four Points as outlined at Florence, not the more multifarious and culturally biased precepts laid down by Kollonich's ecclesiastical bureaucracy. In this regard, the Protestant reported that Teofil agreed simply to substitute the Pope for the Patriarch in Constantinople as the head of the church, to administer the Eucharist only under one species, to observe certain rules of abstinence, and finally not to allow future priests to have wives after the Orthodox custom. Otherwise, this early source reports Baranyi suggesting and Teofil accepting that, the "religion of the Greek Church...would not be disturbed." With this preliminary understanding worked out to both sides' satisfaction, "Teofil responded that he would readily assent" to the Union with Rome.[16]

1697 marked the year that the process of the Union with Rome formally began for the Romanian Orthodox of Transylvania. Though the maneuvers would be drawn out for some four years, due to the nature of the negotiations and a change in the occupant of the Metropolitanate, all parties recognized from its inauguration what was at stake. At a meeting in Vienna in 1697 with the Catholic proponents of the Union, the prominent Transylvanian nobleman Miklos Bethlen described the move to integrate the Orthodox within the Roman Church as "being directed against the three religions of Transylvania." Along with Governor George Banffi he maintained that what Stefan Apor and the Jesuits were attempting amounted to "an especially forceful attack on the Calvinist religion."[17] In this view, of course, they had correctly gauged the situation. The Roman Catholic-Habsburg cooperation regarding the Romanian Union fitted nicely into the long term dynastic effort to undermine Magyar political power in the region. And, of course, it would give them the stage from which to proclaim the official verdict that with the complete return of the Romanians to Rome Roman Catholics then constituted a "majority" in Transylvania. As happen repeatedly such statistics, whether applied to Habsburg political agenda or to the comprehensiveness of Romanian participation in the Union, were at best non-modern in their methodology and quite often simply a statement of preference as to how a given party would like to interpret reality.[18]

By the year of the initial synod (1697) formally dealing with the Union of the Orthodox Romanians with Rome, then, the impositions of the Calvinist Superintendent as summarized in Teofil's conditions for appointment gave eloquent support to the Catholic case; namely, that "only through Union with the Church of Rome could the true faith [i.e., the Romanian "law" or "*lege*"] be saved from the Calvinist danger." This litany struck a particularly responsive cord among the clergy the Jesuit were addressing, finding there willing recipients of Roman

Catholic proselytism. As with their Metropolitan so too the priests and protopopes had their "personal reasons" (e.g., "to escape the status of a serf") for acquiescing in the Jesuit sponsored ecclesiastical merger. The added factor of having one of the more talented and resolute members of the Society of Jesus on the scene in the person of Baranyi provided the decisive factor. Even hostile sources consistently reported his unique influence on the upper clergy and on the final course of events culminating in the definitive expression of the Union by the first decade of the eighteenth century.[19] The contemporary Jesuit history from the residence in Alba-Iulia where Baranyi was stationed contained a yet more glowing evaluation of the situation and the priest's impact on the development of Orthodox-Roman Catholic bonds. Besides detailing a partiality for Union with Rome on the part of the Orthodox leadership, this Jesuit chronicle likewise characterized the link between the Metropolitan Teofil and Baranyi as being that of close associates. Clearly all the major players in this ecclesiastical-political arena, Protestant and Orthodox and Catholic, perceived the role of the Society of Jesus as being a major, if not principal, determinant in the ultimate resolution of this matter. For their part, the Orthodox soon to be Uniates would also over the next three generations see in the Jesuits a paramount sculptor in the etching out of the church's administrative and liturgical life.[20]

Under these pressures and with all these concerns to be resolved, Metropolitan Teofil decided in 1696 to meet in Alba-Iulia in February of 1697 for the purpose of discussing a "return to the Roman Church." The bishop and the twelve archdeacons assisting him in Alba-Iulia, though eager to accomplish their "personal reasons" for the Union, did not come to this stage without preparation or calculated aforethought. To understand their participation in the process carried out between this point and 1701 as well as the criticisms forthcoming from Catholics of the Latin and Greek rites afterwards, one must be apprised of the provisos they set forth initially. However, ignorant and unskilled they might have been, they did have a most definite bargaining position from which they were not willing to deviate. As the *quid pro quo* for the Union with Rome, Teofil and the archdeacons requested of Leopold the satisfaction of three stipulations. First of all, both ordinary clergy and the monks of the Order of St. Basil had to enjoy every advantage and right not only of Catholic priests, but likewise any others that the Calvinist, Lutheran, or Unitarian ministers might possess. Secondly, every Uniate parish priest should have a rectory in the village that he served. Finally, in their new ecclesiastical structure in contrast to the Protestant they had been exposed to since the mid-sixteenth century, the bishop alone should possess the authority to control the clergy. They specifically wanted to exclude lay intervention from the relationship of the Metropolitan and the local pastors. The appropriate link of clergy and hierarch was to be one of clear cut dependence and lines of authority. Obviously the meddling of the Calvinist Superintendent had left a caustic impression which the prospective Uniates did not wish to see replicated in their new ecclesiastical environment. Such oversight, if not outright tutelage, had galled them in its Calvinist form and would do so again when it reappeared unexpectedly in a "jesuitical" guise.[21]

In this Synod of 1697 preparatory to the initial act of Union, Bishop Teofil summarized for his archdeacons the bad conditions under which he and his predecessors in the Metropolitanate had had to operate under. Most especially he emphasized the inroads made by the Reformed Church and the overweening position attained by the Calvinist Superintendent in their Orthodox Church. In the light of what they intended to escape from, the representatives of the Orthodox clergy of Transylvania along with their bishop likewise discussed the impending Union with Rome in the context of dangers to their rite. Having experienced considerable travail in this regard under the Superintendent, they now specified that in no way was their Eastern Rite and the attendant church discipline to be altered. The move to become Eastern Rite Roman Catholics should not bring in its wake modifications in the canonical basis or liturgical expression of their church. Though agreeing to the Union, these Orthodox clerics prefaced their compact with several narrative prescriptions in the hope that their intent would not be misunderstood or misconstrued. While willing to accept the Four Points as established at Florence, they adamantly maintained that these were not to be added to "under any pretext." They also reiterated their claim to be full fledged citizens (i.e., "*patriae filii recepti*") rather than simply "tolerated" as well as to enjoy the full range of benefits accruing to the Latin Rite clergy.[22]

In the declaration flowing from this discussion and the decision to accept the Jesuit proposed Union with Rome Teofil and the archdeacons listed four binding criteria by which to judge their commitment. They promised to "embrace and observe" only the Florentine Four Points, which were not to be interpreted to mean anything further in the way of endorsing the customs of the Latin Rite. They expected to receive any and all preferments allowed the Latin Rite clergy. Romanians were to gain access to Roman Catholic schools and all types of employment without being subject to any prejudice. Finally, the financial needs of the Uniate Archbishop and his household were to be guaranteed.[23] Although a significant number of Uniate youths would indeed be educated by the Jesuits both at home and abroad (including Vienna and Rome), the other three stipulations framing Teofil's and his clergy's acceptance of the Union with Rome would become issues bitterly contended in the eighteenth century. The educational foundation laid for a Romanian intelligentsia and ultimately for a nationalist ideology tinged by "Latinism" would not suffice for the disappointment surrounding the failure to realize those other three demands. Teofil's exposition in favor of the link with Rome presumed both an attachment to the Eastern Rite as the visual crux of his flock's faith as well as an intense dislike of all things Magyar. In procuring the archdeacon's support, then, he encountered no resistance on the doctrinal level. Dogma *per se* remained unintelligible for these men and left them quite unconcerned. What did move them and their parishioners, and would continue to agitate the Uniate and Orthodox worlds from this point on, was the status of the Eastern Rite. Whatever these twelve archdeacons thought they had committed themselves and their church to in 1697 they certainly had resolved to maintain the entire traditional structure of their church. Where religious feasts, the church calendar, vestments, law, or the liturgy came into play, they had contemplated no changes and wished none. An almost "instinctive mistrust" compounded by Calvinist catechization moved them to couch their approach to Rome in such careful terms. Given the interpretation that would later be put on their adherence to Rome and the almost cavalier disregard of their stipulations regarding the preservation of their rite, their foreboding had ample and persistent vindication.[24]

In the third and final session of the Synod of 1697 Teofil and his clergy took an oath to reunite with Roman Catholic Church on the basis of the Four Points and sought from Emperor Leopold the benefits already detailed. Adding to the controversy stemming from this first phase of the maneuver towards Rome the Latin original and subsequent Romanian renderings have the Metropolitan and all his clergy ("*clerus universus*") accepting the Union and the Four Points upon which it was built.[25] Considerable debate would result in the development of the

Uniate Church in the eighteenth century and in the even more partisan atmosphere of the nationalistic modern world over the informed, if not "unanimous," quality of this vote. Even greater rancor and consternation resulted from the comprehensiveness of this claim to represent the entirety of the clergy. However, given the frequent reiteration of their fundamental negotiating stance and the furor that would develop in the eighteenth century, there can be no doubt that Teofil and the Synod adopted the Four Points alone, and certainly not the Tridentine Mass and all the cultural baggage of the Counter-Reformation in the Latin West. Whether they could be deemed skilled theologians or even adequate masters of the Latin of the texts employed, the Orthodox Romanians of Transylvania unquestionably avowed their determination on the cultural-religious issue of preserving the Eastern Rite in the future Uniate Church. Just as obviously they expressed their plan to limit their endorsement of things Roman to the Four Points as laid out in the Bull of Union (*Bulla Unionis*) of July 6, 1439. If as charged later by many on all sides the Orthodox delegates at this Synod of Union did not possess the linguistic skills or dogmatic training to plum the depths of their commitment, they undeniably understood enough to delimit what they were willing to give up. On the basis of the Bull issued by the Council of Florence they accepted the Latin definition of the Trinity in the *filioque* clause, the reality of purgatory, the Pope as supreme teacher and administrative head of the united church, and the cultural component of using only unleavened bread in the Eucharistic service. As far as the promulgated position of Rome, this was sufficient. As far as the Romanians now Uniates were concerned, this was the outermost marches of their willingness to accommodate Western cultural biases or doctrinal preferences.[26]

Since the Western estimation of the nature of the Uniate obligation (at least, as demonstrated by both ecclesiastical and secular officials of the Habsburg dynasty) came to encompass considerably more than the Four Points, the dispatch with which this Union was achieved must be stressed. In the debate leading up to the Synod of 1697 Roman Catholic agents of the Habsburg administration as well as of the organized Church indicated their accurate perception of the almost total lack of education and formal religious instruction among the Romanian Orthodox. To alter this situation sufficiently to prepare the general population for an informed conversion would have taken a measure of time and effort that the Viennese dynasty could not afford to allocate to itself. Rather than such a slow and yet unsure process, the decision was made to proceed along the route of offering "material prerogatives" first to gain the clergy, and then perhaps the people, for a Union with Rome.[27] Reinforcing this position, of course, stood Cardinal Kollonich's success with the 1692 Union of the Ruthenes with Rome. Built upon the Jesuit evaluation that the doctrinal contents of Orthodox and Roman Catholicism possessed a virtual identity ("*...die bis auf geringe Abweichungen fast durchgangige Gleichheit der griechisch-orientalischen und romischen Glaubenslehre....*"), a similarly ill-trained group of clerics had become Uniates. Once reunion became a fact, though, the Four Points served only as a foundation for further dogmatic demands, while the cultural ingredients of rite assumed a far more crucial guise in the mind of the Latin Rite Roman Catholics, a role that stood diametrically opposed to the initial and abiding Romanian position. Unfortunately, the Latin Rite representatives displayed a penchant for downplaying theological differences and later insisting on their significance, for superficially acquiescing in the Romanian attachment to the cultural embossed liturgical tradition of the Eastern Rite, that would haunt the Transylvanian Uniate Church from its inception to the present. This approach received a characteristic Latin endorsement by a twentieth century Jesuit historian who wrote that "The dogmatic questions [i.e., for a Union between Orthodox and Roman Catholic] created no difficulty" ("*Die dogmatischen Fragen machten keine Schwierigkeiten.*"). Politically, perhaps, they did not. For ease and speed of culmination, obviously they could only hinder the endeavor. But the Latin Rite would very shortly see the Uniates as the equivalent of "rice Christians," while the Uniates would feel cozened. They had not anticipated further exactions for the privilege of Union with Rome. And they had most insistently repudiated any that might adulterate the character and expression of the Eastern Rite church services. If the Romanian Uniates as later charged had been ignorant and feckless, their Latin Rite mentors exhibited a glibness and haste that tainted the Union. This combination of cultural-jurisdictional factors would serve from the very beginning as a fecund source of factional and subsequently nationalistic disputes between spokesmen for Roman Catholicism and Orthodoxy.[28]

That these issues of culture and rite had been glossed over and would return to plague the Romanian Union with Rome could not have been missed by the Latin Rite emissaries who dealt with Teofil. For besides the Romanians own insistence on these factors and the example of the Union of Munkacs only a few years prior, they also had the pattern provided by the sixteenth century Union of Brest-Litovsk. In 1594 a Ukrainian-Ruthenian Uniate Church came into existence, one which like that of Munkacs later served as a prototype for the Romanian version. Most prominently delineated in that settlement was the express understanding "...that the rite should be maintained and that the Uniate Church should be free from the direct interference of Latin church dignitaries...." Even if the negotiations with Apor and Baranyi begun under Teofil are only seen as the commencement of a more drawn out process of reunion with Rome, it still remains quite clear that this "tentative" initiative had as one of its declared, non-negotiable preconditions the inviolate status of the Eastern Rite. Words on documents, even formerly bitterly disputed words such as "*filioque*," could be tolerated if the patina of customary church culture remained inviolate.[29] Teofil's oath to the Union as taken before the Jesuit Baranyi in Alba-Iulia, while including the Four Points and the material advantages to be forthcoming, did not mention rite in either the Latin or Romanian texts. But there can be no doubting this framework of overriding allegiance the legacy of Eastern Rite ecclesiastical culture. The only possible wedge by which the unwelcome ritual-cultural influence of later times might be inferred would be the coda added by Teofil to the Four Points; namely, that the Romanians agreed "...to receive, affirm, and believe everything which the Holy Mother Roman Catholic Church receives, affirms, and believes." This adamantine obstinacy in rejecting any and all substitutions of Latin Rite mores for Eastern traditions stands out not merely as the most consistent ethnic based position on the subject, but also that of the major Romanian historians, even those educated as a result of the promised access to Latin Rite schooling.[30]

Since the somewhat acrimonious disputation carried on between 1697 and 1701 by the various Transylvanian denominations as to whether or not Teofil truly "reunited" with Rome must be traced, the Vatican's appraisal can provide some much needed perspective. The archives of the Congregation for the Propagation of the Faith in Rome contain a document from the summer of 1697 maintaining that the Romanian Uniates (formerly Orthodox "schismatics") had "converted" once Teofil subscribed to the "customary [or "ordinary"] profession of faith." It also repeats the rather optimistic claim that the bishop "with all his clergy" had made this transition. Though where the generality of the Transylvanian Romanians were concerned this bulletin displayed far greater hesitation, noting merely that "many other thousands of persons" had accepted the Catholic faith. It did not, as more partisan observers in the area would do, claim that the entire nation could now be considered Uniate. Noteworthy also regarding Rome's viewpoint the "customary [or "ordinary"] profession of faith" required to become Roman Catholic found adequate satisfaction in a rather prosaic acceptance of the Four Points by the Romanians. Rome did not exact, as those closer to the scene would shortly do, a more elaborate dogmatic litmus test or extensive acculturation to Western ecclesiastical traditions.[31]

The Jesuit history for the events of 1697, written at their residence in Alba-Iulia, specifically stated that the Romanians had become Catholic by accepting only "the Four Points of the Council of Florence." This first hand, contemporary witness to the mentality and actual progress of the negotiations leading to the Union with Rome likewise substantiated the newly coined Uniates assertion that they were promised "the integrity and purity of the Greek Rite." This same source continued on to explicate the avowal that all of Teofil's clergy had joined him in this passage to Roman Catholicism. The Society of Jesus' interpretation of the actions of the 1697 General Synod (i.e., "*sobor mare*") centered on the canonical principle that that body had "legitimately represented" all of the Romanian Orthodox clergy in Transylvania. "Juridically," therefore, it could be inferred that the entirety of the schismatic ecclesiastical structure in the province had embraced the Union with Rome. Such a legalism might prevail in a structured dispute, but in this environment it could, and did, lead to endless debates and indignation which have persisted into the twenty-first century.[32] Indeed, some such doubts seem to have entered the minds of the sponsors of the Synod of reunion almost immediately. At the conclusion of that meeting Teofil and the archdeacons sent a petition by way of Baranyi to Cardinal Kollonich. In that missive they "humbly asked that all the points in their former letters" (i.e., the privileges of the Roman Catholic clergy, the integrity of the Eastern Rite, and their acceptance of the Four Points) be expeditiously and formally recognized. In short, they sought ratification of their status as full fledged Catholics of the Eastern Rite of that singular basis. At the same time, however, as if carefully preparing for an expected onslaught of criticism, this entreaty was introduced by a further rationale for asserting the adherence of "the whole clergy." This additional exculpation reinvoked the theme of synodal legitimacy, going on to profess that "…even the absent must be considered to have juridically consented…" to the Union with Rome.[33] While placating the canon lawyers, such cramped reasoning found something less than a compliant reception in the ethnic and denominational turmoil resulting from the Union. It also laid the foundation for extensive review and repudiation on nationalistic grounds in the last three centuries, at which time such nicety of argumentation came to be seen as at least tendentious and more often as blatantly self-serving. While allowing the Union's mentors the equivalent of a public relations bolt hole, this ploy did not serve its intended purposes of deflecting procedural criticism or sapping the emotional reaction to Western encroachment. It did substantiate subsequent allegations of disingenuousness.

The emergence and then apparent success of this Habsburg underwritten Union with Rome alarmed the Calvinists, threatening as it did their overall predominance in Transylvania. Throughout this contest for the political weight, if not minds, of the Romanian Orthodox the Reformed Church took the position that they had been dragged away from the fold through the use of force. Venting no little spleen the Calvinists proclaimed that the Union was the product of "various deceitful stratagems" on the part of the Roman Catholics. In seeking to have the Emperor nullify the Romanian Union with Rome the Calvinists throughout this period alleged that their church now suffered persecution at the hands of the Catholics. They further asserted that the Romanians should be left in the "ancient union" they enjoyed under Reformed supervision.[34] In this context of contested reunion with Rome Teofil died suddenly in July of 1697. Redoubling their efforts to hang on to the Romanian church and, if possible, to augment their influence over this population, the Calvinists thought the Catholic initiative might be cut short by the loss of such a key figure. Since Leopold had yet officially to confirm the result of Teofil's and Baranyi's negotiations, they had every hope of success. Perhaps, more to the point and to the realism of Calvinist expectations of undercutting the Jesuits, the Orthodox Romanians of Transylvania continued in their dependence on their earlier religious mentors and under the surveillance of the Reformed Superintendent.[35] Of similar interest was the suggestion that foul play on the part of the rejected Calvinists had somehow come into play. The most distinguished modern version of a Romanian *Who's Who*, though perhaps echoing both nationalistic and sectarian grievances, phrased this reproach delicately, simply saying that Teofil had died "not without the suspicion that he might have been poisoned." Even a more dispassionate Western historian commented that "Within a few months the newly reconciled metropolitan was dead, probably poisoned by the baffled Calvinists."[36]

However the Romanian bishop met his end, in the summer of 1697 the putative Romanian Union with Rome had yet to receive any official confirmation by the secular authorities. The series of decrees from the hand of the Emperor formally accepting the Uniates within the Roman Catholic Church and theoretically confirming their preconditions would not begin for another year. In the meantime, the five generations long tradition of Calvinist control and selection of a metropolitan's successor remained firmly ensconced. The Jesuits and their Romanian partisans would have to start afresh in their efforts to lay the organizational foundation for the Union with Rome. Though as contemporary histories testify the Jesuits considered the Union a *fait accompli*, there remained the problems of ensuring that Teofil's successor sanctioned the Union and securing Habsburg officialdom's recognition so as to obtain the needed bureaucratic underpinnings for permanence. Only this time around the Calvinists had been alerted and resolved to use their institutional controls over the Romanian Church to preclude any further erosion of their distinctive standing in Transylvania.[37] Thus in the spring of 1698 Banffi, as was the conventional procedure for such cases, on the recommendation of the Calvinist Superintendent named Angel Atanasie to the post of Romanian Metropolitan. Atanasie came from a priestly family of the village of Ciugud in the vicinity of the Metropolitan see of Alba-Iulia. A product of the Calvinist school located there, he made the journey to the Danubian Principalities in January of 1698 to be consecrated bishop of the Romanians of Transylvania by the Metropolitan of Bucharest. In addition to embracing him as the candidate supposedly most disposed to further Calvinist aims, later Romanians historians have also charged that representatives of the Reformed Church also intervened in the selection process to prevail upon the Metropolitan in Bucharest to overlook Atanasie's youth.[38] Whatever factors or forces interposed themselves to ensure the choice of Anghel Atanasie he did follow the well established pattern for the seventeenth century in his expedition to Bucharest for formal enthronement as Metropolitan of Transylvania. For the hundred years prior to this most Orthodox bishops of that province had done similarly returning from their sojourn among their ethnic and religious compeers with both felicitations and presents indicative of the close relations transcending the barrier of the Carpathians. The tradition for the succession to the Metropolitan dignity in Transylvania, then, called for the culling of a single individual by the synod and subsequently for the secular authorities to confirm that person. Once this stage had been achieved, the bishop-designate did as Atanasie in 1698 journeying across the Carpathian Mountains to be consecrated in the Wallachian capital. Even if the vested self-interest of the Reformed Church did come into play with the choice of Atanasie, the Calvinists had carefully allowed for the prescribed forms and sensitivities.[39]

From the point of view of the Habsburg authorities and of institutionalized Catholicism in Transylvania, then, Metropolitan Anghel Atanasie appeared to have all the characteristics of a Calvinist protégé. Contemporary reports from Wallachia even insisted that Calvinist magnates had had to overcome the reluctance of both the prince and metropolitan in Bucharest to endorse Atanasie by the outright purchase of his consecration as bishop. The supposition that he would therefore be their creature came to mind immediately, if the observer was Catholic and/or pro-Union with Rome. Despite all these appearances, however, the Jesuit Baranyi continued his work among the Romanians and particularly with Atanasie to effect the Union. At the same time he labored to obtain the necessary support and documentary legal foundation from both Emperor Leopold and Cardinal Kollonich to complete the Romanians' rapprochement with Rome. These principals in the Catholic establishment, as well as the factions they represented, would continue to be suspicious of the Protestant educated Romanian bishop. But at the same time, they likewise persisted in the view that a "greater doctrinal disparity existed between the Orthodox and the Calvinists than between the Orthodox and the Catholics." Even given their leeriness as to the reliability of the new Metropolitan, these same Roman Catholics thought that the greater affinity between themselves and the Eastern Rite Christians should of itself lead to a permanent Union with Rome. Unfortunately, this somewhat tentative judgment on the Romanian religious leader would result in a hierarchical misappraisal of his quality and furthermore in an insistence on bureaucratic safeguards for the Union that would prove debilitating and productive of inter-Rite conflicts.[40]

On the other hand, Baranyi and his fellow Jesuits throughout the entire process spoke out in Atanasie's favor and in defense of his sincere support of a Union with Rome. Furthermore they rallied to his cause when his character as well as his motivations were challenged, claiming that he observed "all virtues and the commands of God." Some modern Romanian historians, especially those critical of the Jesuits and the entire process leading to the Union with Rome, have charged that Atanasie and Baranyi had "come to an understanding even before the trip [for Atanasie's consecration] to Bucharest." The none too subtle implication was that obviously the Calvinists had not only misjudged their man and the situation, but had failed to receive an adequate return on the coin they had expended.[41] For his part, despite the testimonial of his Jesuit mentors, Atanasie in his recently assumed role as Romanian Metropolitan for the Orthodox of Transylvania found himself caught in a vice. The Calvinists magnates at the apex of the province's established order, the Roman Catholics of the Emperor's party, and the Orthodox of the Danubian Principalities all squeezed him in an attempt to secure their own aspirations. In commenting upon the series of awkward power relationships Atanasie had inherited from Teofil, one modern observer offered the understated judgment that these interest groups "made the situation difficult" for the bishop. Atanasie's conduct in trying to maneuver between these pressures did not add to his prestige or assuage his critics' concerns over his true intentions. The Orthodox hierarchy in the Danubian Principalities, even before his consecration, were fully aware of the situation in Transylvania. Because of this the Metropolitan in Bucharest, speaking for his church as a whole, required Atanasie to read, accept, and sign a twenty-two point instruction aimed at stemming Western ecclesiastical influences on the Transylvanian Orthodox community. Atanasie's oath to support the positions outlined in this document supposedly committed him to repudiate "the double danger of Calvinization and Catholicization." The Wallachian Metropolitan expected by this set of instructions to guarantee Atanasie's dedication in resisting the "primary" peril symbolized by the Calvinist Superintendent. But he also expected a determination from the Transylvanian bishop not to allow any success to accrue to the "secondary" threat of the Church of Rome. In specifying the anxieties of the Orthodox Church in the Principalities, this instruction directed Atanasie's attention not simply to the heresies of Calvinism or the grab for power by the Roman Catholics. He was alerted most especially to refuse to sanction any attempt to induce a schism or to allow the traditional Eastern Rite to be contaminated by "liturgical innovations." This instruction captures our interest not only as a failed warning from the Romanian Patriarchate, but likewise as a notice that Eastern Rite adherents traditionally have placed the integrity of their church's visible characteristics on the same treasured plane as theological purity and ecclesiastical unity. Not only did Atanasie not live up to his pledge, but his mentors for the Union – with very rare exceptions – did not understand or value the importance of this profound ethnic/ denominational devotion to all the attributes of the Eastern Rite.[42]

In this complex of competing loyalties and pretensions Leopold's motives and character came to play a crucial role. Having received some little formation for the priesthood and having been influenced by the Society of Jesus for years, he had acquiesced activity in the Jesuit missionaries who entered Transylvania in contravention of standing statute and precedent. While Cardinal Kollonich undoubtedly stood out as the principle architect of the Union's final form, the Emperor translated this background into a series of actions that facilitated the goals of the Jesuits and the Primate of Hungary. In doing so he acted in part out of a vague sense of largess towards the Romanian community, an altruism colored to a significant degree by his expectation that the Orthodox, if given a choice, would unquestionably elect affiliation with Roman Catholicism. Constrained as he was by both the political realities of the Catholic Church's diminished presence and prospects in Transylvania as well as by the untouchable constitutional status of the four received religions, a Union between Rome and the Romanians constituted the only key to the problem. This was "The single route by which the emperor could aid the Romanians on the ecclesiastical as well as the political venue. …At the same time this was the solitary route by which he could help the Catholic Church in Transylvania…."[43] On April 14, 1698 Emperor Leopold issued a decree to the government of Transylvania based on the lineaments of the 1692 Munkacs (Ruthenian) Union with Rome. This proclamation (which would have to be reiterated on August 26, 1699) stated that any Romanian Greek Rite priest who recognized the Pope and the Four Points would be considered to have completely satisfied the "conditions for union" and legally to possess all the privileges of Roman Catholic priests. The text also specifically indicated that those making this passage to Roman Catholicism were likewise making a "profession to observe the Eastern Rite as Catholics." In a move to mollify the expected resulting religious-political turmoil the Emperor went on to allow for the adhesion of Orthodox priests to any of the other received religions of Transylvania or for such clergy to remain in their present religious status. In all instances they would participate in the preferments of the sect to which they declared their allegiance.[44]

As might be anticipated the entrenched Calvinist authorities in Transylvania both resisted implementation, even *de facto* recognition of this imperial edict, and attempted once more to stress the long standing relationship of the Romanians with the Reformed Church. Besides the insinuation of the possible use of force to ensure their vested interests, they would claim from this point on that, given Leopold's text of 1698, the Romanians could indeed unite with them as well as with the Roman Catholics. However fair and patently obvious from the text of Leopold's decree, this was simply a ploy on his part meant to divert the most likely and forceful ire generated by the change in the Catholic Church's as well as the Orthodox Romanians' status.[45] The true political intent of Leopold and the overall ecclesiastical motivations came more unabridgedly to light in the content of a personal note of the Emperor's delivered secretly to the commanding general of Habsburg forces in Transylvania. Leopold first explained that due to the importunate pressures brought to bear by the Calvinists, he had had to expand the scope of his decree directed at the Romanian Orthodox to include the possibility of their union with any of the four received faiths. Having said this, the Emperor went on to order his commander to employ "...all his force to hinder any possible Romanian attempt to unite with any but the Catholic religion."[46]

In this struggle to institutionalize the Romanians' Union with Rome and to guarantee its longevity, the Emperor received support not merely from Cardinal Kollonich and the assorted Jesuit missionaries like Baranyi, but also from the Jesuit Provincial Gabriel Hevenesi. Such support would prove vital in fending off Protestant inroads as well as in shepherding the newly minted Eastern Rite Roman Catholics through the factious initial stages of incorporation with their new ecclesiastical home. The mentality involved here emerged most clearly in a letter of June 2, 1698 from Emperor Leopold to his religious emissary Cardinal Kollonich. This dispatch attempted once more to spell out what was being agreed to so as to prevent any later misunderstandings or exaggerations. The Emperor's stance was considerably more moderate and limited vis-à-vis the Uniates than would be that of Kollonich once the bureaucratization of the Eastern Rite in Transylvania began. Here even more explicitly than in the decrees of August 23, 1692 and April 14, 1698 to which he made reference, Leopold declared the Uniates to be officially recognized once they had acknowledged the position of the Pope and accepted the Four Points of the Council of Florence. He lent greater specificity to the Uniates' future legal claims by stressing that they now possessed a right to whatever privileges Latin Rite priests enjoyed whether these were defined under canon law or the statutes of the Kingdom of Hungary. These technicalities out of the way, the Emperor then offered his "favor and special protection in all matters…to all those now returning (or who would return in the future) to the Roman Catholic Church." This "special protection" was detailed to mean a threat to unleash the judicial arms of both church and state against anyone who might interfere with the new rights the Uniates enjoyed as now being classified as members of one of the "received religions" under the province's constitution. A Uniate reading this document would have had to be pleased, since at the time it appeared to offer both assured rights and the prospect of enforcement. Here that Uniate would have found himself disappointed very early on. Furthermore, by the early eighteenth century re-reading this letter and reading between the lines with some hindsight, he would probably have been disturbed by the structure of Leopold's language which projected a parallelism between being Roman Catholic and belonging to the Latin Rite. Perhaps, this was coincidental or a merely slip in a letter emphasizing other points and concerned with what seemed at the time to be the pressing difficulties presented by Calvinist recalcitrance. But, by the first decade of the eighteenth century, it would have turned out to be precisely the *modus operandi* by which Cardinal Kollonich institutionalized Jesuit surveillance of the Uniate Church and, in the view of many Romanians both Uniates and Orthodox, sought to render the Eastern Rite more Western in tone and expression.[47]

In the fall of 1698, then, Atanasie and his archdeacons met in a General Synod at Alba-Iulia to take an oath of loyalty to Rome and to confirm their position as Eastern Rite Roman Catholics before Baranyi. This synod that began on October 7th and lasted until the 24th resulted in a series of decrees spelling out the nature and depth of the Romanians' commitment to live as Uniates. These decrees have survived in both Latin and Romanian forms and are of considerable interest in their different emphases. The fact that the Latin ones were probably written by the Jesuits rather than by the freshly coined Eastern Rite Roman Catholics (who by all contemporary estimates were educationally simply not up to such a daunting t ask) also helps us understand the various forces at play. In both the Romanian and the Latin translation of what the Uniates pledged there was no doubt that Atanasie and what clergy were present made a solemn profession of faith accepting Roman Catholicism on the basis of the Four Points. Strikingly, in the Latin documents coming out of the General Synod, in the Metropolitan's letter of October 24th seeking a diploma of official recognition from Emperor Leopold, and in Jesuits' own summary of what had transpired a marked and repeated emphasis was placed on the fact that the Romanians had "spontaneously and of their own volition" (i.e., "*libere and sponte*") elected to accept the chance for a Union with Rome. Missing from the Latin transcriptions of the proceedings and decisions of the General Synod of 1698, however, were the extensive and conspicuous conditions for Union with Rome relative to the Eastern Rite. The fact that they can be found in the Romanian language versions and not in the Latin may simply reflect the interest and concerns of the scribe involved. But, the Romanian renditions do more fully and accurately mirror the pre-Union sentiments of the Uniates and are, in this author's view, a more credible witness to the mentality of those making the solemn commitment before Baranyi to live and die as Eastern Rite Roman Catholics.[48]

Whereas the Latin documentation limited itself to a formula of acceptance and profession of faith, the Romanian clearly spelled out the Uniates' provisos. They were to receive the privileges of Latin Rite priests, all the customs of the Eastern Rite were to be treated as sacrosanct, and the position of the Uniates bishop was not to be compromised. In reading the list of qualifications set forth by the Romanians one can not help but be struck by their specificity and prescience. This were not only the items that they had the most concern for as they emerged from their century and a half of Calvinist tutelage, but the exact ones that would be contested and a prolific source of bitterness until the time of the suppression of the Society of Jesus in 1773. The Uniates insisted as part of the price of their welcoming the Union with Rome that they receive more than a vague, generalized assurance that their Rite would not be impinged upon. They specified that all the ceremonies, holidays, and attitudes of the Eastern Church were to remain as they were at the time of the Union. Looking back on the subordination of their church and its leaders to the Calvinist Superintendent, they likewise claimed a guarantee that the bishop's authority would not be compromised and that Atanasie's successor must be selected by the Synod. While "it pleased the Synod" to allow Baranyi to report the progress of the Union and their profession of faith to Vienna and Rome in the more convenient Latin translation, they obviously did not intend for their pre-conditions to be emended or expurgated. Their concern in this regard would not have been alleviated fully, even if they had been able to read the language involved, to know that the official Latin document entitled "acceptance of the [Romanian] Union" did contain references to their "suspicion of alterations of the Rite" and to the fact that "acceptance of this formula of Union shall in no way detract from the integrity of the Greek Rite." But tacked on to even this Latin document there stood out a Romanian rendered insistence on preserving everything then found in the Eastern Church's liturgy and traditions as well as the integrity of the Romanian bishop's administrative authority.[49]

The issue of the language of record for the Romanian Union with Rome assumed greater importance because of the way the Jesuits officially reported the Synod's actions. Besides not finding there the detailed list of Romanian expectations (particularly where the integrity of the Eastern Rite was concerned), one also discovers a much broader evaluation of what the Uniates had committed themselves to than was encompassed in the Romanian versions. In the "Annals of the Dacian Mission" the Society of Jesus reported a more sweeping acceptance of things Roman Catholic than Atanasie's profession of faith and agreement with the Council of Florence's "Four Points." Cardinal Kollonich was informed that the Metropolitan and his archdeacons had "freely and willingly... admitted, professed, and accepted everything which the Roman Catholic Church admits, especially the 'Four Points'." Given the Westernizing and patronizing mentality the Cardinal seems to have been possessed by, this more ambitious if embellished rendering of the Romanian position helped lay the cornerstone for Kollonich's restrictive administrative stance towards the Uniates and their considerable despondency with the day to day implementation of their church's liturgical and bureaucratic policies. In its own letter (dated November 16, 1698) to Cardinal Kollonich the Synod stated in the first place that it accepted the privileges enjoyed by Catholic priests and then that a profession of faith had been made before Father Baranyi. Beyond the perennial point of the *quid pro quo* which the Uniates expected and the almost offhanded reference to their profession of faith, the Synod said nothing about a more complex definition of the Union or of the recognition of anything beyond the "Four Points." What the Synod did do was ask the Cardinal for help against the Uniates' "adversaries" and that he might write the Habsburg commanding general in Transylvania (Graf Jean Louis Rabutin de Bussy) in the same vein. Just over a week later (November 27, 1698) both Bishop Atanasie and his Jesuit mentor Baranyi wrote to solicit assistance for the new Eastern Rite Roman Catholic, Atanasie to the prefect of the Transylvanian chancellery and Baranyi to Cardinal Kollonich. While the Romanian bishop simply informed the provincial administration of his followers' new status and that he now presumed its protection and recognition of Uniate privileges comparable to those of other Catholic priests, Baranyi described for the Primate the opposition to the Union by the "heretics" and the urgent need for official support from Vienna.[50]

This last plea of the Jesuit missionary assumed critical importance. Although the Romanians had from their viewpoint fully committed themselves to everything they had been informed was required of them, their constitutional status of Orthodox and "tolerated" had not changed. For this purpose a diploma from the hand of the Emperor would be required, or more exactly the central government in Vienna had to pronounce for all concerned, especially the Protestant opposition in Transylvania. on the new juridical status of the Uniates. This political as well as clerical process would drag out over the next three years. The delay, once the former Orthodox had pledged themselves to the supposedly definitive formula of the "Four Points" and the preservation of the "Romanian" character of their church, was not only unsettling but in the long run a portent of the circumscribing of their goals.[51] For in the course of this protracted process for all intents and purposes the Union was not simply being political recognized, but also informally reinterpreted. Despite the fact that contemporary Jesuit witness confirmed the Romanian position that their commitment was limited to a public profession of faith and the Florentine "Four Points," they would in the course of these three years find themselves viewed as suspect by Latin Rite

Catholic and Protestant alike. Clearly, the Latin documents forward to Vienna and to Cardinal Kollonich did not qualify as "translations." Rather they constituted a somewhat optimistic précis of the Jesuit-Orthodox interactions combined with an interposition of some of Kollonich's ideas on the process of reunion in general. Given the incompleteness of the bureaucratic process and the later conflict as to what exactly transpired, the common denominator accepted by all was that at least the "Four Points" had been embraced. More to the point of the infighting that would go on later and the mixed bag of contrary interpretations, the kindest thing to be said is that the Jesuit party "presumed" that the Uniate profession of faith constituted a shorthand for the more generous expatiation in their document. On the Romanian part, their document was twice as long as the Jesuit one sent to Kollonich and Vienna precisely because their concerns were riveted on the privileges to be obtained and the continuance of their traditional form of worship. They in turned "presumed" that the imperial edict "for the preservation of [and/or reverence for] the Greek Rite" not only meant that literally, but also created a bulwark preventing all further intrusion of Western influences.[52]

To resolve these problems, to signal official approval and at least the prospect of enforcement, Baranyi sought to have Vienna's *nihil obstat* and *imprimatur* promulgated in the form of an imperial decree. Besides meeting Romanian desires and undercutting Protestant objections, this proposal and its source are of interest for the later course of the Union as well. Given the control of the Uniate Church by the Society of Jesus during the eighteenth century, Baranyi's suggestion for the diploma at this time was quite significant. His summary of the Synod's actions was sent to Gabor Hevenesi, S.J., who at another time would hold the office of Jesuit Provincial, but at this time functioned as Cardinal Kollonich's confessor and counselor.[53] Most significantly Cardinal Kollonich, with his dual ambitions of consolidating Habsburg control over Transylvania while at the same time effecting a definitive settlement of the Romanians' Union with Rome on the basis of his personal theological predilections, became the fulcrum for further action. The Leopoldine Diploma of 1699 came from his pen. He in short set the tone for the legal foundation of the Uniate position in Transylvania and exercised a determining role in predisposing the nature of that Rite's reactions to the Latin Rite. This decree issued by the Emperor but reflecting the Cardinal's political and ritual preferences likewise convinced the representatives of Transylvania's ruling classes that unless they acted promptly and determinedly "...the Union of the Romanians [with Rome] would sooner or later revolutionize the constitution of the province." It would also raise the level of the Uniates' anxiety over their new status, since they had acceded to Baranyi's blandishments only on the basis of the "Four Points" certainly not on anything like the Cardinal's estimation of what reunion should entail.[54] As the Romanian Uniate movement entered its early, critical phase of formal establishment on a constitutional basis and the working out of the canonical specifications of its relationship with the Latin Rite, the two parties at least conversed on skew lines, perhaps even pursued converse aims. Meeting in the Synod of 1698, the Romanian Orthodox priests under Atanasie's leadership obviously wanted the privileges of the Latin Rite priests promised by Leopold. But anything beyond the "Four Points" enunciated by the Council of Florence would, in their view, be a matter for further negotiations. Undoubtedly, the long conversations with Baranyi as well as the protracted character of what can only be depicted as bartering for improvement in their social lot reinforced in their minds the arbitration aspect of the exchanges with Rome's representatives.[55]

Unfortunately for the Romanian stance, Cardinal Kollonich had by this time decided to consolidate a Union that up to this point remained not merely ill-defined in his view, but one accomplished only "in principle." He wanted matters settled once and for all, and quite specifically on his unique terms. His approach as well as his position stood out in direct variance to those of the putative Uniates. He viewed the Romanians' Union with Rome, and the grounds on which it was founded, as totally a concession from the Vatican. Whatever the Synod's Romanian text of 1698 spelled out or was in the Jesuits' view obliquely implied in the Latin, the Cardinal insisted that the Romanians' commitment encompassed more than the exactions worked out at Florence. Directly opposed to the position of the Uniates, and probably to that of Rome, Kollonich maintained that adherence to the "Four Points" alone would not suffice. What came across most clearly to contemporary Romanians and to later observers was the Primate's extreme lack of trust. On the basis of that absence of certitude regarding the Uniates' motivations and faithfulness to the Latin model of Catholicism Kollonich pursued an approach strongly hierarchical, even monarchical, in his administrative rulings.

The standard he chose to employ in treating with the Uniates was that of the Council of Trent, not that of the Council of Florence. This approach, of course, not only heightened the traditional Western suspicion of Eastern Christians, but also brought with it the additional vigor of a combativeness arising out of the Counter-Reformation. Whether arrived at on his own or due to the influence of the Jesuits, Cardinal Kollonich wished to exact an "obedience to the Pope" that entailed more than the expected separation from the hierarchical structure and theology of Eastern Orthodoxy. His version of "obedience to the Pope" also smacked of the military deference promised by a Jesuit who had achieved the status of a "professed" priest through taking a special fourth vow (i.e., a second and more demanding vow of obedience superceding that taken at the end of the novitiate). Twentieth and twenty-first century Romanian historians, and not necessarily only the hostile or nationalistic, have seen these attitudes of Kollonich's as not merely harsh but unprecedented in the handling of a people supposedly returning to the fold. As a twentieth century Jesuit has put it so succinctly and ominously for the immediate future of the Romanian Uniate Church, Cardinal Kollonich not only rejected as the basis for reunion "...the decisions of the Romanian General Synod, but deliberately ignored its wishes." These desires, of course, entailed both a Florentine profession of faith permitting the maximum retention of Eastern Rite mores and the more mundane warranty of gracious treatment of the Uniate clergy and hierarchy.[56]

On February 16, 1699 Emperor Leopold promulgated the diploma that had been induced by Baranyi and formulated by Kollonich. The tactical thought behind the document centered on acting "in favor of the Union" by providing for its formal legal execution coupled with the "binding force" of the Emperor's endorsement. Sadly for the Uniates Leopold had to keep political as well as religious considerations in mind, attempting to balance between offering support to the new Eastern Rite Roman Catholics while not impinging on the peculiar constitutional status of Transylvania. The Diploma of 1699, then, did not have the appearance or tone of a direct answer to the Romanians' negotiating stance for Union with Rome and was not even unmistakably addressed to them. Indeed, it made no reference to the actions of their Synod, which had so laboriously worked out the stipulations framing their profession of faith.[57] Speaking in his legal *persona* as Emperor, Leopold declared that

> any Romanian, Greek, Ruthenian schismatic…resident in Hungary, Croatia, Slavonia, or Transylvania…wishing to effect a Union and return to the Holy Roman Church…must admit, profess, and believe all that Holy Mother Roman Catholic Church [does]… expressly the Four Points…. We…declare that those of the Greek Rite united with the Holy Roman Church shall as a Church and as individual ecclesiastics…enjoy the same privileges and immunities as the faithful of the Latin Rite of the Holy Roman Church.[58]

Leopold then went on to "firmly order" the faithful execution of all the favors that had been promised to one and all who embraced union with Rome. The length and detail of this proscription of all impediments "under any pretext, open or hidden" to the Uniates' new preferments read well. But it likewise conspicuously anticipated the opposition to come and did not mention the specifics of Rite or administrative autonomy so prominent in the 1698 Synod's position papers on the Union.

The Leopoldine Diploma of 1699, then, presented for the authorities of Transylvania a generic endorsement of the Uniate movement, but did not name the Romanians of the province or expressly sustain their conditions for re-union. Whatever the generalized promise of support to an unnamed audience considering a union with Rome, the Transylvanian established classes clearly saw the threat to their position and determined to do everything possible to frustrate the Romanian Uniate effort. If they could not do so openly without violating the diploma and risking a clash with the Emperor, then they would seek other means. Lest one miss the extent and depth of the opposition to the Romanian Uniate cause it would be well to remember that the Roman Catholic magnates joined those of the Calvinist, Lutheran, and Unitarian "received religions" to try to limit, if not completely thwart, it for economic reasons. If unchecked in the attainment of the promised exemptions from the exactions of the serfs among whom they lived and worked, the Uniate movement might remove a significant number of clergy from an estate's roll of laborers. There would, of course, be a concomitant reduction in an individual magnate's wealth.[59] In like manner the Roman Catholic clergy of the Hungarian lands recently liberated from Muslim Ottoman suzerainty were thoroughly ethnic in their mentality and inclined towards local autonomy in their politics. The Magyar princes of the church shared the secular magnates' distaste for the new "German" centralized government and a proclivity for interpreting even ecclesiastical matters in light of their nationality. Thus, in 1699 the Vicar General of the Transylvanian Roman Catholic church twice asked to be excused from any participation in instructing the Orthodox interested in Union with Rome. Among the ostensible reasons this Magyar ecclesiastic proffered for such recalcitrance in coping with the Romanian Union with Rome and its propagation were an ignorance of their language and the "uncultivated nature of the people." Kollonich and the Jesuits would obtain little if any assistance from this quarter.[60] In both instances, of course, history and jurisdictional anxieties spoke loudly. The Protestant magnates had for generations voiced their resistance to the Catholic Habsburgs with the rejoinder "Better a Muslim than a worshiper of idols!" In Transylvania the late seventeenth century political equivalent for Protestant and Catholic magnates alike would have been "Better Ottoman sovereignty than Habsburg!" Specifically on the Catholic front, neither the secular magnates nor the princes of the Church displayed any inclination to tolerate a religious union that would undermine their status or power. The magnates viewed their faith as one of the prime supports of the serf owning system from which they profited. The Union's extension of privileges to their ordained serfs constituted a serious challenge to the aristocracy's economic and social well-being. In turn the creation of a Greek Rite Roman Catholic diocese in Transylvania seemed to the Latin hierarchy unacceptable, both for canonical-jurisdictional reasons as well as as a devaluation of their own station so recently regained after one hundred and fifty years of Protestant usurpation. This competition for place would result not merely in the already discussed reluctance to aid the Romanian Uniate movement, but eventually in the subordination of its hierarchy to that of the Latin Rite. The stature and authority of the Uniate bishop would have to suffer a certain derogation to allow the Latin clergy reclaiming its prominence in Transylvania a primacy of place similar to that pledged to the Pope.[61]

Whatever the potential defects of the Leopoldine Diploma of 1699 from the Romanian point of view, it served to bring into sharp focus the apprehensions and discontents of the ruling elements of all four received faiths in Transylvania. The estate structure of the province had been determined, since the beginning of the Uniate movement in 1698, to protect themselves economically as well as religiously. The non-Catholics wanted to be sure that their respective denominations received, on the basis of the Emperor's decree of April 14, 1698, their fair share of the Romanian population as prospective "converts." This edict permitting the union of the Orthodox with any of the four "received faiths" they were not willing to allow to be read as benefiting only Rome. Perhaps, even more pressing, regardless of which sect the Romanians might unite with, the resolution granting them equal status with that group's clergy had devastating potential. For the provincial tax rolls offered the specter of several thousands priestly families suddenly being freed from the burdens of serfdom. Looking past the venerable facade of the diploma, these men of all religious persuasions could glimpse damage to their economic interests as well as the turbid secret of the Habsburgs' centralizing political agenda.[62] These forebodings would seem to have been fully justified, since later historians have labeled the 1699 diploma of Leopold's as possessing "epoch making significance." Unless legal undermined or subjected to procedural limitations, it granted the Romanians their first recognition as having an official, constitutional existence within the structure of the Transylvanian political and religious order. The Uniates, then, found themselves at the pivot point of a heated altercation between Vienna and the Transylvanian feudal lords that would stretch the length of the eighteenth century; namely, to what extent would the Habsburg efforts to govern the province from the imperial capital and as a decidedly Catholic state succeed. The "Romanian question" presented, therefore, the possibility of interpretation as well as manipulation from several sides that did not have the Uniates' advantage in first place, if in mind at all.[63]

In view of the resistance encountered by the Diploma of 1699 Leopold had to enter the lists again that year in the late summer ordering his commander in Transylvania (General Rabutin) "in every way and manner" to ensure the rights of the Romanians to unite with the Roman Catholic Church. The Emperor expressed his "highest displeasure" at the fact that many had attempted

> to dissuade the Romanians from the Union with the Catholic religion through every kind of means, pretexts, and machinations, even threats...and to force them to join one of the non-Catholic religions to the great disadvantage and prejudice of the Catholic religion.[64]

The general was to protect those Orthodox wishing to become Uniates from "all hazards" and in so doing accomplish the Emperor's true intention: the multiplication of the number of Catholic adherents in

Transylvania. On that same day (i.e., August 26, 1699), Leopold also wrote to the governor of the province remonstrating against the pressures being exerted to frustrate the Romanians' Union with Rome. This Latin document, when compared to the German one sent to Rabutin, resounded at least as peremptorily ordering that the original diploma be "exactly observed." Besides the strikingly curt tone sent to the Transylvanian Diet through the governor, this message differed from that sent to Rabutin in not candidly highlighting the risks to Catholic interests in the region. Whatever the 1699 diploma's rhetoric of allowing the Romanians to choose among Calvinists, Catholics, Lutherans, and Unitarians as churches with which to unite, these epistles like Leopold's earlier one on the subject clearly demonstrated his resolve to stabilize the Transylvanian political situation in his favor through the use of religious policy. The purported choice of any of the four "received religions" remained a fiction indulged in by both sides for reasons of convenience.[65]

Neither the diploma of 1698 nor Leopold's various letters changed the nature of the opposition to the Romanian Union with Rome or to the centralizing tendencies of the Viennese government. While the Emperor continued to seek his ends through these means, the Transylvanian Diet remained at least as tenacious in their efforts to frustrate both. The Catholics with Leopold's backing determined to insist not only on the political potential of increased numbers through Romanian adherence, but also on a commensurate gain in power in the Diet and provincial administration. With the growing political weight of the Viennese central government in the back of all the interested parties' minds, the Emperor decided to address even more emphatically the issues of proportional power for Catholics in Transylvania and the necessary prerequisite of equating the Uniates' constitutional status with that of the larger body of the Roman Church. On September 5, 1699, then, he issued the so called "Puncta Leopoldina" in an effort to accomplish these ends. Coupled with a general proscription of any inequality of treatment of Catholics by Protestants (especially by Calvinists), Leopold specifically ordered that one of the three candidates for provincial office required by his diploma of 1691 must be a Roman Catholics as must be one of the three custodians of the Transylvanian seal. On the economic front he enjoined that Catholics no longer be obliged to pay any portion of the tithe to Protestant ministers and that they have access in equal numbers to the markets and other business opportunities of the area. All of these points he addressed prompted "by the complaints of the Catholic estate…and to ensure justice and equality…."[66]

Reacting to these initiatives of the Emperor's and their own concerns the delegates of the established orders in the Transylvanian Diet met in the early fall of 1699 to act on the conditions of any Romanian union. Supposedly their response would be one that "exactly observed" the letter and spirit of the imperial diploma. However, the tone and intent of their actions as a body were presaged in an earlier letter addressed to Leopold in July. In that preface to their official action the representatives of the *status quo* informed their Emperor that the Romanians were both ignorant and insincere, that they "simply wish to evade the laws of Transylvania, …and are neither Catholic nor truly Uniate." On September 27, 1699 the Transylvanian Diet both determined its official policies towards the Uniates and reported the same to the Emperor. By way of a preface, it proclaimed that Orthodox priests had the right to unite with the Catholic Church, with any of the other faiths of the province, or to remain what they had always been. In each instance the priests were to enjoy complete liberty to live according to the norms of the dispensation they chose. Interestingly this document establishing the legal status of the Uniates, one written by those hostile to both the Habsburgs and the Union with Rome, picked up on the cardinal Romanian point of the negotiations; namely, the continued use and integrity of the Eastern Rite. While this fundamental demand of the those becoming Uniates was ignored in the Latin language documents of the Emperor and the Jesuits, their Calvinist opponents in the Transylvanian Diet recognized the Uniates' right to join with Rome and to preserve their "Greek customs [i.e., rite]." Then, after a somewhat confused rendering of the Florentine "Four Points" as the sole criteria for Union with Rome, the Diet began to lay down those safeguards it deemed necessary to prevent the Union from undermining their position economically, politically, or socially. It established a *numerus clausus* limiting the number of Romanian priests per village as well as the bishop's authority to ordain priests "lest they multiply" and in doing so undermine the feudal manor owners' vested interests. Finally, on top of some economic fine tuning regarding payments on an estate, the Diet specified that any individual wishing to be a Romanian priest had to study in a school of the religion with which he wished to unite. If he did not, "then he could not be a priest."[67] Given the educational level and prospects of the Romanians, this created a considerable obstacle should it be enforced. Ironically, in creating this facade of acknowledging the Emperor's will while pursuing their own ends, the Transylvanian Diet provided independent verification of the Romanian insistence that they united only on the basis of the "Four Points" and with a guarantee of the sacrosanct status of their Eastern Rite traditions. Representatives of the Latin Rite would very shortly challenge both assertions.

By 1699, then, the Uniate movement was embroiled in a triangular dispute between Latin Rite Roman Catholics, the Transylvanian estates, and the Romanians claiming to have united with Rome but only on their own terms. At the center of the confrontation, and in large part summing up the issues (religious and political), was the character and career of Angel Atanasie, the Uniate bishop. Perhaps, the best introduction into this phase of the contest is to highlight the Calvinist sense of betrayal with its resultant rancor and sense of increased political assailability. While hailed by some modern historians as the architect of the finalized Union with Rome, the spokesmen for the Reformed Church could not but feel gulled by Atanasie. They had educated him in their schools, selected him to be the Romanian bishop, and then through their influence and financial resources managed to have him consecrated in Bucharest. Between this domination of the Orthodox hierarchy and decades long supervision over the rank and file, they thought themselves "the legitimate masters of the Romanian Church...with a rightful claim on the loyalty of the new bishop...." The Calvinist bargaining position in the fall of 1699, then, became one of not recognizing Atanasie's corporate attempt at Union with Rome, but rather to demand personal declarations regarding denominational status. To undercut the decisions of the Romanian Synod, they would require each individual to state a preference.[68] If their political posture encompassed the right of every priest to choose any one of the "received religions," the Protestant demeanor towards the person of Atanasie entailed assaulting his character and motivations. In addition to depicting him as "avaricious" the prime tactic called for questioning his sincerity. Ultimately, not only the Protestant opposition but Latin Rite Catholics as well would pose this query, Rome eventually even investigating his consecration as a bishop. The vilification went to the extent of alleging that the bishop was a "fornicator" who struck a deal with Baranyi to effect the Union. If Atanasie delivered the Romanian people to Rome (which the bishop did not suggest he could do), then Baranyi would lend his assistance to compensate for the charges being leveled by Atanasie's opponents.[69]

Throughout his career, even after the Union with Rome was definitively settled, Angel Atanasie would be portrayed as cleric who being poorly educated and weak in character found himself maneuvered into this alliance. Buckling under the "continual Catholic pressure" he broke his word to Orthodox and Protestant alike. This line of attack was pursued originally by those opposed to the Union itself. The suspicion generated by these specific points, however, would be picked up by Latin Rite Catholics, serving as the background for Cardinal Kollonich's severity towards Atanasie as well as for the jaundiced view many outsiders would hold of the Uniate Church in general.[70] The far more common charge, and one that contaminated not only the Uniate bishop but everyone who followed him into the bond with Rome, centered on Atanasie's acceptance of Baranyi proposal for purportedly purely materialistic reasons. For many contemporaries as well as for modern critics of the Uniate movement, this summed up the prime motivation of all concerned, the bishop simply serving as a model for those who followed him. "Atanasie and a part of his people and clergy left the religion of their forebearers and embraced that of the West *only* [emphasis added] from material motives, and not from conviction." Having sworn to remain Orthodox and having taken the coin of his Calvinist masters, then, Atanasie was charged with accepting for the basest of reasons a Union he did not fully comprehend or affirm.[71] Contemporary documents attest to this approach, one in which the motivations and character of the bishop were attacked and then the resulting opprobrium transferred to the Union as a whole. In one such report Atanasie was described as a "bishop who having no other income other than that he could derive from his priests, ordained one and all indiscriminately for the sole purpose of obtaining additional income." This same record also championed the view that, since the Catholic party in Transylvania was the weakest of the denominational groupings, in order to increase their numbers they recruited into the Union with Rome "...priests lacking in religious zeal...whose only interest was in liberty [from economic exactions], most of whom were coarse people who did not even know their faith...."[72]

Atanasie and his church attempted in the course of 1699 to have confirmed their status as true Roman Catholics of the Eastern Rite. With this barrage of attacks, however, not only did they encounter Protestant (most notably Calvinist) hostility, but also Latin Rite Catholic suspicions. Kollonich and others looked askance at the Union and its leader due to the century and a half of Calvinist impact and the residue of Reformed Church "religious propaganda." While the misgivings of their Latin Rite mentors would take bureaucratic and enduring form shortly, at this juncture the Protestant onslaught seemed the most dangerous.[73] While meeting opposition from all three Protestant sects, the most serious practical hindrance came from the Calvinist Superintendent's office. The Lutheran and Unitarian churches had not had the close association with the Orthodox that the Reformed had nor did any sense of a commitment on the Romanians' part exist in their view. The Lutheran Church had evolved into an ethnic enclave not permitting Romanian participation, while the Unitarian evidenced a theology totally incompatible with Eastern Christian sensibilities. These sects provided support for the more militant and larger Reformed element. The Calvinists in 1699 and afterwards felt threatened as a faith, as a "national" group, and as a socio-economic factor under siege by the prospect of a burgeoning Roman Catholicism reinforced by the largest single ethnic component in the province. They determined to hinder the Romanian Union and the consequent flowering of Habsburg-Catholic power by every means at their command. The Transylvanian Diet's restrictive interpretation of the Emperor's diploma constituted one of the immediate results of these attitudes. The magnates of Transylvania whatever their religious inclination, even Roman Catholic, were prone to place their economic interests in the forefront and to resist the Union. The sectarian rhetoric and the legalisms often remained just that, the real focus being the debilitating effect of the easily predictable loss of the revenues generated by a large body of clerics perhaps now to be excused from such payments.[74]

More agitating and damaging over the course of time, however, was the opposition from the Orthodox hierarchy outside of Transylvania and from that portion of the local Romanian community that chose to remain in the Eastern Church. This schism, both ethnic and religious, would cause immediate turmoil in the province that reached a peak in the mid-eighteenth century. Its relics, in terms of bitterness and polemics, can be seen even in the first decade of the twenty-first century. The Orthodox hierarchs of Eastern Europe have only recently expressed their opposition and distress at the Vatican's policy of re-invigorating the various Uniate Churches of the region in the post-Communist period. At the point of Atanasie's embracing of the Union with Rome the Romanian Prince Constantin Brâncoveanu, ruler of the Ottoman controlled area between the Carpathian Mountains and the Danube, attempted to undermine the bishop's action through his political and financial resources. The prince displayed particular resentment at Atanasie's willingness "to trample" on his consecration oath to remain within the Orthodox Church.[75] The broad base of this institutional indignation at the perceived Roman Catholic intrusion into the an Orthodox sanctuary appeared also in a letter of complaint which the Metropolitan of Bucharest (Teodosie) sent to Patriarch Adrian of Moscow. Presaging the grievances of his twenty-first century counterparts in tone if not verbatim, Metropolitan Teodosie reported that yet another offensive by Rome had begun, one aided by the House of Austria and the Jesuits. In asking for assistance from the Tsar as well as from the Patriarch, the Romanian religious leader left no doubt in their minds that the Union represented a major and "imminent Catholic danger." He specifically accused Rome of conduct that featured every "defilement,... lure,... tyranny...to convert [the Romanians] into enemies of the Holy Eastern Church...." To gauge properly the animosity that this Orthodox generation would pass on even to the present, the reader should remember that the Union was categorically labeled a "seduction" and the term Teodosie employed for "defilement" can also be translated as a sexual violation. This letter to the Russian Patriarch laid the foundation for and captured almost exactly the rhetoric of a tradition of Orthodox hostility present to this day, one that categorized the Union achieved by Atanasie as "a deception foisted on the weak and the ignorant...."[76]

The Orthodox Romanians of Transylvania demonstrated a far more long-lived resistance to the Union with Rome that did their religious brethren mentioned in the preceding two examples. The framework for the popular demonstration against Atanasie's actions which began in 1699 and grew into widespread discontent in the eighteenth century found its basis in the legalistic rationale that the Orthodox Church did not exist once the Union was complete. Thus from 1701 on Cardinal Kollonich and the Habsburgs would maintain that, since the Romanian bishop had acted as the administrative head of his church, no Orthodox ecclesiastical structure remained. The reasoning here approximated the "*cuius regio, eius religio*" settlement of the mid-seventeenth century, only for contemporary Transylvanian purposes the translation would have been "whoever's diocese, so too his faith." The managerial decision of Atanasie, interpreted for political and religious reasons as a mass conversion, became then a "dogma of state" with at least as much emphasis on the politics of the situation as on the spiritual condition of the Uniates. Any assertion to the contrary or claim to be other than Uniate would for two generations be treated as "apostasy."[77] As background to such accusations, the level of education among the Orthodox Romanians, even the clergy, did not approach that of their Western peers. Since the mass of the people were considered far too ignorant and difficult to persuade to anything resembling the "Four Points," the Habsburg authorities in both the religious and secular venues decided to target the priesthood. In view of the immediate hostile reaction, a rejection that would grow in scope and vigor in the eighteenth century, it becomes very difficult to see the avowal that "every Romanian" converted as anything more than a political extrapolation or a form of hagiography.[78] Whatever the numbers involved, this "dogma of state" led to a battle over statistics that has poisoned the historiography of the subject from that time onward as well as further embittering the relations between Orthodox and Catholic. Given the technical expertise possessed at the time, obviously nothing like a modern survey of attitudes based on a representative sampling existed. In place of such there exists claim and counter-claim often more polemical than scholarly in nature. For example, a Jesuit witness proclaimed that in 1699 "the greater part" of the Romanians were Uniates,[79] while a more modern apologist asserted that "all" Romanians had become Uniates by that date.[80] The offsetting contentions have ranged from the assertion that only Atanasie and his coterie of archdeacons embraced Rome through perhaps a few lay people doing so to a charge that the Jesuits even faked documents forming the basis of the Union.[81] The contemporary Romanian Orthodox contention has been that the "fiction" of a total conversion of the Orthodox to the Uniate Church served to justify depriving their forebearers of any formal ecclesiastical structure for sixty years. Since "the entire Romanian people had passed to the Union," no Orthodox bishopric would be necessary or recognized in Transylvania from this point until the reign of Maria Theresia.[82]

Since the Habsburgs chose to address their political goals in Transylvania and the social status of the Romanians through the mechanism of religious policy, perhaps this "fiction" made some sense at the time. But, besides inducing yet another element of tension into the relationship of the dynasty with the provincial diet, it at the same time severely complicated dealings with the Romanians. For at most one half of the Romanian Orthodox population seems to have sought union with Rome, a fact apparently borne out by the extensive disturbances that began early in the next century and reached a peak by the mid-eighteenth century. The problem, of course, appeared in the shape of that other fifty-plus percent that had either by deliberate choice, if at all educated, or through the inertia of folkloric default chosen to remain in the "old faith."[83] At this point in the progress towards Union with Rome the antagonism that would become endemic erupted into a pronounced struggle along religious lines between Romanian serfs who either had or had not become Uniates. The Orthodox view, then and now, contended that only the Uniate priests profited from this situation, the antagonism being defined from the beginning as one generated by those who had deserted "the faith of their ancestors." This emphasis upon the lack of "a true Union" because only the clergy received the promised privileges would become standard fare for the Orthodox opposition in little more than a generation as well as a staple of nineteenth century romantic nationalism and the historiography that grew out of it.[84] Whatever the rhetoric of either side in this controversy, a considerable portion of the Orthodox Transylvanian population "pronounced themselves for the old belief." The priests who elected to go with the bishop did so on the understanding that the preconditions he had forwarded would be met. In this they were especially concerned, as would be all Uniates and Orthodox during the period under study, that "'their rite stay on the spot,' or in other words suffer not a single change…." Even if there had not developed the subsequent discord and tussle over the issue of the Eastern Rite, great feeling existed on the Orthodox side from 1699 until the present that "moral compulsion" rather than persuasion had been the effective agent of change in this instance. This suspicion likewise influenced the concern for their Rite and their interpretation of all Latin Catholic actions affecting it. The result, of course, was a marked resistance on the part of a large portion of the Romanian population, which if not at first then later would approach the "massive opposition" seen by the modern nationalistic historian. This same type of critic focused on the lack of contemporary Romanians witnesses testifying to the motivations and enthusiasms leading to the Union, a complaint perhaps misplaced given the educational and social level of the average Romanian of the time.[85]

From the start, then, the Uniates and the Latin Rite authorities fostering the Eastern Rite church ran into the same adamantine resistance to conversion which the Calvinists had encountered, one that brushed aside perceived persecution just as easily as the proffered privileges. At the head of this opposition stood the monks of the Order of St. Basil for whom the Romanian people had a special affection and extraordinary respect. They were able to turn this relationship with the laity into a striking sway directed at "protecting the ancestral faith...against its enemies…." Also influencing the mentality and actions of the Romanian populace were the parish priests who, while most often not well educated, demonstrated a profound religiosity that included that same love for the traditional liturgy and a "fanatical" adherence to Orthodoxy. By Maria Theresia's time these qualities would have not only generated extensive, even violent, dissent but also an Orthodox migration into Ottoman territories which was large enough to worry Habsburg officials.[86] Adding to the fratricidal conflict over the sensitive issue of preserving the Eastern Rite that would rack the Romanian community for most of the eighteenth century, the peasant found himself the recipient of none of the privileges promised to the Uniate priests. Given the nature of the feudal regime in Transylvania, he could only look forward to an increased personal burden as the landlord shifted the payments the clergy were excused from to his back. The "contemporary system of collective responsibility" generated yet another source of bitterness to supplement the social-political struggle between the two segments of the Romanian population. Sharing the Eastern Rite but divided by economic as well as confessional concerns, this ethnic schism would require that the secular as well as ecclesiastical authorities of Habsburg Transylvania continue their role as guardians of the Uniate Church well into the eighteenth century. Leaders such as Stefan Apor who had initiated the bureaucratic side of the Union movement would now be called upon for a more generalized secular support.[87]

This advocacy Atanasie and the newly coined Union would need urgently. Both now came under increased criticism for economic reasons as well as due to accusations of insincerity. While the economic opposition cut across sectarian lines, the Calvinists led the assault based on an alleged lack of *bona fides* which would subsequently be picked up by

Latin Rite Catholics and used as a justification for encroaching on the affairs of the Eastern Rite. Removal of Calvinist supervision and, more specifically given Romanian concerns relative to their ritual, interruption of a century and a half of foreign influence constituted one of the earliest and most important results of the Union with Rome. If in the eyes of the modern nationalistic Romanian historian the Union did nothing else, it impeded any further "Calvinization" or "Magyarization" of his forebearers. For this espousal of Roman Catholicism in Eastern vestments reasserted "the ethnically Latin origin and character" of the Romanians.[88] The abrogation of such long standing prerogatives, even without the further essential consideration of economic factors, would have quite sufficed to move the Calvinists to action. They occupied, however, an uncomfortable position in that in attempting to salvage their preponderant influence over the Romanian Orthodox Church they could not appear to be attacking the Emperor or his stated policies. More politic was a course directed at the quality of this "conversion" and manipulation of Catholic apprehensions about the probity of the new Uniate bishop. As already seen, the Calvinists had presumed Atanasie to be their man. What education he had he received in their schools. Moreover he attained the episcopal dignity solely through their intervention. *À propos* to maligning his character and undermining the Uniate position with both Imperial and Catholic authorities the Calvinists could bring up the oath which Atanasie, like his predecessor Teofil, took upon assuming the post of Romanian bishop for Transylvania. In that commitment, Bishop Atanasie promised not simply to accept the control of the Calvinist Superintendent, but also to champion "the Calvinization of the Romanians." That the leaders of the Reformed Church and their partisans in the Transylvanian chancellery were shocked and enraged should not surprise nor should their determination to undermine the protégé who had failed in gratitude and rejected their culturally oriented presentation of Christianity.[89]

In the fall of 1699 in response to an official letter from the Calvinist chancellor of Transylvania, Miklós Bethlen, Atanasie wrote to the provincial authorities protesting his sincerity. In declaring the canonical validity, based upon good faith, of his and his church's Union with Rome the bishop made great play of his loyalty to the Catholic Church. Speaking for himself and the General Synod of the Uniate Church, Atanasie asserted (in the language of the Latin version written by the

Jesuit Baranyi) that they had "sincerely and with free will" accepted the Union under the terms of Leopold's diplomas. Aside from the direct refutation of the Calvinist charge of duplicity, the bishop's letter has significance because it indicates once more in a forceful fashion that the Romanians had embraced the Union with Rome under a very specific regime; namely, the Florentine "Four Points," the administrative autonomy of their church, and most of all the integrity of the Eastern Rite. Theirs could not be, in any dispassionate light, interpreted as an unconditional reunion nor an open-ended one, one that lent itself to further embellishment according to Latin Rite notions of what might be proper.[90] Unfortunately, the fact that this letter of Atanasie's was Jesuit-authored because of his and his clergy's ignorance of Latin laid the basis in the view of many modern nationalistic Romanian historians for the institution of the Jesuit "Theologian." This churchish factotum commissioned to supervise the Uniate hierarchy due to its perceived lack of sound training, and according to some critics its dearth of dedication to things Catholic (more specifically, Roman), would inherit the ecclesiastical sovereignty exercised by the Calvinist Superintendent. He would also garner the same suspicion and resentment enjoyed by that Reformed Church official for what, by Romanian standards, constituted a similar encroachment on the dignity and independence of the Uniate Church. Initially the reaction would be one of fear for the liturgy and traditional usages of the Eastern Rite. By the nationalistically minded modern period, this pervasive complaint would turn into a far more aggressive accusation that through the "Theologian" and other mechanisms the Roman Catholics planned "to absorb" the Uniate Church making it indistinguishable from Western Christianity. The distorting impact of such culturally generated supervision can be gauged by remembering that often during the Society of Jesus' nearly eighty year association with the Romanian Church, before and after the Union, it was seen as supportive of the Eastern Rite. But the trust enjoyed during the time of Teofil and Atanasie, when Jesuit solicitude for Greek Church mores was aimed at the Calvinists, was first undermined and then in many quarters lost due to the bureaucratic position of the "Theologian" as the representative of intrusive Western influences.[91]

This missive of the Uniate hierarchy to the Transylvanian estates should interest us, however, for more than its expected reiteration of theological purity of intention. Chancellor Bethlen's letter, as a political and economic as well religious response to the Union with Rome, delimited the manner in which the Eastern Rite Catholics might express their new corporate identity. Most importantly, among other provisions regulating the Uniate Church in Transylvania, Bethlen formally broached the topic of restricting the number of Romanian priests permitted in each village. This did not represent an attempt to alter the nature of the Eastern Rite liturgy or to change village customs, though eighteenth century ventures in the same direction would be seen as such. Rather it signified an awareness of the loss that might be incurred by increased number of priests completely excused from the financial exactions usually paid by Romanian clergy. Traditionally each village contained a far larger number of priests than either Latin Rite Catholics or Protestants would have deemed appropriate. Partially these numbers were dictated by the nature of the service. But Bethlen's prohibition of "excess" priests reflected the Romanian youth's inclination to seek the priesthood in significant numbers because Orthodox priests under the feudal order had been relieved of the corvée obligation. Ordination provided a road by which to escape from the worst of the serf's lot. Some Transylvanian villages ended up with as many as six to ten Orthodox priests because of this theological safety valve from the pressures of the Old Regime. Under the Uniate dispensation, in which yet more attractive inducements to the priesthood were to be offered, Bethlen and the estates he spoke for had to be anxious about further flight from the financial depredations of the existing feudal order. By seeking to circumvent the Uniate expectation of enjoying the same number of priests per village as did the Orthodox, the Magyar Chancellor sought to employ a more politic weapon against the Union and Habsburg centralist policies than mere obstruction. Though an economic point well made, when the same issue surfaced in the hands of Latin Rite Catholics, it also took on some of the trappings of animosity towards the Eastern Rite. The Uniate as well as the Orthodox of the eighteenth and later centuries could not but take umbrage at the Western condescension contained in the stereotypical observation that they "were less fastidious in the selection of their priests than were the Catholics of the Latin Rite." Even when the adherents of the Eastern Rite acknowledged the financial motivations and the educational deficiencies of some of their clergy, the hauteur of such remarks came to symbolize their status as perceived second class Catholics of questionable ardor. Once they too had an educated clergy some of whom had been trained in the West, Latin commentaries of this ilk would transcend the galling to become unacceptable. Such residue, acutely remembered even in the twenty-first century, helps explain much of the exasperation of the relations between sects as well as rites then and now.[92]

By 1699 although having to all outward appearances fully endorsed Union with Rome according to the strictures of the Council of Florence, Bishop Atanasie found himself attacked by the Protestants and yet not unreservedly welcomed by the Latin Rite hierarchy. His faith and character along with the aspirations of his clergy would still have to undergo considerable scrutiny before satisfying the Cardinal Kollonichs of his world. The same session of the General Synod that had responded to Bethlen's letter likewise protested the investigatory nature of the Chancellor's measuring of the Uniate movement. For some three centuries the Romanian Eastern Rite Catholics' repetition of their devout willingness to accept all of Rome's preconditions for reunion has seldom been sufficient to allay their opponents' suspicions or occasional enmity. Those with economic agenda as well as those irritated by denominational or ritual issues persisted in imputing to them the mentality and ethics of "rice Christians." But Atanasie and the Synod did try again. Having once pointed out that they had accepted Union on the basis of the "Four Points" contained in the Emperor's diplomas, they proclaimed furthermore that this action was taken "...of their own free will, without concession to human respect, solely because of their love of the uniquely true and salvific religion...." They went on to maintained that they wished "to remain in and serve...that Union," vowing that they had no intention "of either lapsing from the Roman Catholic Church or joining any other religion opposed to Roman Catholicism." Whatever amelioration of the attitudes of their adversaries that could be accomplished by words Atanasie and the Synod essayed. It would not be enough for either Latin Rite Catholic or Calvinist. Atanasie, as an individual, would be accused from the very beginning of being openly duplicitous, of admitting to his confidantes that he had espoused the Union "only for appearances" as had his priests only for the advantages they could gain. Shortly, on the basis of similar intimations, he would be accused for apostasy.[93]

To undercut such suspicions and opposition the Uniate bishop called yet another Synod for the first week of September 1700. His goal here centered on giving the clerically inspired and endorsed Union the impress of a more general folk enthusiasm. In so doing he might refurbish his own image, foil the intrigues of the Transylvanian elite, and finally obtain the Emperor's definitive sanction of the Eastern Rite Roman Catholic Church. Such a chorus of reaffirmation of the Romanian collective commitment to Rome was seen as the best practical defense against entrenched opposition as well as the most effective way of achieving Vienna's official recognition. This meeting, held at the episcopal see in Alba-Iulia drew not only a greater attendance from the clerical elite of the Uniate church, but also over a thousand ordinary priests drawn from every Romanian village in Transylvania. The hope being, of course, to present a facade of widespread, general acceptance which would preclude further carping from either Latin Rite Catholics or Protestants regarding the religious foundation of the movement towards Union with Rome. But even with this manifest political intent and the by now almost *pro forma* incantation that they were acting "freely and of their own will," these delegates to the Synod of 1700 still adhered to their original bargaining position. They accepted Union with Rome only on the basis of the "Four Points" and "nothing else." Likewise they insisted that their Greek Rite and church discipline "remain as it has been until now."[94] Whatever they hoped to obtain from the Habsburgs and the Transylvania estates they clearly and consistently would not consider any adulteration of their traditional modes of worship and church governance.

The month following this Synod Atanasie wrote to Cardinal Kollonich imploring his assistance against the Calvinists, begging in short for the status he believed the Uniates had been promised in Leopold's diplomas; namely, to be indeed treated as Catholics. He knew he was swimming against the tide in this instance. For in the spring of 1699 he had received a set of guidelines specifying how the Emperor's invitation to Union would be interpreted by local authorities. This "Instruction" severely circumscribed the number of individuals allowed to enjoy the privileges of the Catholic clergy, specifically limiting the number of Uniate priests in a village. More to the point of the deeply ingrained opposition, Roman Catholic as well as Protestant, to the Uniate Church was this document's *caveat* that "…all those wishing to enjoy…such privileges, had to sincerely unite with the Roman Catholic religion; for those who might be deemed guilty of fraud, would not be able to avoid his Majesty's severe reproof…." Cardinal Kollonich's attitudes stood out even more as the determinative factor where Bishop Atanasie's career as well as the structure and lineaments of the Uniate Church were concerned. Eight months prior to Atanasie's plea for support Kollonich had sent him a decree outlining what the Uniates could expect from the Cardinal's office and illuminating for them in no small measure his sentiment towards their church. In his capacity as Primate of Hungary the Cardinal ordered that the number of Romanian priests in a village be restricted, that the youth of that nation be admitted to Roman Catholic schools so as to produce a better educated priesthood, and that the Uniates were to have the same status and access to the law as did Latin Rite Roman Catholics. To understand the cultural clash that would characterize the relationship between the two rites as well as the jurisdictional jockeying that would continue into the modern world it must also kept in mind that this forceful "resolution" by the most important Roman Catholic cleric in the eastern marches of the Habsburg Monarchy likewise severely limited the autonomy of the new church. Although encouraging the education of Uniate young men and guaranteeing them admittance to Jesuit and other institutions, Cardinal Kollonich similarly commanded that no Romanian be ordained "without first being tested not only by Romanian clerical examiners, but also by Latin Rite priests appointed by the Vicar General."[95] He trusted neither the basic commitment nor competence of the Uniates, an aversion reinforced by both ecclesiastical tradition and folkloric considerations. In the end the result would be the installation of the Jesuit "Theologian" at the side of the Uniate bishop to ensure his *bona fides* and the appropriate acquiescence to Roman cultural sensitivities as well as to church discipline.

The continuing background to this struggle for final, definitive legal recognition of the Uniate Church and Atanasie's stewardship consisted of the split in the Romanian community, a rupture reflecting not only approximately half that group's determination to remain Orthodox but also a rejection of many villagers of their priests' accommodation with Western Christianity. While this atmosphere of generalized Romanian opposition to the Uniate Church would persist well into the eighteenth century, indeed becoming even more violent before Maria Theresia's reinstitution of an Orthodox hierarchy in Transylvania, by 1700 this ethnic schism had found a focal point in the commercial association of Braşov with its intense devotion to the Eastern Church. This community would in many ways sum up the new century's opposition to the Uniate Bishop and his church by accusing him of hypocrisy and recasting their cherished Eastern Rite.[96] In June of 1700 the leaders of the Orthodox Church in that southeastern Transylvanian town wrote to the General Synod that they did "not wish to know anything about the union with the Church of Rome" and furthermore that they would not readmit to their community any priest that had accepted the "Four Points." They were most specific in their rejection of the Uniate Church citing their refusal to embrace any other rite. By the following year the Orthodox of Braşov sent Atanasie an even more explicit letter declaring they would not accept the Union with Rome under any circumstances, that to acknowledge the "Four Points" not only introduced variation into their traditional rite but also made one a "Papist." In a like vein that transmitted their absolute recalcitrance they also wrote to both the Governor of Transylvania and to the Emperor asking "to be left in peace" and "in their ancient orthodox faith."[97] Such correspondence not only alerted Leopold to their dissatisfaction and to the putative nature of the proclaimed universal union of the Transylvanian Orthodox with Rome, but at the same time reinforced the resistance and leverage of the province's established orders. The Protestant and Roman Catholic who opposed the Union for economic or political reasons could now point to the extensive Orthodox resistance as well as to the doubt it cast on Atanasie's and his followers' true motivations. The fracas had sufficient extent and volume to bring itself to the attention of the Catholic authorities in Italy within the twelvemonth. From this point on Braşov as a focus of Orthodox repudiation of the Uniate movement and as a reproach to those who had entered the world of Western influences would remain a constant in the cultural-political life of the Transylvanian Romanians.[98]

1701, then, stood out as a critical year for the Uniates. In that pivotal twelve months they would finally obtain the official recognition they had so long sought from Emperor Leopold as well as experience the full weight of Cardinal Kollonich's administrative authority and cultural predispositions towards Western norms. The Cardinal's receptivity to the accusations from all sides against Atanasie's actions and character would later express itself in the limitations imposed upon the Uniate bishop's autonomy and the fundamental structure of his church. Looming large in Kollonich's view was the suspicion of continued Calvinist influence over Atanasie. The Cardinal was well aware the Romanian's Calvinist education, his ties to the Reformed Church's administration, and the promises he had been compelled to make in order to obtain his episcopal see. If these evaluations of Atanasie's person are then put into the context of Kollonich's general views about the Orthodox, there emerges not merely an inaccurate, but a quite jaundiced theoretical opinion of the entire group the Cardinal had just allowed to enter his church under the guise of a reunion with Rome. For in the spring of 1701, at the very time when so many lasting and crucial decisions were being made about the Uniate Church, he wrote to the Congregation for the Propagation of the Faith detailing his distrust of all such persons. In that letter Cardinal Kollonich made the sweeping claim that "schismatic bishops are either atheists or men without faith…and guilty of simony." With this gentle introduction he went on to generalized on the moral and canonical turpitude of the Orthodox hierarchs ending up questioning the "validity" of all Orthodox consecrations and ordinations. Even more ominous for the relations between the rites and the future of the Uniate ecclesiastical organization, Kollonich also passed on to Rome the sort of scurrilous misrepresentation that all too often contaminates contact between cultures. With all the prestige of his position as Primate and as the authority on the scene, he reported to Rome a series of "errors" supposedly characteristic of the Orthodox Church and all those such as Atanasie who emerged from its ambience. While detailing quite real distinctions between Catholicism and Orthodoxy, Kollonich also regaled Rome with simple cultural differences or perceived slights (e.g., "they do not allow Latins to celebrate [Mass] on their altars") as well as gross overgeneralizations (e.g., "the Eastern Church permits divorce at the whim of the marriage parties with no reference to the reasons"). Finally, Cardinal Kollonich's basic attitude towards the world of Orthodoxy and the rite from which his new charges, the Romanian Uniates, had emerged encompassed the wildest misunderstanding or perhaps even calumny. For he charged in his letter to the *Propaganda Fidei* that, on top of everything else, "[Orthodox] confessors oblige their faithful to kill Latins, promising them that this act would result in the remission of their sins."[99]

In this context and before this ecclesiastical superior Bishop Atanasie would be called to Vienna in 1701 to give an account of himself and his prospective stewardship of the Uniate Church. Influential modern Romanian historians have termed this sojourn in Vienna and the bishop's treatment by Cardinal Kollonich a "catastrophe" and a "purification…by inquisitorial examination" which would ultimately "humiliate" bishop and church alike. Although both the Habsburgs and institutionalized Roman Catholicism in that monarchy wished to consolidate and strengthen the Uniate movement, in the first year of the new century the approach taken was a comprehensive assault upon Atanasie and his church. The Uniate ecclesiastical structure was seen as in bad repair and certainly not capable of withstanding the opposition of both Calvinist and Orthodox churches. The bishop was deemed of fundamentally bad character, probably insincere in his commitment to Roman Catholicism, and obviously not up to the demands of his office where spiritual and theological training were concerned.[100] Behind this facade of dispute over Atanasie's morals and devotion to Rome towered a matter of far more transcending importance, one that would shape the development of the Uniate Church from this point on as well as the nature of the opposition it would meet at the hands of its former Orthodox brothers down to the present time. Would the Union with Rome and the details of its working out be interpreted from the Romanian or Viennese point of view? More specifically, could Atanasie and his supporters cling to the Florentine interpretation of the requirements for reunion (i.e., only the "Four Points") as embraced by the General Synod? Or would Kollonich's views prevail, a set of opinions that mandated all the Counter-Reformation rigor of the Council of Trent and a corresponding emphasis upon each individual's commitment. The fact that Atanasie and his flock sought socio-economic improvement as well as liaison with Rome complicated their lot and increased the suspicion with which they were viewed in Vienna. To remedy the unclear nature of the Union with Rome, to make it conform more strictly to the Tridentine views of Cardinal Kollonich, and to ring the Uniate bishop about with sufficient safeguards to ensure his *bona fides* Atanasie was in 1701 called to Vienna to be interrogated and then reconsecrated. Kollonich had managed to maneuver the Emperor into accepting his views on both the bishop's person and the deficient formula of the Romanian commitment. Now the oath that would be required of the Uniates and the subsequent interpretation that Cardinal Kollonich as well as those of like mind would be able to place on it would reflect the tone of Trent rather than of Florence. The differences were not simply substantial, but also reflected in a causal fashion the cultural incoherencies existing then and now between the two rites. Kollonich had won, but in the process guaranteed a generational long conflict over the integrity and dignity of the Romanians' cultural expression of their Christianity. As would be pointed out with all too rare a frequency, this would indeed prove to be a pyrrhic victory.[101]

In February of 1701, accompanied by the Jesuit adviser Karl Neuräuter, Bishop Atanasie journeyed to Vienna to begin the process that would eventually grant official corporate existence to the Uniate Church as a sanctioned if not comfortably conventional part of Roman Catholicism. Unfortunately, in the dispute over the character of the Uniate commitment and the politically sensitive nature of their status, the trade-off would be the abandonment of the laity. Only the clergy would receive the promised privileges. In addition the profound alterations demanded by Cardinal Kollonich in the quality of the oath taken by the Uniates would in the long run constitute at least as great a peril to the Union with Rome as the entrenched opposition of the Transylvanian elites. Without the moderating influence of a few influential individuals like the Jesuit Ladislaus Baranyi the strictures imposed by the Primate would have been even more crippling to the new church. Under the prodding of Cardinal Kollonich the Viennese Court had decided to compel Atanasie to relinquish a union based on the Florentine concept of a "meeting in faith" between the two Christian sects and to opt instead for the Council of Trent's "penitential return to the true faith and to the law of the Church." This latter approach not only demonstrated a lack of feeling for the Uniates' extraordinarily deep devotion to the culture of the Eastern Rite, but also laid the groundwork for the difficulties including outright revolt that would plague the Uniate Church throughout the eighteenth century. The procrustean bed into which Kollonich forced the Romanians had as much to do with a significantly more authoritarian conception of ecclesiastical organization as it did with theological or even liturgical discrepancies.[102]

At the end of the first week of April 1701, Atanasie took an oath comprised of some sixteen propositions summing up all of these factors, one remarkably similar in intent and tone to that the Calvinists had subjected him to. This vow also encapsulated the substance and tenor of the "canonical cleansing" ("*purgatio canonica*"), technically a "canonical demonstration of innocence from criminal charges," which the Romanian bishop was constrained to endure. Both pressure and the promise of various marks of honor were required to ensure his acceptance of and then compliance with this vastly altered scenario for the Union with

Rome. Interestingly, perhaps even ironically, the Latin Rite authorities who were questioning Atanasie so vigorously as to his motivations and sincerity, apparently saw no discrepancy between this mode of action and the use of such extraneous means of compelling assent. The mentality was reminiscent of that which initially sought the Romanians for reunion despite their "ignorance," but then subsequently criticized their uninformed, incomplete endorsement of all things redolent of Western culture's version of Catholicism. Cardinal Kollonich and other Latin Rite authorities seemingly wanted it both ways; namely, a conveniently quick "conversion" for political purposes and at the same time one hundred percent educated sincerity on the part of the Romanian Uniates.[103] Similarly in this instance the stated purpose of having Atanasie repeat yet again his commitment was "not to disturb the tranquility of the Greek Rite Uniates, ...but rather to nurture and consolidate that group...." Kollonich did ask the Uniate bishop to accept a number of items that were to be expected. Having once again proclaimed his sincerity and the *sine qua non* condition of his clergy's participation in all Catholic perquisites, Atanasie accepted Cardinal Kollonich as his legitimate ecclesiastical superior. In like vein he promised obedience to the reigning Pope (Clement IX), to remove the name of the Patriarch of Constantinople from the liturgy, and to make a complete break with the Orthodox Metropolitan of Bucharest and other such schismatic church leaders. From this point onwards he could admit to his residence no one who was not a "Roman Catholic or Uniate" (Calvinists and "schismatics," i.e., Orthodox, were excluded by name as were women as a category). Not surprisingly he had to vow to erect a school where the instruction would be in Latin and Romanian as well as to encourage the frequenting of the sacraments by the Uniate laity.[104]

Sadly, for the relationship between rites and denominations right down to the present time, Kollonich's exactions from the Uniate bishop did not stop at this foreseen and understandable juncture. Atanasie had to reiterate his "profession of faith according to the publicly prescribed form of the Council of Trent." Furthermore he promised to require the same of each and every one of his clergy under pain of not being allowed to enjoy the privileges promised by the Emperor. Far more damaging to his position and to the interaction of Catholicism and Orthodoxy even into the twenty-first century, Atanasie had to admit that the orders conferred by the Eastern Church were "in a great many cases" questionable, indeed that often the Orthodox ecclesiastics concerned were "neither true nor legitimate priests and bishops." Because of this in his oath Atanasie "prayed" that he might be re-ordained a priest and reconsecrated a bishop. Once having received Roman Catholic orders, the Uniate bishop expressed his desire to re-ordain all clerics previously brought into the priesthood by either himself or his predecessors. Besides the obvious affront to the Uniates and the Orthodox, this stipulation of Cardinal Kollonich's cannot but surprise the informed reader, since it flew in the face of the Vatican's expressed policy dating back to the mid-seventeenth century. Furthermore, the reasoned bias behind this stance of Kollonich's with its markedly deleterious effects upon the Romanians would, of course, have applied to all other Uniate churches in Eastern Europe. Thus, in 1699 the Congregation for the Propagation of the Faith reported that the Ruthenian Uniate Bishop Johann de Camillis of Munkacs had declared his determined opposition to such re-ordination and re-consecration as a marked danger to the Romanian Uniate movement, one that could possibly cause "a mass return to schism." By the summer of that critical year of 1701 the *Propaganda Fidei* ruled that bishops such as Atanasie had been "validly but illicitly consecrated" and should not be reconsecrated. Unfortunately, Cardinal Kollonich had already acted both apodictically and prematurely in this matter. Lasting harm to the Uniate Church as well as to relations between Catholicism and Orthodoxy had been done. Even if he had not acted so swiftly there is no reason to believe that the Cardinal would have accepted this repetition of the *Propaganda Fidei*'s decision on the legitimacy of Orthodox orders any more than he had been willing to acquiesce in that tribunal's verdict on what constituted an sufficient profession of faith; namely, the norms of Florence rather than those of Trent. He simply chose to ignore the Vatican's chosen forum for determining these issues. Being at the scene and having Leopold's ear guaranteed the adoption, if not the wisdom or ultimate success, of his policies.[105]

Though not quite as long-lived in their detrimental impact on the Uniates as this attack on Orthodox orders, Cardinal Kollonich acting in his administrative capacity as Primate of Hungary did compel Bishop's Atanasie's acceptance of two structural concessions, one relating to the inculcation Western norms of competence and the other pertaining to Vienna's influence over the selection of future Uniate bishops. Both would exacerbate Romanian sensitivities for most of the eighteenth century. The first, the imposition of "a Roman Catholic priest as theologian and counselor," Atanasie petitioned for in his prescribed oath. He described this religious bureaucrat as being necessary because of the Eastern Rite's "many errors contrary to the councils and canons of the Universal Church that had crept in over the centuries under the Turkish yoke." On a more personal level, he also implored the creation of this post of Latin Rite "Theologian," a position of significant power that everyone (in Rome as well as Transylvania and Vienna) anticipated would be filled by one of the Jesuits already active in the province, because of his "lack of instruction and experience." This Jesuit "Theologian," however, possessed far more influence over the Uniate episcopal see than would ever be tolerated in the Latin Rite, whatever the character of the bishop might be. Without the "Theologian's" presence and prior permission Bishop Atanasie could not convoke a Synod, ordain or issue an edict of excommunication, transfer or award an ecclesiastical distinction to one of his priests, or communicate with any Orthodox official. Besides being required to pledge "to act honorably, not despotically," the Uniate prelate had "to embrace and follow the advice of the 'Theologian'...in all church matters." These "church matters" over which the Jesuit would have final say included the right "to censure" books, to oversee the general administration of the diocese especially legal issues, to determine the appropriate fees for all services rendered by the Uniate clergy, to audit the financial affairs of the see, and finally "to correct" the bishop as required by circumstances. In addition to putting up with all of this interference, Atanasie had to announce that he would "willingly receive...and act upon" the admonishings of the "Theologian," both as these applied to himself and to the Romanian church.[106]

As one modern Romanian historian has so pointedly observed these strictures of Cardinal Kollonich imbedded in Atanasie's oath to the Union, perhaps most importantly the creation of the Jesuit "Theologian," treated the Romanian bishop as "a delinquent and were without precedent in the history of the religious unions."[107] Equally unique, and reflecting the same severe attitude of admonition towards the former Orthodox now supposedly so eagerly desired as Uniates, was the Cardinal's "Instruction" naming the Jesuit Karl Neuräuter as "Theologian" to Bishop Atanasie. Once again as in the lengthy vow analyzed above, the complex of conflicting attitudes produced a detailed document reminiscent of the lists of conditions imposed on the Romanian prelates by the

Calvinist Superintendents. Here, Kollonich instructed Neuräuter that as "Theologian" to the Uniate bishop he would be dealing with a people both "ignorant" and swayed by the baleful influences of "barbarians and heretics." The daunting task set for the Jesuit, then, was to root out ecclesiastical abuses and "errors in matters of faith…in the laity, the clergy, and even in the Bishop…and in doing so to prevent a relapse into schism by a people so inclined…." Specifically, the Jesuit "Theologian" received directions to instruct the bishop and to observe that good order was maintained in the episcopal residence. If upon examination the Jesuit determined that Atanasie was not living up to his various promises, he was to caution him to do so. Neuräuter also had the obligation to scrutinize the administration of the Uniate diocese, among other reasons to ensure that Atanasie did not act "despotically." If and when a Synod should be convoked, the "Theologian" was to be present at the bishop's side to guarantee good order and, if it should prove necessary, to side with the clergy against the bishop. As promised in Atanasie's deposition before Cardinal Kollonich, the "Theologian" obtained the power to censure all printed literature and any correspondence with "schismatics." Besides having the right to examine all Romanian candidates for the priesthood, the Jesuit "Theologian" possessed an absolute veto over who could be ordained and the authority to prevent the Uniate bishop from creating too many new priests and thus an "inconvenience." On a more positive note, this Latin Rite official also received Kollonich's charge to promote schools for Uniate youth and to help ensure that Atanasie's clergy did indeed succeed in enjoying the same privileges as other Catholic clerics. But even this ameliorating aspect of the "Instruction" was undercut by Cardinal Kollonich's closing remark. Here he warned the "Theologian" that the fourteen points covered in this guide to dealing with the former Orthodox only covered the more important problems. Neuräuter and his successors were to use their "prudence" in addressing any other particulars that might arise in guiding this congregation that had so recently returned from schism. This sweeping grant of power over the Uniate Church was limited only by the suggestion that, in cases of doubt, the Jesuit "might have recourse" to the Primate's office in Strigon. Adding to the preponderant prestige of this office within the structure of the Uniate Church would be the fact that final papal approval of Atanasie's episcopal dignity would be coupled with the office of this "Latin Theologian" designated to stand observantly at his side.[108]

The second of the structural changes inspired by Kollonich's investigation of the Romanian hierarch in Vienna was the alteration of the method of selecting Atanasie's successors. In contrast to the selection by the Grand Synod which had been the norm in the past, even if such an individual had to have had the sanction of both the Calvinist princes of Transylvania and of the Superintendent, now the Synod could only propose three candidates to Vienna for consideration. After the submission in writing of the names of these individuals to fill future vacancies in the Uniate Church's leadership, the determination as to who would be the Romanian bishop would be made by Rome and Vienna. Beyond the control to be exercised by political and religious factors outside of the Uniate Church's sphere of influence there existed the added problem of the selection process becoming overly protracted. When the lack of suitable Romanian candidates or jurisdictional squabbles entered the picture, such difficulties might slow the procedure. Indeed, over the next two plus generations the Romanian episcopal see in Transylvania would be vacant for twenty-five years. This "calamity for the Uniate Church" also allowed not merely for drift in the supervision of the Romanian rite, but also permitted the Jesuit "Theologian" to step into the episcopal vacancy as "Director" of the diocese. However well meaning and efficient this may have been, it would obviously aggravate the already suspicious Romanians and their sensitivities as to the integrity of their Greek Rite.[109]

This whole process supposedly was designed to encompass not only the "cleansing" ("*purgatio*") aspect of Atanasie's confrontation with Cardinal Kollonich but also an element of "reconciliation." Unfortunately, any adjustment seems to have been on the side of the former Orthodox and amounted to propitiation on a grand scale. Atanasie's oath, the "Instruction" to the omnipresent Jesuit counselor, and the abrogation of the Synod's ability to choose its bishop all seemed to indicate that the Latin Rite would insist on conformity whenever possible. The quality of Cardinal Kollonich's rigor in these matters seemed somewhat incompatible with his political/proselytizing intentions, even given his suspicions about the Orthodox Church. After the death of Teofil, the initial Uniate bishop, he had written to the movement's secular sponsor Stephen Apor "urging him to guide the Romanians however possible into the Union with the Roman Catholics, and thus to complete that Union." The mentality involved perhaps can be explained by Kollonich insinuation that "inestimable thanks" would be garnered in Rome and Vienna by bringing the Romanian Union to a solidly satisfactory fruition.[110] As already intimated and as would later be worked out in bitter detail, the imposition of these conditions on Atanasie and the Uniate Church revealed a considerable "shortsightedness" on the part of the administrations of both Cardinal Kollonich and Emperor Leopold. Between 1701 and the suppression of the Society of Jesus in 1773 Rome would often lack the ability to act as a countervailing force against the cultural myopia of Vienna and Strigon. As a result tensions would emerge in the Uniate Church and in its relations with Latin Rite authorities that found their origin in the *sui generis* judgments of ecclesiastical leaders like Cardinal Kollonich rather than in any liturgical or theological mandate from the Pope.[111] The direction in which the Primate of Hungary was moving may be seen from his letter of December 17, 1701 in which he petitioned the Congregation for the Propagation of the Faith to allow Latin priests to transfer to the Greek Rite. The rationale offered centered on these priests teaching Romanian youth and thus leading them to the Union. To understand this request, besides keeping in mind the already ubiquitous Jesuit sway through the presence of the "Theologian" and the other Jesuits stationed at the episcopal see in Alba-Iulia, it should be understood that the Cardinal by "Latin priests" specifically meant that primarily Jesuits were to change rites. In seeking this multiplication of influence Western influence he wrote not only the Vatican, but also the General of the Society of Jesus, believing that the Jesuits "were the most suitable for this work." The interesting portion of this request centers, however, around "the winning to the Union" of Greek rite young men. Under the terms of the Romanian Union with Rome only children of Uniate families were to gain access to the type of education enjoyed by Latin Rite Roman Catholics. Thus Jesuit influence, whether these clerics remained Latin Rite or switched to the Greek Rite, could reach only Uniates, the already "converted." If though the intent was liturgical instead of denominational or educational, then the use of priests steeped in and partial to the Latin Rite presented a apt facade behind which to intensify the cultural impact of Western Christianity.[112]

Lest this conclusion seem to mirror the markedly nationalistic perspective of some modern Romanian historians or to have too much the flavor of an anachronism, it must be remembered that a strong but minority point of view supporting this contention existed among the

Jesuits of the time. Gabriel Kapi (the Jesuit superior for the Dacian mission) and Christophorus Gebhard (superior of the Jesuit residence in what was then Hermannstadt, now the modern city of Sibiu) both thought Cardinal Kollonich was acting inadvisably in his treatment of Bishop Atanasie. In March of 1701 the Jesuits wrote to the Primate agreeing that Bishop Atanasie was suspect and in all likelihood insincere in his protestations of loyalty to the Union with Rome. But they also thought the plan of action contained in the Romanian leader's oath before Cardinal Kollonich and in the instructions to the Jesuit "Theologian" would ultimately be harmful to the Uniate movement. On the most basic point of continued contention between the Latin and Greek rites from Kollonich's day until the twenty-first century, the two Jesuits adamantly maintained that there could be no doubt as to Orthodox orders. Atanasie had indeed been validly ordained a priest and consecrated a bishop, even if according to a cultural idiom not entirely palatable to Cardinal Kollonich. Furthermore, despite the widespread problems with faith and morals among the Uniates, they argued that

> ...it is sufficient at this time to labor for the substance of the Union; that to attempt to eradicate even all of the grave abuses of the Romanians would be most dangerous and patently impossible. Therefore it would suffice to have the bishop and others make a profession of faith in the Union, if they declare their allegiance to the Church of Rome...and promise to practice the Greek Rite according to the norms approved for their region by Rome....[113]

The culturally judicious appraisal of the two Jesuit superiors also manifested itself in their statement that there would be plenty of time to amend the inappropriate customs and beliefs that had crept in due to the influence of an uneducated and perhaps occasionally remise clergy. Even in this critical view they quickly added that the failings in question were repugnant to Christians in general and in no way peculiar to either the Greek Church or to schismatics. Kapi and Gebhard refused to sanction the sort of calumnious rumors about the Orthodox which Cardinal Kollonich had reported to Rome and which stood as the motivating background to many of his actions vis-à-vis the Romanian Uniates. In this balanced approach a Uniate would only be concerned by their offhanded remark that they "perhaps, might also correct the [Greek Rite] liturgy," a prospect that would suffuse Jesuit-Uniate relations for the next seventy years.

The two Jesuit superiors displayed an equal candor and acumen in relating for Cardinal Kollonich their views on the foundation of the Union, the quality of the Uniate bishop, and the institution of the "Theologian." However weak the Union and even admitting the highly questionable nature of Atanasie's commitment to it, Kapi and Gebhard recommended that he be confirmed as Uniate bishop. They also counseled against any use of force to support the Union with Rome. In their judgment the use of the attractive potential of the privileges granted to the clergy would be sufficient to entice adherents to the Uniate movement. They likewise advised that Cardinal Kollonich should confirm Atanasie in his possession of the Romanian episcopal see, lest major disturbances damaging to Roman Catholic interest and the civil order in Transylvania take place. The most insightful comments made by the Jesuits, however, centered on their rejection of the notion of a required "Theologian" peering over the Uniate bishop's shoulder, even though this office with its obvious power and discretion would fall within the purview of the Society of Jesus. They argued that this official was "neither expedient nor necessary." Kapi and Gebhard rightly judged that the bishop and Romanian people would find it unpleasant as well as difficult to have the "Theologian" thrust upon them, especially since two possibly competing sources of authority would then be in residence in Alba-Iulia. Even more interesting and revealing was the two Jesuits' analysis of why this arrangement was not required at all.

> [The "Theologian"] is not necessary, because it is quite sufficient that the [Romanian] priests are fully committed to Father Baranyi or to his successor or to any other of Our [i.e., the Jesuits'] priests in Alba Julia. For it is a certain fact that more of the priests are dependent on Baranyi now than on their own bishop...this dependency is less obvious to the Romanians, and therefore less repugnant [than the "Theologian"].[114]

They also thought that any danger Atanasie's character and lack of profound attachment to the Union might entail could easily be adverted through the use of the General Synod at which Jesuits would always be present. "For it is certain that many of the priests are opposed to the bishop; many are friends of the Union." In concluding their remarks on the "Theologian" the two Jesuit superiors demonstrated a marked prescience regarding the interaction of these two structural changes imposed by Cardinal Kollonich on the Uniate Church. If Atanasie ever had to be removed (and, by implication, in all future cases of selecting a bishop under the new regulations), they strongly urged that the transition be made "without delay." Though thinking in 1701 about the avoidance of public disturbances should Atanasie have to be dismissed, their caution in this regard would easily encompass the extraordinary damage done by twenty-five years out of the next seventy-two in which a Jesuit "Theologian" bearing the title of "Director" substituted for a missing Romanian prelate.[115] Only intimated, but present and again extremely accurate as an instinctively felt prognosis, stood the Jesuits' anticipation of what this post of "Theologian" might do to their initially favorable relationship with the Romanian clergy. By the suppression of the Society of Jesus in 1773, and the concomitant disappearance of this ecclesiastical functionary, the empathy that had existed between Uniate bishop and Jesuit in the time of Teofil had long since evaporated into fractiousness and even enmity.

Whatever apprehensions there may have been on the part of the Jesuits as the primary guardians of the Romanian Uniate Church, these remained secondary in 1701 to more bureaucratic and culturally oriented considerations. The results of the miscalculations being made at this point would only manifest themselves gradually, though with a growing petulance, over the next several generations. Some continue to be felt today. At the end of March, with the authenticity of Atanasie's profession of faith having finally been properly documented according to Vatican specifications, Cardinal Kollonich formally and legally confirmed him as the Uniate bishop of Transylvania. Emperor Leopold, acting at the same time, both ratified that confirmation of his episcopal status and ordered his installation as a fully sanctioned Roman Catholic prelate.[116] All three clearly understood that the Jesuit "Theologian" complemented Atanasie's oath of commitment to the Catholic Church as an essential part of the bishop's engagement. The Jesuits for their part clearly comprehended that the Cardinal would not have proceeded with Atanasie's enthronement without this guardian of faith, morals, and Western ecclesiastical culture firmly planted behind the bishop's throne. The Emperor likewise commanded the Transylvanian authorities to support the Uniate Church and its new bishop. Along with these efforts to strengthen the Romanians' Union with Rome, Leopold at this time issued his second diploma on the subject which constituted the definitive legal establishment of the Uniate Church. The Romanian people now had in the context of the Uniate Church their sole forum for cultural and political expression in the province of Transylvania. But, if at this juncture Bishop Atanasie and his supporters did obtain the solid legal foundation for the Union with Rome that had been sought for half a decade, in the judgment of influential modern historians they lost at the same time the prospect for autonomy which had helped impel them out of their Calvinist tutelage.[117] The effect of the Second Leopoldine Diploma of 1701 would be to write into stone their subordination to the Jesuit "Theologian" and to a culturally partial Latin hierarchy. So strongly felt has this sentiment been in the nationalistic historical writing of Romania that Atanasie's acceptance of this diploma has been described as

> leading to a system of patronization over the Uniate Church of such pervasiveness and to such weakening of the episcopal power through subordination to an all powerful Theologian, that the reuniting Romanian national church shrank to the status of a simple Catholic diocese or branch church. In addition the Uniate Church's subjugation in this fashion today cripples its beating of wings and hybrid position, which seeks to join the East with the West but which serves neither the enhancement of its reputation nor the enticement of new, respectable followers.[118]

The Second Leopoldine Diploma (1701), serving as it did both political and religious purposes, became the public relations/constitutional foundation for the Habsburgs' claim to domination in Transylvania. In creating a Uniate Church putatively the equal of Latin Rite Roman Catholicism, Leopold gained the legal advantage of henceforth being able to assert that the entire Romanian population of Transylvania had accepted the Union with Rome. After 1701, "in the official opinion of the Viennese Court the Greek [Orthodox] Church no longer existed in Transylvania." Given the unrelenting opposition by the other "received religions" and by their political opponents, this stance had considerable leverage to offer the Habsburg partisans.[119] However, it far exceeded both what can now be determined of the statistics of "conversion" by the Orthodox and even Bishop Atanasie's contemporary embroidery on the reality of his jurisdictional situation. The Uniate hierarch, despite having perhaps the best of vested reasons to overestimate the reach of his church, limited himself to the hyperbole of declaring that "at least 200,000 souls" had opted for the Union with Rome. Most obviously, this diploma demonstrated once again the enormous influence that Cardinal Kollonich had over the Emperor. Leopold's emendation to the Transylvanian constitution and to the religious situation of the Romanians turned Catholic reflected not only the original Uniate diploma inspired by the Cardinal, but also the Hungarian prelate's subsequent statements of position on the whole range of topics affecting this new ethnic branch of Catholicism. As in virtually every other decision made relating to Transylvania in the last quarter century of Leopold's reign, Kollonich's guiding counsel in this constitutional schema for the future of the Uniate Church stood out as the decisive factor.[120]

The fifteen article Diploma of 1701, once again highly reminiscent of the minutely detailed contractual bonds insisted on by the Reformed Church when installing a Romanian metropolitan, had as its doctrinal preface an insistence on the Florentine "Four Points." But from this point on, if the matter be viewed from the perspective of the negotiations and commitments acceded to by that date, the fifteen articles represented at least more circumscribing glosses if not outright additions to what was originally asked of those returning to the Catholic Church. For the most part the various provisions simply reiterated either the 1699 diploma which emanated from Kollonich's office or the dictated oath prescribed for Atanasie or the Cardinal's charge to the Jesuit "Theologian." But now Emperor Leopold spoke formally and legally to bind the authorities in Transylvania to accord the Uniate clergy every privilege enjoyed by the Latin Rite clergy, to forbid the imposition of feudal dues on them, and to insist that all properly accredited laity also be counted as Catholics. He continued to call for a new catechism to replace the old Calvinist tainted version, for regulation of fees for religious services, and for schools for male Uniate children. But beyond these proscriptions, the Diploma of 1701 imposed constraints on the Uniate Church not broached in Teofil's time and now promulgated as binding preconditions for the much desired change in the Romanians constitutional status. Leopold did, indeed, declare that Uniate Romanians could no longer be classified under the medieval constitutional category of "tolerated," but must now be treated as natives of Transylvania. As the price in ecclesiastical autonomy and structure for these concessions he imposed on the Uniate Church Kollonich's two innovations to the basic framework of the then existent Romanian hierarchy; namely, a new selection process for the bishop and the mandatory Latin Rite "Theologian."[121]

As part of the 1701 settlement, and therefore binding politically as well as religiously on the Romanians, the Uniates now had to submit to the Emperor the names of three "suitable and deserving" candidates for the episcopal dignity. The possibilities for delay and manipulation under this schema for choosing Atanasie's successors exceeded to a marked degree even the past incursions of Calvinist authorities into the administrative life of the Romanian Church. Most significantly, in the course of the eighteenth century this process would be the occasion for almost a generation-long hiatus in native leadership for this neonate branch of ethnic Roman Catholicism. The impact on cultural consciousness as well as on the genesis of antipathy towards the most visible symbol of this interference, the Society of Jesus, would be considerable and long-lived. The background for the change from admiration for individual Jesuits to disdain for the Order itself stemmed from the 1701 diploma's imposition on the Uniates of the "Theologian" (though the Jesuits were not named in the document). Due to the ignorance, inexperience, and propensity for creating scandal of the Uniate bishop and his clergy the Emperor wrote into his diploma of 1701 a mandate for this doctrinal steward. For the next seventy-two years, the Society of Jesus would provide a guardian who had to report to the Primate of Hungary, but who had been given specific responsibilities by the head of state. According to the Emperor's guidelines, then, the Jesuit "Theologian" was entrusted with the peremptory power to decide the norms by which a particular Romanian could be judged to be or not to be a Uniate (and thus enjoy the entitlements promised in the Diploma of 1701). When such an individual was permitted to make a profession of faith, thus becoming a Uniate and the possessor of highly valued privileges, that oath had to be taken in the presence of both the bishop and his "Theologian." This Latin Rite custodian received the obligation of censoring, before the fact, the bishop's letters to all Orthodox and other non-Catholic leaders (religious and secular), lest the Uniate's *bona fides* be called into question. The "Theologian" furthermore had to watch out that the bishop did not ordain "more priests than were necessary" and in general insure that the Romanian prelate did not abuse his administrative powers. Finally, echoing the sweeping grant of power contained in Cardinal Kollonich's instructions to the "Theologian," Leopold placed the Jesuits filling that office on the same level with the Uniate bishop in so far as supervising the execution of this diploma was concerned.[122]

With the promulgation of Emperor Leopold's Diploma of 1701 the initial phase of the Romanians' Union with Rome reached fruition. Technically they now composed part of the Roman Catholic Church. Constitutionally they had achieved the status enjoyed by the four "received" religions in Transylvania. They no longer labored under the burden of the pejorative categorization of "tolerated" with all that term meant for their rights and potential permanence of residence in the province. But politically and where Rome's bureaucracy came into play their fate had not been fully worked out yet. Now the frustrations and tensions of Jesuit trusteeship and the continued opposition of Transylvania's established orders would come glaringly to the surface.

III
Jesuits and an Ethnic Hierarchy

Back in Transylvania from the exacting experience in Vienna, Bishop Atanasie returned to his see in Alba-Iulia with the episcopal dignity confirmed by his religious and secular superiors as well as with a display of honor as compensation. With some considerable show he was installed as the Uniate hierarch on June 25, 1701. Attesting to his endorsement by Emperor and Primate, besides the new Leopoldine Diploma of that year with its greater exactitude and legality, the Uniate clergy and laity noticed the conspicuous presence of the Jesuits instrumental in this entire Union process. Ladislaus Baranyi who initiated the Latin Rite participation in the movement and so influenced Metropolitan Teofil along with the new "Theologian" (Carolus Neurauter) came to witness the consolidation of the Society of Jesus' missionary effort among the Orthodox. Also present was the Jesuit superior of the province, Gabriel Kapi, who with such acute foresight had counseled Cardinal Kollonich against imposing either the reception of Latin Rite orders or the "Theologian" on the Uniate bishop.[1] Unfortunately, behind the facade of this obviously satisfying public spectacle, the perceptive observer such as Kapi could still detect the cultural and organizational problems covered over by the rhetoric of the second Leopoldine diploma and the ornate ceremonial for installing a new bishop. The Calvinist opposition to the loss of a century and a half of preponderant influence over the Romanian church had not lessened simply because Leopold and Kollonich now pronounced themselves canonically content with this former client of the Magyar Reformed Church. In addition to this continued pressure from without, the freshly minted Uniate Church faced the reality of the Romanians' ethnic schism. For not only was the Habsburgs' legalistic stance that the Orthodox population had simply disappeared not accurate, but even Atanasie's more modest estimate of the extent of adherence to his church proved optimistic. From the moment of his return to the province sizeable pockets of resistance among the supposedly "converted" manifested themselves. Rejecting the

Union with Rome and renouncing Atanasie's sway over them, these Romanians proclaimed their determination to persevere in Orthodoxy. Their antagonism centered on their fear that the Uniate bishop was embarked on a course that required the renunciation of the Greek Rite and their personal transformation into "papists."[2]

Emperor Leopold's second diploma on behalf of the Romanian Uniates, then, became the framework within which most of the future political and cultural struggles of that ethnic confession would be fought. In the face of entrenched sectarian and civil antipathies, the formerly Orthodox Transylvanians encountered the challenge of transforming this putative Habsburg emendation to the province's constitution. Unfortunately, the protracted campaign to obtain the tangible implementation of the privileges detailed in the 1701 diploma as well as to obviate its detrimental articles such as the introduction of the Latin Rite "Theologian" into the fabric of the Uniate Church would in the course of the eighteenth century consume all of the energies of Atanasie's successors.[3] Despite the pomp and circumstance accorded him as well as the legal basis for his optimism attained through this more formidable imperial decree, Atanasie soon discovered that *de facto* recognition of these changes in the status of the Romanians would be difficult if not impossible to come by, when the Transylvanian authorities were involved. These entrenched, vested interests manifested their displeasure through a manifesto issued by the Diet proclaiming that the Diploma of 1701 violated the province's existing legal scheme. Most particularly they protested not only the ecclesiastical innovation represented by the Uniate movement, but more importantly the alterations it occasioned in the established "political and national" constitution of the region. This combination of church and civil transformations in the Romanians' favor were seen not simply as novelties but more ominously "as a great danger to the state" as it then existed in Transylvania.[4] Regardless of the Emperor's wishes as expressed in the 1701 diploma or the muted nature of their ability to resist outright an improvement in the Uniates' condition, the members of the Diet steadfastly refused to accord anything resembling a full or guileless acceptance of the imperial edict's provisions. For traditionally access to a privileged status in Transylvania had remained tied to ethnic as well as to religious considerations. It was well and good that the Romanians were now a type of Catholic, but they still did not belong to one of the three nations (Magyar, Saxon, and Szekler) which had for centuries monopolized the province's aristocracy. For the Emperor now actually to implement as opposed merely to promulgate such alterations in the traditional constitutional order exceeded the acceptable. Indeed, such a policy would amount to a second, political-social "reformation" that would be resisted violently. After all Leopold pledged in his diploma of 1691 to hold sacrosanct and integral the medieval system of three nations and four accepted religions. His promise had included all the laws supporting that system. They were to be "considered as fundamental and unalterable."[5]

As Bishop Atanasie returned to his diocese, then, both he and his people suffered under the illusion that the Leopold's issuance of the 1701 diploma constituted, in both theory and practice, the bedrock of their new status. Unfortunately, the remainder of the eighteenth century would prove that this was simply a unilateral act on the part of the Viennese court that did not automatically or necessarily elicit a comparable willingness on the part of the ruling classes in Transylvania to abide by the diploma's letter or spirit. Despite repeated imperial directives the governing estates would be consistently successful in circumventing both the supposed rights of the Romanians and the expressed will of the monarch. These privileged elements, including Latin Rite Roman Catholics, through interpretation and legalistic recalcitrance would guard their material and political interests with such tenacity as to more than hold their own against the imperial as well as the Uniate episcopal court. To truly rank and then act on the Uniates' promised position as "sons of the homeland" ("*fiii ai patriei*") would have impressed on the imbedded constitutional structure of Transylvania a new and "revolutionary character." This disparity between what had been guaranteed by Vienna, what was anticipated by the Uniates, and what was realistic to expect given the Diet's opposition would determine all future disagreements between these parties. This triune *contretemps* foreshadowed not only continued impediments generated by those seated in the Diet, but also throughout the eighteenth century a diluted Habsburg interpretation of the rights granted to Atanasie and his successors. Despite the initial high hopes and later the almost scriptural exegesis performed on the Diploma of 1701 by the Romanians, their aspirations based on Leopold's commitment would not see a practical expression.[6] The stratagem embraced by all concerned with the Uniate movement (Habsburg, Jesuit, and Romanian alike) centered on the illusion that making the Transylvanian

Orthodox into Eastern Rite Roman Catholics would serve to distract their opponents from the true intent involved. Somehow the Magyar Calvinists and others were not supposed to interpret this granting of equality to the formerly Orthodox and the concomitant improvement of the Habsburgs' political position as the constitutional revolution that it was. While some contemporaries and later historians analyzed this maneuver as "the only way" to circumvent the existing constitutional order and its defenders, they sadly underestimated the perspicuity of their opponents. For the Union with Rome, if honored in deed as well as in rhetoric, was clearly understood by all to be inimical to the established scheme of precedence in the province. Indeed, "Not one among the 'political nations' or received religions, not even the Catholics, wanted the Uniates to become 'a fourth political nation' as the Romanians postulated was their right according to the diploma of Leopold."[7] The Protestants preferred, and subsequently encouraged, Orthodoxy as a less objectionable alternative to the political encroachments of the Union with Rome. Hauntingly in the background to the half century effort to reestablish an Orthodox bishopric for Transylvania, then, was a Calvinist stratagem to employ this struggle to exert once again their control over a sizeable portion of the Romanian population. In the process they could likewise weaken the position and prestige of the Uniate bishop.[8] The Catholics for their part have been largely interpreted by later, and usually nationalistic, Romanian historians as being willing to accommodate the Uniates only if the price of assimilation were paid in full; namely, that Romanian culture and rite had to be fully "Latinized."

The impenetrable barrier which Atanasie and his church were about to encounter, an obstruction never to be completely overcome, was the privileged classes' exclusive acknowledgment of those rights which were expressly defined in terms of historic legal precedents. The novelties contained in the 1701 imperial diploma simply did not meld with the Transylvanian protocol of earlier diplomas, royal patents, and legislation by the Diet. Regardless of their sectarian affiliation, then, the members of the three "political nations" adhered steadfastly to the factional tenet that constitutional tradition alone mattered, regardless of what Vienna had promised to the Romanian converts to Catholicism. Obviously, by dangling "membership in the Catholic estates not only to priests but also to laymen" the Emperor had dramatically increased the menace to the aristocracy's control over the region. Openly or in a subterranean fashion, and whatever their ethnicity, the nobility had to oppose this religious-political innovation. Moreover, as the privileged orders clearly understood,

> Leopold was offering [in the 1701 diploma] more than he could or wanted to deliver. He had no intention of emancipating the Romanian peasants; he regarded them as instruments for changing the religious, not the social or political structure of the principality.[9]

In the modern era, nationalistic and official historians have presented even more jaundiced evaluations of this opposition and the equivocal nature of the Viennese Court's support. Besides asserting the hyperbole that "the Romanian Church had exchanged the constitutional yoke of the Calvinist for the absolutist one of the Catholics," such critics have also pointed out in a more balanced manner that the Habsburgs never intended to execute their pledges to the Uniates, having instead other goals in mind.

> The [Viennese] Court did not make this concession with the thought in mind of implementing it literally. Indeed, it [i.e., the Diploma of 1701] had only been issued as a matter of necessity and with a political purpose. The text of this concession could confer a double advantage: on the one hand, it could represent a new bait for the Romanians binding them reliably; on the other hand, it could be utilized as a new, directly felt threat against the political nations.[10]

This ploy gave the Habsburgs the unanticipated prospect both to increase vastly the numbers of Catholics in Transylvania and at the same time better compel the fidelity of the "political nations" of Magyars, Saxons, and Szeklers. This form of "divide and conquer" permitted the Habsburgs to intertwine religious and political antagonisms, amplifying the resulting disharmony to their own advantage.

While the legalistic struggle described above with its ethnic and social overtones raged between the Transylvanian estates, Leopold's court, and the Uniate hierarchy, that portion of the Romanian peasantry unwilling to accept the Union with Rome also made itself felt. Even though the official stance of secular and religious authorities prescribed that the Orthodox Church no longer existed in the province, this patently did not correspond with the facts. As the leading element in this resistance, and a symbol of the even more widespread dissatisfaction to be found among large numbers of the Romanian community, the Orthodox of Braşov and the surrounding areas proclaimed their displeasure and determination to avoid the "papists" in loud and most decided terms. Beginning with the installation of Atanasie as the Uniate Bishop of Transylvania the Orthodox Romanians of southeastern Transylvania led the opposition to any dalliance with Rome and in doing so presented Viennese authorities with a foretaste of the failure of the Habsburg policy of prematurely publishing their church's obituary. In "protecting the faith of their parents and ancestors," these religious traditionalists protested both what they saw as an escalation of the original terms of the Union with Rome and a continuous effort to make them into Latin Rite Catholics.[11] One critic observed at the time of Atanasie's acceptance of the episcopal dignity that many Orthodox Romanians had not reconciled themselves to entertain the basic "Four Points" of Florence, much less the more extended interpretation now being placed on them by Latin Rite ecclesiastics. He likewise pointed out in a trenchant fashion that the Habsburgs authorities, religious and secular, were well aware of the nature of the motivations compelling what acceptance of the Union as there was among the Orthodox. Indeed, he stated categorically that it was impossible that they could "persuade themselves…that the Romanian priests had embraced the Union out of love of the Catholic religion…." In his letter of complaint to Emperor Leopold this same antagonist of the Union claimed that "the Catholic priests simply used" the grievances of the Romanian clergy, then leading them to the "Four Points." Concerning the prescriptions of Florence relative to establishing a Union with Rome, this contemporary continued on to say that "they were either not mentioned; or if they were mentioned, they were interpreted differently and in an obscure manner so that the Romanians did not understand them…." By 1702 the Transylvanian authorities were sufficiently worried about this "rebellion" by the non-existent Orthodox of the province to comment on the continuous tumult that it was producing.[12]

Very quickly, however, the opposition of the Orthodox community transmuted itself into something considerably more widespread and virulent than lists of grievances. Nor did its leaders remain content to observe that they had had a different perception of the nature of the Union with Rome than the Jesuits and Transylvanian administration. Indeed, they "neither understood, nor wished to receive, the Union in the sense in which it was executed…." by the Habsburg religious and secular bureaucracy.[13] In 1702 the Metropolitan of Bucharest (Theodosius), the Patriarch of Jerusalem (Dositheius), and the Patriarch of Constantinople (Callinicus) all condemned and excommunicated Atanasie. The most moderate reproaches leveled at the Uniate prelate focused on "the comedy" of his consecration and his lack of respect for the oath he had taken. In embracing the Roman Church he had rejected his "Mother, the Eastern Church" as well as both cultural and doctrinal fundamentals dating back to the Fathers of the Church. More indicative of the vehemence felt by the Orthodox, lay and clergy, was the Patriarch of Constantinople's pronouncement that Atanasie had shown himself to be a hypocrite. For acting duplicitously, Callinicus relegated him to damnation and, at least from the Orthodox hierarchy's point of view, removed him from the office of bishop. In attempting to instigate what from the Catholic perspective amounted to sedition, Theodosius presented himself as the only legitimate Romanian prelate for Transylvania. To properly gauge the depth of feeling reflected by these Orthodox hierarchs, and more importantly the popular agitation that would characterize much of the Romanian community during the eighteenth century, an awareness is required of the fact that labels and appearances perhaps more than tenets governed the throng's reaction to the Union with Rome. The leaders of the Orthodox world denigrated Bishop Atanasie as "a false metropolitan, a betrayer of the faith, and a new Judas." This emotional, and occasionally wrathful, rejection of the Uniate Church and its spokesmen would endure for generations, in some instances well into the present century.[14]

Part of the irony of this repudiation by the Orthodox ecclesiastical structure centered around Atanasie's being described as a "false metropolitan." For he and his successors, in one of the few cases where the prescriptions of Leopold's various diplomas actually saw fruition, lost that distinction. Rather than bearing this administratively and symbolically important title, Atanasie and his successor now became simple bishops. In the view of later Romanian historians this change in ecclesiastical nomenclature signified far more than the Uniate prelate's subordination to the Primate of Hungary and the Church of Rome. They regard this alteration in status as a "degradation" and as directly linked to the humiliating tutelage the Uniate bishop had to endure at the hands of the Jesuit "Theologian." Their interpretation of that extensive control of the "Theologian" included not simply his peering over the bishop's shoulder, but their contention that the Union (administratively and doctrinally) endured as a continuous process of redefinition according to the Society of Jesus' unilateral dictates. More than having lost a mere ecclesiastical distinction, the Romanians had been compelled to forfeit their ancient process of selecting church leaders (i.e., the Synod's choice of a single candidate for the episcopal office).[15] But more disturbing to the Orthodox than the mere unprecedented nature (either in terms of previous experience with Calvinist supervision or the normal pattern for Roman Catholic ecclesiastical structure) were the implications of this total suppression of the previous Romanian church organization. The suspicion would persist for generations that the ultimate intent was to subvert Uniate culture and further an entirely new schema of denominational sensitivities among the recent converts from Orthodoxy. While this sensitivity on the Romanians' part would come into play all too frequently during the eighteenth century and the Jesuits' tenure as their spiritual custodians, in the spring of 1705 the Pope had to address such an occasion, one highlighting the Uniates' anxieties and the all too common Latin condescension towards the Eastern Rite. At that time Clement XI wrote Cardinal Kollonich rejecting the Hungarian prelate's request to allow some few priests (presumably Jesuits) to change rites. Clement refused, pointing out that such transfers would weakening the Eastern Rite Roman Catholic Church. He foresaw quite accurately that the remaining Orthodox of Transylvania would play upon the Uniates' fear of a progressive cultural and liturgical taint resulting from this contact. Perhaps, most interesting for later observers, and granting a better insight into the discernments of both the Latin and Greek rite parties, was the justification offered for such ecclesiastical relocations. Latin Rite missionaries were to be allowed, "where necessary," to assume the Greek Rite. However, "whenever this necessity dissipated," they were have "the liberty" of returning to the Latin Rite. The hauteur of the missionary mentality as well as the transparent disregard for the inherent worth of the Greek Rite could not be missed. Uniate and Orthodox Romanians alike would, all too often during the eighteenth century, emerge from contracts with Latin Rite representatives with the distinct impression of being considered second rate, suspect, and prime candidates for "conversion."[16]

From the viewpoint of the Uniates' the selective vision of their patrons and the discrete enforcement of the Emperor's diplomas reinforced their anxiety on the issue of ritual and cultural differences. If the Habsburg authorities had somehow managed to miss the recalcitrance of the Transylvanian estates vis-à-vis Romanian rights, they surely could not overlook the outright promulgation in 1703 of the provincial leadership's refusal to count Romanian priests among the privileged elite of the province.[17] What has consistently struck the perceptive contemporary and the nationalistic modern observer is the way the Catholic authorities managed to pick and choose their points of pressure on the Uniates and Transylvanian administrators. They did the practical. They did not seriously threaten the hegemony of the groups that had enjoyed it, when Vienna succeeded Istanbul as overlord of the region. But they did insist on the letter of the diploma where the status of the Jesuit "Theologian" was concerned. In the fall of 1701, after the initial reactions of all parties would have permitted the knowledgeable in Rome and Vienna to discern accurately the forces aligned against the Uniates' promised prerogatives, the Congregation for the Propagation of the Faith issued a detailed pronouncement on Bishop Atanasie's immediate, functional responsibilities regarding the powers and living of the "Theologian." Besides being concerned with something other than what truly moved the Romanian Uniates at this juncture, their purported equality of status with the clergy of the political nations, this missive from Rome lent yet greater foundation to what would become one of the most galling of irritants generated by their change of religious allegiance. Only the recurrent threats to their cherished Eastern Rite would surpass the pervasiveness of Jesuit control and the economic burden of maintaining the "Theologian's" household as a focal point of discontent and potential alienation.[18]

If such failures to enforce the Leopoldine Diploma of 1701 and the specter of cultural encroachments by the Latin West had not presented Bishop Atanasie with sufficient difficulties at the start of his reign, in that same year he also found himself under surveillance by the Uniate priesthood. Along with some Roman Catholic and Protestant authorities, these men wondered about his sincerity and the damage his perceived ambivalent attitude might do to the Union with Rome. These priests were in particular agitated by the suspicion that Atanasie continued to maintain contact with Orthodox leaders, most importantly with the Prince of Wallachia. As already seen, the Uniate prelate was expressly forbidden such correspondence. He would have had to circumvent not only this proscription, but likewise the dictate that all episcopal mail be vetted by the Jesuit "Theologian." Such short cuts, if not morally and canonically questionable actions, not only fed the misgivings of his own clergy, but reinforced the already dubious reputation that Atanasie enjoyed among the influential and powerful of the Habsburg Monarchy. They certainly did not help his standing with the Roman Catholic hierarchy and estates.[19] To begin his pastoral activities as the new Uniate bishop for Transylvania and obviously to try to stanch the outright opposition as well as the more subterranean suspicions mentioned, Atanasie meet in synod with his clergy in 1701 after his return from Vienna. Besides discussing the promulgation of the latest imperial diploma and Cardinal Kollonich's letter of instruction to the Romanian clergy, the Romanian prelate also set the stage for another profession of faith. As a demonstration of his Catholic intent and to accommodate that portion of his clergy that had been absent, Bishop Atanasie planned another occasion for the Uniate priesthood to pledge its faith to Rome. But, as had been his lot coming out of the sessions in the Habsburg capital, the Romanian priests would be asked by Atanasie to go beyond their initial concept of the Union with Rome and the original formulation derived from their conversation with the Jesuits. They too, as had their bishop, had to make an oath tailored after the norms of the Council of Trent. This more rigorous, Tridentine requirement reflected both an increased cultural as well as doctrinal rigidity on the part of the Uniates' sponsors. For Atanasie it would, hopefully, assuage the criticism he received from all quarters in that it would substantiate his protestations of *bona fides*.[20]

In the meetings held with his clergy in each of the next two years, Atanasie continued this practice of addressing not merely matters of normal episcopal concern, but likewise comporting himself in such an irreproachable manner as to belie the harsh critiques of Catholic, Orthodox, and Protestant alike. During the General Synods of 1702 and 1703 he and the Uniate clergy solemnly deliberated on the purported failings of the Greek Church as well as on those doctrinal issue which Cardinal Kollonich considered pertinent and pressing. At this critical moment in the development of the Uniate Church and its relationship with its Latin Rite trustees, Atanasie again found himself subject to a scathing and tumultuous attack by the Orthodox hierarchs of the Ottoman Empire. Interestingly, at this juncture where the Metropolitan of Bucharest (Theodosius, who also claimed the Transylvanian episcopal see as Metropolitan of that province and its entire Vlach population) sought to move the Romanians to sedition against their bishop, Atanasie did even more than cloak himself in a seemingly exemplary effort to follow the spirit of his agreement with Vienna. Despite the reluctance to accept the Jesuit "Theologian" and the even more bitter confrontations over that personnel issue that would shortly eventuate, the Uniate prelate specifically sought the presence of current occupant of that position (i.e., the Czech Carol Neurauter, S.J.) at the 1702 General Synod. Although Cardinal Kollonich had wanted Neurauter at the side of the Uniate bishop because of Atanasie's glaring lack of learning, the Primate of Hungary had also in mind the Romanian's reputation and somewhat questionable *curriculum vitae* to date. But while Neurauter had been delayed in taking up his position at the Uniate episcopal see due to his service to the Habsburg commanding general in Transylvania, Ladislaus Baranyi of the Society of Jesus had temporarily filled the office of "Theologian." Now, however, Bishop Atanasie specifically entreated that the popular Jesuit, a favorite of his, be allowed to begin his duties as "Theologian." In addition to the warm personal ties here, Neurauter had the added attraction of being thoroughly knowledgeable about the Greek Church. In his appeal to the Habsburg general for Neurauter's reassignment, Bishop Atanasie supposedly referred to the Jesuit as "my angel Raphael." Whether or not the new "Theologian" possessed the healing powers which the archangel has traditionally symbolized, the Uniate leader urgently required not only his learning but his political astuteness and affiliations as well. The Jesuit would bring to Atanasie's household and his efforts to consolidate the Uniate ecclesiastical structure the patronage of both the religious and political magnates of Transylvania. Hopefully, these qualities would serve to help remedy the disregard and suspicion the Uniate bishop labored under.[21]

With the Jesuit's analeptic qualities present at the General Synod of 1702, Bishop Atanasie turned to concerns reviewed at Vienna and reflected in the documents issued by both Leopold and Kollonich. Addressing these he aspired to help his church and his own standing. He, his clergy, and the Jesuit Neurauter now discussed improving the level of Uniate culture by enhanced schooling and religious publications within Transylvania. They likewise began exploring the possibilities of an entirely new level of education (secular and sacred) by sending select young men for training in Tyrnava, Vienna, and Rome.[22] Emperor Leopold, for his part, promulgated a series of diplomas in 1701 and 1702 having the political intent of undermining the attacks on Atanasie and placing the attachment of the Transylvanian Romanians to the Union with Rome in a more favorable light. In the document of December 12, 1701 he reiterated his statement of March 19 that no force was to be used in the matter of religious allegiances. Besides the obvious purposes of precluding any violent reaction to such harassment, the Habsburg monarch wished to emphasize the sincerity of those who had embraced Rome. In his diploma of January 29, 1702 he pursued this tack yet further reaffirming the earlier promise that every Romanian had "complete liberty" to unite with any of the four received religions of Transylvania or, if they so chose, to remain Orthodox. Indicative of this line of political design and of the recalcitrance of the Latin Rite civil authorities of the province Leopold wrote on February 13 of that same year to insist that the terms of the Romanian Union with Rome be honored in all specifics.[23]

Having analyzed at such length the Latin Rite Catholic and Protestant opposition to the Uniates, as well as the modern Romanian accusation that the Habsburgs had largely dealt in illusions in their beguiling of the Romanian adherents of Rome, perhaps a little perspective is needed. That these factors were at play all are agreed upon. That discontent over non-fulfillment of the Leopoldine perquisites and the status of the Jesuit "Theologian" would fester have been hinted at and will be seen in detail. However, the Romanians were not singled out exclusively for such manipulation. Nor were they alone caught in a larger web of countervailing pressures which robbed them of the promised package of socio-religious benefits. In November of 1703 the Serbian Metropolitan Arsenie Czernovich wrote Emperor Leopold, sounding all too similar to the Romanian Bishop Atanasie. Metropolitan Czernovich complained that the privileges guaranteed his people in the 1690s had not been forthcoming. Also among other difficulties experienced his church had been severely challenged in its efforts to practice and preserve the Greek Rite. These and other rights stood out as the same sort of items tormenting the Romanian Uniates and stimulating questions as to the quality of their commitment to Rome. Unfortunately, the Serbs obtained an analogous response to that received by the Transylvanian Uniates. On November 22, 1703 Leopold responded to Metropolitan Czernovich's petition asking him to be patient and promising that eventually "the promised privileges would be scrupulously respected."[24] Even if known however, this would have been cold comfort for Atanasie's flock and probably not mitigated the growing tide of discontent that would trouble the Uniate movement up to and past the dissolution of the Society of Jesus in 1773.

The year 1703 also brought to the forefront an additional factor affecting the disgruntled elements among the Romanians and the circumspection with which the Habsburg had to address their concerns. The political equation in Transylvania now became more complicated, turning extremely violent with the revolt of Ferenc Rákóczi II. Lasting from 1703 until the Peace of Szatmár in 1711 this Magyar led revolt against Habsburg rule not only devastated the entire region, but likewise had an enormous impact on the Romanians and their Union with Rome. The representatives of the Magyar estates had become by 1703 extraordinarily dissatisfied with the continuous exertions by the Viennese court to plant firmly the absolutist flag of Habsburg control in a Transylvania so recently won from the more cavalier domination of the Ottomans. Along with that attempt by the dynasty to enlarge the scope of its provincial supervision, the traditional authorities in the province felt repelled by attacks on their privileged social status and freedom from taxation. Adding an acerbic edge to this dispute, whose violence would devastate the region for almost a decade, the latter day "Counter-Reformation" with its Jesuit leadership and emphasis on "re-Catholicization" lent an impetus and staying power to the revolt that reverberated with the viciousness of the "Wars of Religion."[25] On the eve of the outbreak of Rákóczi's rebellion, Graf Jean Louis Rabutin de Bussy (the commanding general of the Habsburg forces in Transylvania) reported that the more widespread, popular discontent derived in large measure from the skillful propaganda of the Magyar ruling class. Whatever the exactions demanded by the imperial administration, the burden of these was vastly increased by the far more burdensome financial charges imposed by the nobility's cupidity. The line taken by the Magyar gentry, and fed to the peasantry, resounded to the effect that all of these exactments occurred due to the Emperor's will. The peasants' hatred focused on the German led administration imposed by the Habsburgs. Rabutin summed up the impact saying that the province's magnates were endeavoring, successfully, "...to render this [German] nation loathsome throughout the province." He further advised the Viennese Court that he expected those opposed to Habsburg rule to continue and to aggravate such tactics.[26]

If Rabutin's insight and talents represented one of the keys to the Habsburgs retaining their position in Transylvania, the participation of the Romanians as an ethnic-religious group stood out as another decisive variable in that equation. Among at least a portion of "that embittered people" a desire to oppose visibly the Union with Rome and the perceived resultant threat to the Greek Rite resulted in support for their former Calvinist overseers. "The political-national opposition of the Magyars combined with the confessional resistance of the Romanians" to offer Leopold a decisive and costly challenge to his hegemony in Transylvania. Indeed, the Habsburgs would be so hard pressed in this contest that at least temporarily the Uniate Romanians would find themselves courted. Though not in the long run determinative in obtaining for them execution of all the promises in the Leopoldine diplomas, for the moment the special emissaries of the Viennese administration both protected and cultivated the adherents of this newborn ethnic offshoot of Roman Catholicism.[27] Unfortunately, such last minute solicitude for these Greek Rite neophytes did not placate the remaining Orthodox believers of Transylvania. Along with their Magyar Calvinist overlords, these inveterate disciples of the Eastern Church joined in what quickly became a "*Volkskrieg.*" More threatening from the point of view of Vienna, the number and geographic spread of these fanatical opponents of the Union with Rome increased continually. They simply would not remain mute to accommodate the political-religious schema of the Habsburgs nor submit to what they discerned as incessant pressure to imitate their kinsmen by accepting all that was now read into the "Four Points." The ferocity and extent of this resentful Romanian resistance would by the end of Rákóczi's revolt have had the effect of once and for all dispelling the notion that no Orthodox presence endured in Transylvania. By 1711 only the most opinionated and narrow-minded of Latin Rite Catholics still attempted to maintain that position. But that lesson as well as its eventual aftermath at mid-century of reestablishing an Orthodox hierarchy would be hard-learned and even more difficult to acknowledge.[28]

During this desperate struggle of some eight years, then, the Habsburg Monarchy found itself distracted by serious disturbances in the area of foreign policy. It simply did not enjoy the luxury of being able to single-mindedly concentrate on Ferenc Rákóczi at a time of great anxiety over developments in France, Spain, and Poland. "The general European situation impeded the Emperor's discretion in the use of force" at this juncture where the Magyar insurgents accused him of capriciousness in his handling of their constitutional rights and traditional provincial freedoms. Vienna even experienced a slight frisson with the apprehension that the contretemps with Rákóczi might occasion a Ottoman bid to undue the settlement arrived at in the Treaty of Karlowitz.[29] Adding to these justified forebodings was the status of Habsburg forces in the region. In this climate of intimidation from abroad and critical challenge from domestic foes the imperial army in Transylvania would be hard pressed to prevail over the combined forces of the Magyar-led privileged estates and the disgruntled Romanian peasantry. General Rabutin, as the primary shield for Habsburg policies in Transylvania, had at his disposal neither adequate fortifications nor munitions. Furthermore, his limited supply of troops did not suffice to garrison the important cities that had to be held, staff the frontier, and yet competently confront Rákóczi in the field. In the mostly non-Catholic forces arrayed against him (i.e., the "*Kuruzen*"), Rabutin encountered not only the to-be-expected Protestants but also Orthodox Romanians. These latter felt themselves forced into allying with the very groups that had so dominated them through the legalisms and mores of the traditional Transylvanian constitutional order. Yet, at this point, defense of their rite and reaction against a perceived Jesuit-led missionary movement drove them into Rákóczi's ranks. The Imperial loyalists (i.e., termed "*Lobonzen*" and mostly drawn from Latin Rite Catholics) went against an insurgency that had been significantly augmented by the very population Vienna had counted on to tip the political balance in its favor.[30]

Though sparked primarily by Protestant outcries against Catholic Habsburg encroachments, this rebellion also set Romanian against Romanian (Orthodox *Kuruzen* v. Uniate *Lobonzen*). One modern commentator observed that this civil war for most of its duration exhibited qualities that were "all too barbarous." Indeed, for the Uniates the turmoil and lack of guaranteed protection reached the point that Bishop Atanasie had to flee to the imperial held city of Hermannstadt on the southern border of the province. For Rákóczi's promise to all who followed him that "the entire country will regain its liberty and privileges" galvanized the non-Uniate Romanians' sense of aggrievement and desire to resist forcibly further encroachments on their traditions or established patterns of worship.[31] Rather than endure the chance of either having to neglect their ancient "law" or perhaps even being compelled to abandon it, the remaining Orthodox of Transylvania turned to what would become the standard options of Romanian peasant opposition. The more tenacious of these would be the process of emigration into the Danubian Principalities which would continue for as long as the Jesuits served as the Uniates' mentors. At this point early in the eighteenth century, however, the discontented threw their lot in with the Magyar forces of Rákóczi rather than risk the perils of a Catholic culture oriented towards Western ecclesiastical norms. The ensuing civil war produced enormous consequences for the province as a whole and for the situation the Romanian Uniates would enjoy for most of the remaining portion of the eighteenth century.[32] Their participation in this struggle for "the Magyar nationality and Transylvanian separatism" opened a new vein of more visible recalcitrance on the Romanians' part. Along side the great landed magnates (even those who espoused Roman Catholicism) and the far more numerous Calvinist gentry, they joined Rákóczi's crusade to supplant Habsburg hegemony. Whether or not removal of Viennese domination in the province would indeed have resulted in "equality of rights for all religions" and "a more durable religious peace" remains debatable. The appeal of such a sweeping restructuring of Transylvania's "political, economic, cultural, and social" landscape along with the religious tableau could not but appeal to those affronted by the fact or perceived failure of the Union with Rome.[33]

Unfortunately, for both the Magyar insurgents and the discontented Romanian Orthodox of Transylvania the revolt of Ferenc Rákóczi failed. In doing so it inflicted terrible damage upon both the province and the position of the Romanians. By the time that Rákóczi's "War of Independence" ended with the Peace of Szatmár of April 30, 1711 almost twenty percent of the population had perished as a result of either war deaths or the ravages of plague brought on by the depredations of the campaign. The physical damage to the province assumed commensurately calamitous proportions. To end this carnage the Habsburgs agreed with the dissidents who undercut Rákóczi in his absence, signing a treaty which he could never accept. At Szatmár Vienna bought peace at the price of guaranteeing the continued existence of the feudal order in Transylvania. However it might affect groups like the Romanians (Uniate or Orthodox) the traditional social, religious, and constitutional structure received an imperial sanction that would last the century. The Magyar element that abandoned Rákóczi's struggle for sovereignty did forswear independence, but obtained in exchange unchallenged mastery in the political arena. Unanticipated by the Magyar magnates of Transylvania, however, would be the boon provided to the imperial bureaucracy by the subsequent and unprecedented period of peace. Despite the Peace of Szatmár's underpinning of its privileged status, that feudal territorial elite shortly found itself constrained by "a paper power" emanating from Vienna, a bureaucratic cataract against which it saw itself as "defenseless." The transformation being worked on Transylvania by this calculating process of regulatory aggrandizement afforded the authorities at the center of Habsburg officialdom a quieter but no less substantive advantage than the one supposedly won by the Magyar gentry at Szatmár.[34]

For the Romanian Uniates and their church the consequences of Rákóczi's "War of Independence" and the Peace of Szatmár were equally profound. A modern compatriot, one inclined to see the entire Union experience in a uniformly favorable light, thought that only the eighteenth century's repeated and prolonged vacancies in the office of the Uniate bishopric had a comparably ruinous impact. Under the terms of the treaty "the liberty of the received religions was confirmed...and the constitution of Hungary and Transylvania was guaranteed."[35] One of the minor ironies of this period consisted in the signing of this pact, and thus the confirmation of the Romanian status quo in face of the entrenched privileged estates, in the present-day Satu Mare region. The Orthodox of the area had felt themselves singled out for a most intense Jesuit evangelistic effort and consequently had provided a disproportionately large segment of the Romanian volunteers who had flocked to the insurgents' banner. Neither they nor their Uniate brothers had any reason to be happy with this outcome. In addition, despite a Catholic "victory" the Romanians of the Roman Catholic Eastern Rite had had to be satisfied during the course of the war with such symbolic acts as Joseph I's repeated confirmations (e.g., in 1706 and 1708) of the privileges promised in the first diploma issued the Uniates by Emperor Leopold. Nothing had really changed for them.[36] Just as this rebellion, even after the formal termination of hostilities, would continue to agitate the province for years, so too the internal structure of the Uniate Church felt its baneful effects for years to come. By the Synod of 1707 the Jesuit Superior for Transylvania (Andreas Horváth) had become extremely concerned not only by the Romanian participation in the violence of the revolt, but also by the concomitant inroads of a revitalized Calvinist influence among his charges. Roman Catholic leadership, then, foresaw the "extreme" and lingering nature of this disturbance, one that was characterized as "a most serious attack upon the Romanian Uniates."[37]

In this context with its miscellany of the transfer of the primary Habsburg paladin (i.e., General Rabutin) from Transylvania, the unexpected passing of Emperor Joseph I (April 11, 1711), and the Szatmár "stalemate and compromise," the Romanians held yet another synod. But this time one that would directly accentuate the problems arising from the recent civil war and renew the old suspicions of Uniate authenticity. At this fall clerical convocation, an extremely tumultuous assembly held in the shadow of Rákóczi's failed enterprise, Atanasie felt himself pressured to endorse a rejection of the Union with Rome.[38] This "apostasy," which some modern critics have decoded as the temporary demise of the Uniate Church in the fall of 1711, played not only to Protestant interests but likewise to the earlier suspicions (Catholic as well as Calvinist) of Atanasie's sincerity. Unfortunately for this nationalistic and sectarian interpretation, the "reestablishment of Orthodoxy," at least as far as a legally mandated hierarchy was concerned, would have to wait some decades for Maria Theresa's political acquiescence. More immediately the Jesuit "Theologian" stepped in to rectify matters from the Roman Catholic point of view just as Cardinal Kollonich had intended to be the case in his "Instruction." To head off any further resurgence of Calvinist influence among the Romanians as well as to foreclose subsequent accusations of "apostasy," the "Theologian" first of all convinced the Uniate leader of his error. Bishop Atanasie under this determined direction of the Jesuits then "recalled and annulled" all suspect commitments on his part or that of his priests. Secondly, both the bishop and the prominent Uniate clergy reiterated their profession of faith and dedication to the Union with Rome. In his "Protestation" against apostasy Atanasie specifically handed the Jesuit Provincial for Transylvania (Gabriel Hevenesi) his "bond" of honor to be conveyed to Vienna. This solemn pledge proclaimed once more and in categorical terms his compact "to adhere to all the points already subscribed to" by the Uniate Church. Indicative of the damage done by the Rákóczi rebellion and this abortive "apostasy" is the fact that this retaking of vows by Atanasie and the elite of his clergy on November 8, 1711 would not suffice. The reawakening of suspicions dating back to the time of his initial accord with Rome and even further to his original status as a client of the Calvinists would haunt him to the grave. Thus, again in 1712 only a year before his death, the Uniate Bishop along with a much broader selection of his clergy would have to repeat their public profession of faith, hoping that this time their *bona fides* would be accepted by Catholic and Protestant alike.[39]

Once again within the fold of the Catholic Church, the Eastern Rite Romanians found that the military-political turmoil of the Rákóczi era along with the ephemeral "apostasy" of their bishop did not augur well for their institutional integrity. Having conformed to both religious and secular demands for perceptual allegiance, they discovered their hierarchy yet more susceptible to Jesuit influence and outside misgivings. Already, in the persons of Teofil and Atanasie adjudged at best marginally qualified and more often than not of questionable loyalty, all future candidates for Uniate leadership would be compared to the Jesuit "Theologian" with his indisputably better education and doctrinal discipline.[40] And, of course, the end of Rákóczi's insurrection and the "apostasy" of the Uniate hierarch also coincided with the ascension to the Habsburg throne by Charles VI. The new emperor and his advisors had to give special consideration not only to the impact of the recent warfare in Transylvania, but likewise to the internal diversity and hence the weakness of this multi-ethnic state. Continually conscious of foreign policy considerations and the potentially distracting nature of domestic disputes like that of Rákóczi, the court through its growing thread of bureaucratic missives held the disparate sections of the monarchy together. But it had only this mechanism and the territorially specific dynastic claims of the Emperor to assist it in governing. The regionalisms and aristocratic elites of areas such as Transylvania persisted in their own agenda. Thus, the conservative Catholic party, allied with Vienna, set out to regain the ground lost since the inception of hostilities.[41]

This situation epitomized what one modern antagonist of the Viennese Court and the Uniate movement characterized as "the perfidy of the Habsburgs;" namely, what they gave with one hand (the long anticipated privileges promised in the diplomas of Emperor Leopold), they took away with the other (at best dilatory and partial implementation of those perquisites). To such modern critics, and shortly even to the more perspicacious of contemporary Uniate leaders, an obvious trade-off had been arrived at between the Habsburgs and the Transylvanian governing estates. The Roman Catholic authorities in the province would not push for complete execution of the promised Uniate rights and the ruling class in Transylvania would mute its opposition to the Union with Rome. An equilibrium acceptable to both parties would thus eventuate, but one that left the Uniates in limbo.[42] The Eastern Rite Romanians would spend the rest of the eighteenth century performing the equivalent of biblical exegesis on the various diplomas granted them, seldom fully fathoming (or certainly being able to alter) the power balance that made such debating points irrelevant. Occasionally among the men of those generations, and more often among modern historians, the conviction arose that this compromise between Viennese and Transylvanian political ambitions reflected a basic Habsburg judgment on the Romanians. They were and would remain quite simply "an element ripe for exploitation." With the "bait" of the promised privileges and the renewed external attacks after 1711 on basic Eastern Rite liturgical practices (e.g., the Saxon desire to limit the number of priests per village to prevent whole communities from becoming Uniate), the Romanian church authorities would be distracted from the real balance of power in the province. Their lot would be discussed, even disputed vehemently on their part, but not adjusted to suit their convictions.[43]

In this highly agitated and, for the Uniates, potentially compromising situation Bishop Atanasie died on August 19, 1713. In death as throughout his tenure as the Roman Catholic Eastern Rite prelate for Transylvania, he had at his side the "Theologian" to ensure that all went well. Atanasie's passage from the Habsburg scene likewise marked a transition that would have enormous consequences for the contemporary Uniate Church and perhaps even more so for the modern debate (exacerbated since the demise of Communist Romania) over the Latin West's "evangelization" of the Orthodox East.[44] Over the course of the next two decades the Jesuit adviser to the Uniates would find his role enlarged from that of a mere "Theologian" to the effective head of the diocese. For during fifteen of those years the Habsburg authorities had either not appointed a new Romanian bishop or that individual had not yet taken up his official duties. In any case, the Jesuit "Theologian" became for a decade and a half the *de facto* administrator for all things Uniate in Transylvania. These absences of native leadership plus the subsequent one between 1744 and 1754 came to symbolize for the modern Romanian nationalist and historian "a veritable disaster for the Uniate Church." The initial vacancy after Atanasie's demise, then, (1713-1723) constituted not merely a period of Jesuit tutelage from the Romanian point of view, but brought into the forefront such divisive, perhaps even dangerous, issues as the constitution of the new church and the on-going encroachments of Latin influence.[45]

The more perfervid of modern Romanian historians developed a historiography of the vacancies in the Uniate bishopric that declared them to be a conspiracy to undermine the basic character of the Union with Rome. In this angular schema the Latin Rite hierarchy, the Society of Jesus, and the Roman Catholic aristocracy of Transylvania, for their various reasons, combined to keep the episcopal throne unoccupied for long periods of time. The postulated intent, according to this view, focused on facilitating the diminution of the Eastern Rite traditions so dear to the Romanians. Complicating this mix of motivations, the Viennese and Papal courts quite frequently had their own, disparate agenda as well. At the center of the discussion over the genesis and impact of the prolonged absences of indigenous ecclesiastical leadership, however, remained what this nationalistic historiography defined as the "administration and tutelage of the Jesuit [community] in Cluj and the theologian stationed in Blaj."[46] Even dispassionate observers have noted that, when a successor to Atanasie was finally named (1721) and installed (1723), far more had occurred than the simply passage of a decade of outright Jesuit control. By 1723 the Uniate hierarch would no longer possess the customary see in Alba-Iulia as did Teofil and Atanasie, but find himself relegated to a newly founded diocese on the northern slopes of the Carpathians in Făgăraş. Also in marked contrast to his two predecessors in this Union with Rome, the bishop installed in 1723 discovered that his see no longer enjoyed a claim of ecclesiastical independence but fell under the jurisdiction of the Latin Rite bishop of Transylvania. This last factor delineated as clearly as anything could the break with the Orthodox pattern of ecclesiastical government and the encroachment of a rival ritual tradition. In this first, ten year break in native management of the Uniate Church a series of important issues would come to the fore that would help determine the character of that body and eventually of a critical component of Romanian nationalism; namely, the questions of ecclesiastical autonomy, the threat of "Latinization," the dignity of native sectarian folkways, and of Orthodoxy as the posited vital element in the Romanian ethnic equation.[47]

Finally, in 1713, the impact and import of the altered nature of the selection process for the Romanian prelate in Transylvania which was discussed earlier became patently evident. Based on Emperor Leopold's Diploma of 1701 the Uniate Synod now found itself restricted to simply proposing three candidates from which the monarch would choose the one most to his liking. Thus, "the autonomy of the Oriental Rite had shrunk to encompass only the liturgy." And, as will be discovered, many Romanians observing this process then and later had a very real foreboding regarding the integrity of their liturgy as well. For the initial triad of candidates submitted under this new succession stratagem offered a totally Latin visage.[48] The first of these candidates, the Jesuit Franz Szunyogh de Budetgin, served at the time as the "Theologian" attached to the household of the Uniate prelate. A veteran of many years of "missionary" work among the Romanians Szunyogh stood out not only because of his place of importance in the bishop's retinue, but also due to the "Roman Catholic" catechism he authored for his charges (published in 1696 and reissued in 1726). Although the *Constitutions* of the Society of Jesus prohibited its members from accepting any office or rank of ecclesiastical distinction, throughout the order's tumultuous history waivers to this restriction have been forthcoming. In this instance none was granted. But as already seen in the discussion regarding the expediency of establishing the office of the "Theologian," the Jesuits already possessed pivotal influence over the affairs of the Uniate church. Along with this practical consideration regarding everyday preponderance in Romanian church life, there lingered of course the fear of the tenuousness of the Union with Rome. As one later commentator stated, those coming from an Orthodox heritage were characterized by "an instinctive resistance to Protestantism, coming as it did from the West." Where many Romanians were concerned, the operationally imperative factor in this trenchant observation seems to have been not so much the "Protestantism," but rather the origins of any ecclesiastical influence in "the West." Throughout this period the Latin Rite Roman Catholic authorities, both religious and secular, remained quite apprehensive about any movement that might precipitate a return by the Romanians "to schism." A Jesuit bishop loomed rather large as exactly the impetus for such a catastrophe.[49]

The second of the Latin Rite candidates, Wenzeslaus Frantz, had served for more than a decade as Bishop Atanasie's secretary. Moreover, he received the endorsement of the Romanian priests attending the Synod for selecting the new bishop and, most significantly, of the "Theologian" Franz Szunyogh. Both saw him as a educated, honorable individual who knew the Eastern Rite and the Romanian language quite well. In writing the Primate of Hungary, Cardinal Saxonia, to endorse the candidacy of Frantz the Uniate delegates to the Synod emphasized their appreciation of his "insight into our circumstances and rite." Despite the Synod's enthusiastic approval of Frantz, there did develop earnest Romanian opposition to him as bishop on the grounds of his different ethnic background (i.e., Czech-German). While the fear of "Latinization" of the Eastern Rite would continue to stand out as the great *bête noire* for the Romanians (Uniate and Orthodox), in Frantz's instance this was compounded by his Slavic origins. The possibilities of contamination would be doubled with him as Atanasie's successor. As compelling as the censure based on culture and rite might have been from the ethnic point of view, it would however hardly carry the day in Vienna. What probably ended any chance of Frantz's being consecrated the new Uniate bishop was the peroration to Szunyogh's obliquely favorable evaluation of the former amanuensis. After pointing out the same good qualities which recommended Frantz to the Synod, the Jesuit raised the specter of "heterogeneity and disunion" being introduced into the Uniate Church through this man's elevation to the episcopal dignity. By means of the powers granted him as "Theologian," Szunyogh had "intercepted" a considerable correspondence between the Uniate bishopric and "schismatics" (presumably the Orthodox of the Ottoman Empire). Given Frantz's official capacity at Atanasie's court and presumably some complicity in this suspect epistolary connection, his candidacy raised substantial doubts as to the likelihood of "conserving the Union."[50]

Adding the final element to the discord over the choice of Atanasie's successor was the person of Ioan Giurgiu Pataki who would eventually be consecrated (1721) and installed (1723) as Uniate bishop of Transylvania. Though born into an aristocratic Romanian family in 1682, he had been educated by the Jesuits. This exposure to Western ecclesiastical and secular culture took him from the Society of Jesus' colleges in Transylvania to Vienna and then on to Rome. The Jesuits' patronage allowed Pataki to continue his education up to the point of not only being ordained a priest, but also in the process obtaining a doctorate in Theology. By contemporary Romanian standards, then, Pataki possessed far more than average erudition and a significantly wider cultural awareness. Without a doubt he stood out among his peers and reflected in his training all the initial concern of the Jesuits and Latin Rite hierarchy over what they deemed the deplorable quality of the original adherents to the Union. Regarded from the viewpoint of ethnic culture and ritual values, however, and certainly from that of a Szunyogh concerned with the durability of the Union with Rome, Pataki's candidacy presented special problems. Though from a family heritage that was Eastern Rite, he had been ordained as a Latin Rite priest. Perhaps even more indicative of the turmoil his candidacy would cause and its contribution to the perennial Romanian fear of "Latinization" of the liturgy was the fact that he returned to Transylvania in 1710 imbued not only with a fine Jesuit education but also with a simulated Westerner's condescension towards the Eastern Church. Like the Jesuit "Theologian" Szunyogh, Pataki reentered his homeland not simply as a better educated Christian, but rather as a "missionary," a missionary it was feared not merely to the Orthodox on a doctrinal level but also to the Uniates where matters of rite were concerned.[51]

Interestingly in the light of the Romanians' subsequent insurgency against Jesuit sway and their reputed ethnically "instinctive resistance" to Western influences, the initial meeting of the Synod in 1713 had recommended Frantz. The delegates took this action despite the restrictive measures exercised at the Synod by the Society of Jesus. For, in contrast to previous congregations to select a bishop, only the "more senior priests" ("*seniores protopopae*") were allowed to participate on this occasion. Szunyogh later explained to the Transylvanian civil authorities that he took this action in his capacity as "Theologian" for "the most serious of reasons;" supposedly, the danger of a relapse into schism. By the initiative of the "Theologian" with the approval of the Cardinal Primate the decision-making body of the Uniate Church, one virtually representing the larger Synod of former times, became the bishop, the Jesuit representative at the episcopal court, and these "more senior priests."[52] Despite the changed nature of the selection process and the alteration by Jesuit inference of the Synod's composition, a second convocation meeting in the spring of 1714 again petitioned for Wenzeslaus Frantz's confirmation as Uniate bishop. This effort of the Romanians to obtain a compatible prelate would continue into 1715 and a third Synod, but still with no success. Eventually Frantz withdrew his candidacy, probably under imperial pressure incurred by anxiety over the occasion the ascension of a Slav might offer to further alienation of the Romanian people. At the heart of this support for Frantz had been a repudiation of the attempt of Ioan Giurgiu Pataki to become the Uniate bishop. The "more senior priests," culled out by the Jesuit "Theologian" for their judgment and support (if not manipulability) in this grave situation, rejected Pataki for "the disrespect he had shown the Eastern Rite by accepting the Latin Rite." They saw him doing the expedient thing in returning to his native liturgy; namely, performing a political act necessary for his elevation to the episcopal dignity. These delegates to the Synod went on to criticize Pataki for his authoritarian manner and his purported intention of insinuating the Latin liturgy into the Uniate service. In their efforts to denigrate him, they even resorted to the ethnic cultural charge that he no longer spoke his native tongue well.[53]

Pataki in advancing his candidacy had written to the Primate of Hungary, Cardinal Saxonia, expressing his willingness under religious obedience to embrace either the Eastern or Latin Rite. He gave as an explanation his concern for "the salvation of his beloved Romanian people." In that same year, 1713, this Jesuit disciple had also written to Cardinal Saxonia that he wished through his "missionary" efforts to bring his "dear Romanian people…to a true Union." The intuitive trepidation of the Romanian priests, as well as of the modern nationalistic historian, centered on the likelihood that this "true Union" meant "Latinization" and the replacement by subterfuge of the Eastern Rite with Western liturgical norms.[54] Whatever this "instinctive resistance" to Western ecclesiastical influences and to Pataki as their medium, the Uniate "more senior priests" seem to have guessed right about their prospective prelate's underlying cultural ambivalence and distress with the Eastern Rite. In late 1720, having recommitted himself to his native liturgical tradition, he wrote to Clement XI expressing his uneasiness with this transfer of his formal liturgical loyalties back to the Eastern Rite. Indeed, he requested from the Pope permission "to celebrate the Latin Mass." Thus, in 1713-1715 the Romanian protopopes present at the Synod demonstrated great perspicuity regarding Pataki as well as regarding the pervasive Latin disdain for their rite which he had picked up in his travels. In 1705 Cardinal Kollonich, acting in his role as Primate of Hungary, had written Rome requesting that missionaries "in

Greek areas…might have the consolation of saying Mass privately in the Roman Rite." From the Romanian point of view, then and now, there existed a constant thread of conceit that viewed all in the area as requiring the efforts of "missionaries." Besides not allowing for the presence of Christian traditions already on the scene, this missive of the Hungarian Primate made no distinction between Uniate or Orthodox. It emphasized only the fact of the perturbing aspects of the Eastern Rite liturgy. Perhaps, the extent of this aversion for the Eastern Rite, and the encompassing cultural bias that transcended even the aegis of Rome, can best be seen in the comments of Joannes Galdenblad made also in 1705. Of German descent and an adult convert to Roman Catholicism from Lutheranism, this Jesuit protégé of Cardinal Kollonich came late to the cultural contest between the Eastern and Latin Rites. Due to the Cardinal's patronage and expressed wish, Galdenblad exercised his influence in the offices of the Sacred Congregation of the Inquisition. Reflecting his mentor's views, Galdenblad sought a dispensation from the long standing practice of requiring that a change of rites be considered permanent. Use of the Byzantine liturgy should be mandated, according to Galdenblad, only when the "missionaries" were actually in areas where "Greek customs prevailed." Upon return to their homelands, then, these individuals who had been deprived of the solace of the Western liturgy would be permitted "to resume the sacred ceremonies of the Latins."[55]

Since Pataki's training and preferences broadcast this pattern of cultural partiality, the Synod did indeed vote in the interest of preserving their church's folkways and ethnic traditions. Though not yet proven in a juridical sense, the attitudes of this Jesuit educated candidate for the Uniate episcopacy did present a clear and present peril to the integrity of the Eastern Rite. For in this same year of 1715 the governor of Transylvania, Sigismund Kornis, wrote privately to Gabriel Hevenesi the influential Jesuit leader who had recently finished his term (1712-1714) as the Society of Jesus' chief administrator (i.e., Provincial) for Transylvania. Here the master of the secular order in the province confided to a sympathetic religious counselor the sum total of Habsburg intentions with the Romanians and the compelling rationale for underwriting Pataki. Speaking candidly and obviously only for private consumption, Kornis detailed for Hevenesi that

> Catholic government leaders and the Roman Catholic clergy are unanimous in their support of Pataki. Only through him will they be able to achieve what they have sought unsuccessfully for such a long time; namely, that once having been won over by a capable man, the [Romanian] people will be accustomed to accept fully our [Latin] Rite. In this manner the Catholic element [in Transylvania] will surpass in numbers and power the other religious sects.[56]

Unspoken in this exchange, but working powerfully to Pataki's advantage, was the fact that his uncle functioned as a factotum in the Kornis family court. This personalized sense of irritation with the Uniate Synod's choice of Frantz helped frame the governor's zeal for Pataki's candidacy. Most importantly given Kornis' compelling concern with "the future of the Latin Catholics in Transylvania and the political development of the province," he wanted "a tractable bishop at the head of the Romanian [i.e., Uniate] Church."[57] Given the size of the population involved, Pataki became the purported key to stabilizing, and then expanding, Habsburg and Latin Rite Roman Catholic hegemony in their respective fora. With these motivations at play and with the enthusiastic support of their governor, the Catholic estates of Transylvania added their corporate plea to the list of forces arrayed against Romanian cultural continuity, beseeching the Emperor in 1715 to choose Pataki. Sounding very much like the prospective candidate, the Catholic officialdom echoed Pataki's insinuation that no "true" Union existed among the Romanians and that his appointment constituted the key to the aggrandizement of the Latin Rite. Or, as the Catholic political stratum phrased its artful brief, without Pataki as head of the Romanian church "the Union will not be real but feigned, a fraud to Your Majesty's service rather than a means of providing assistance to [our] faith and advantage to the fatherland."[58]

While the various competing factions jockeyed for position and to bolster their candidate for the Uniate bishopric, the diocese remained without the juridically required officer in charge. With the initial 1713 rejection of Frantz by the Viennese authorities, an "interim" administrator drawn from the membership of the Society of Jesus emerged as the solution to this sensitive problem of lack of leadership. The new ecclesiastical functionary would bear the title of "Advocate" ("*Defensor*") or more usually of "Director" ("*Director*"). Even given the fact that this post's origins and jurisdiction had quite different roots and motivations than those of the "Theologian" imposed by Cardinal Kollonich, the demarcation between the two appointments of the Jesuits often blurred. In some cases, a single member of the Society of Jesus would fill both roles. What appeared most obviously to all Romanians was the fact that the same Western religious order that had been tutoring their bishop now oversaw that prelate's powers as well as their cultural and spiritual destinies. The standing given the post of "Director" by the Society of Jesus may be seen by the caliber of men named to it. The first two, Josephus Bardia and Georgius Regai, both came from the official governing class of the Society that provided its own leadership with superiors and rectors of regionally important institutions.[59] During this critical period (1713-1723) each labored among the Uniates as "Director" and on occasion also simultaneously as "Theologian." Thus, by the time the second and third Synods met (i.e., 1714 and 1715) the Uniate priests that persisted in repeatedly nominating Frantz found themselves under the scrutiny not only of this innovative facsimile of the Calvinist superintendent, but also of a new "Theologian" (Gaspar Ujházi) and the Jesuit superior in Alba-Iulia (Laurentius Petz). Though unable to disabuse the very protopopes selected according to Jesuit criteria from their support of Frantz, this cadre of Western missionaries did arrive a determination as to why this was so. In the Jesuits' appraisal the Romanian refusal to renounce Frantz and accept Pataki found its foundation in an ethnically heightened intuition that the Latin Rite bureaucracy was not dealing with them in a forthright manner and did not represent the Emperor's true intent in this instance. On a more personal and patronizing note the Jesuits reported that the recalcitrance on the Synod's part stemmed from the fact that "this is a simple clergy not ruled by supernatural principles, but by transitory necessities." This Jesuit implied superficiality on the part of the Uniates, namely their insistence on actually receiving the privileges promised by Emperor Leopold, though regrettable from the Latin point of view likewise served to emphasize the danger of "both the Romanian clergy and people relapsing into 'the old schism'."[60]

Despite the skillful intervention of the Jesuits, the awkwardness of the transition from Atanasie to his eventual successor Pataki occasioned grave concern among the Catholic and Habsburgs agencies of Transylvania. Contemporary chancellery reports clearly showed marked anxiety over the marginal character of the Romanians' commitment to the Union with Rome and the obdurate refusal of the Synod to accept Pataki.

Statistics from this same period (i.e., 1713-1716) also demonstrated that provincial religious and secular authorities possessed indisputable evidence of the staying power of Orthodoxy. However attractive the postulate inspired by Cardinal Kollonich that after Atanasie's acceptance of the Union the Orthodox Church in Transylvania ceased to exist, the numbers proved otherwise. Although such statistics were often problematic if not tendentious, by 1716 all knew that a sizeable proportion of the Romanian population adamantly clung to Orthodoxy and equally determinedly rejected any and all association with the Church of Rome.[61] Again by that same year the keen observations recorded by the Transylvanian Chancellery homed in on the necessity of quickly anointing Pataki as the only solution to these religious and secular difficulties. For as that synopsis of 1716 opined the Romanians were "not yet sufficiently anchored in the Holy Union and might quite easily backslide." Complicating this stratagem, unfortunately, remained the fact that the very means the Habsburg and Latin Rite officials sought to employ aggravated the situation. Paralleling in time and content these internal insights by Transylvanian commentators the archives also the even more trenchant views of the Apostolic Nuncio to Vienna, B. A. Dusini. Writing in the summer of 1716 this Papal envoy described the seriousness of the predicament as well as sketched in a caustic fashion the reasons for the long struggle over Pataki's candidacy. Briefly and to the point he also limned a cardinal reason for the two-edged character of the assistance Pataki might bring to Rome's and Vienna's apprehension over the Uniates. The Apostolic Nuncio categorically labeled Pataki "a creature of the Jesuits." The challenge, then, amounted to devising a rationale for this "capable" leader without precipitating a mass exodus into schism. How could the Papal and Viennese courts make use of his Roman training and Jesuit affinities without creating yet more Romanian alarm over the issue of "Latinization" of their church? The very personnel and institutions set up to bolster the Union lent credibility, by their ubiquitous quality, to this ethnic fear of loosing culture and liturgy to Western encroachment.[62]

The stakes for Rome and Vienna in stabilizing Pataki's candidacy and at the same time not further estranging the Transylvanian Romanians were considerable. Contemporary Vatican archives gave the Roman Catholic segment of the population as only 30,000, a politically insignificant minority. The same source calculated, probably rather optimistically, the Uniate portion of the province at ten times the Latin Rite number. With this monumental increase in Roman Catholic hegemony at risk, it is no wonder that not only the hierarchy and Jesuit order but also the secular bureaucracy responded as they did. The political situation already described has demonstrated graphically the extent to which both personal and policy factors motivated the Governor of Transylvania, Count Sigismund Kornis, in his support for Pataki. This same administrative apprehension reflected as well in the thoughts of the province's Vice-Chancellor, Joannes Josephus de Kászoni. In advising the Viennese Court on Pataki's candidacy Kászoni insisted that the state of the Union demanded a "more erudite and distinguished man" than the Romanians were likely to choose if left to their own devices. He went on to warn that without a man of such stature, if the Emperor sanctioned the appointment of the "weak bishop" supposedly sought by the Synod, then "the Romanians would become corrupted and attracted again towards schism by either the Protestants or their ethnic kinsmen in the Danubian Principalities."[63] In an interesting effort to advance a procedural objection to the Synod's attempt to select Frantz, and thus to present a more defensible if not persuasive public assessment, the Vice-Chancellor seized upon Szunyogh's having limited participation at the Synod to the "more senior priests." As if this had been the Romanian delegates' design, in 1714 Kászoni offered this lapse in traditional attendance patterns as an invaliding impediment to the Synod's actions. In yet another non sequitur, this representative of Habsburg self-interest argued that, since all three of the candidates evaluated by the Synod had not been "proper and suitable for the episcopal dignity," then the process had to be repeated. Obvious from both the political-religious context and the language Kászoni employed was the fact that only Pataki would be considered "convenient" by those exercising ultimate control over the choice of the new Uniate bishop. However calculating and circuitous these justifications for his candidacy, all agreed that Pataki possessed a fine education and an equally unblemished priestly record. Unfortunately, years of disrupted church life among the Uniates would ensue, despite the patronage he enjoyed "from the Viennese Court, the Transylvanian Governor and chancellery, and the Catholic estates."[64]

In the course of the eighteenth century, all the parties involved eventually learned that the "paper force" of centralization emanating from Vienna may well have circumscribed provincial political discretion, but it did not dissipate the culturally based wariness of the Eastern Rite Romanians. These qualms over Pataki as a conduit for Western influences would become more generalized as an inter-rite antipathy and outlive his guardianship of the Uniate Church. Pataki personally also set the tone for appealing to the specter of possible defections to Orthodoxy as a warrant for financial aid to augment this rhetorically vented political support. He and his successors, however, would find in this more prosaic type of juncture that Habsburg patronage often remained indeed only a "paper force."[65] The regime's determination to pursue its political advantage and the rather peculiar design of preserving the Union through the medium of a "Latinized" Romanian candidate for the bishopric brooked no opposition. Even the Jesuits, with their special insights and relationship with the Uniates, did not stand above the pressures involved. Gaspar Ujházi, the recently appointed "Theologian," had the courage and discernment to speak for Frantz and against Pataki at the 1715 Synod. Echoing in tone the warning issued in 1701 by Gabriel Kapi and Christophorus Gebhard he found little value placed on his thoughtful counsel. Unfortunately, the two earlier Jesuit superiors' carefully reasoned arguments regarding the respect that should be shown the Eastern Rite and the absolute necessity for the immediate naming of a replacement for a deceased Uniate bishop went without heed. Indeed, for his well placed concern and intrepid efforts Ujházi was removed from the post of "Theologian" almost as soon as he had assumed it. Into his place stepped Georgius Regai. But this new "Theologian," soon to be "Director," labored under the conspicuous and singular limitation of being excluded from any communion in the renewed search for a Uniate bishop, "so that there might be no additional obstacle." The pursuit of Pataki's candidacy by the Habsburg and Transylvanian political classes became even more single-minded, allowing not even for sophisticated Jesuit differences of opinion.[66]

By that same year of 1715 Emperor Charles VI, through intermediaries such as the Transylvanian Vice-Chancellor Kászoni, was seeking Papal confirmation of Pataki. Besides the promise of political assistance, Charles pledged some considerable level of economic maintenance as well. In addition, sounding very much like Pataki himself, the monarch sought from the Vatican "a dispensation [for Pataki] to use either rite, the Latin perhaps and also the Greek." Beyond these particulars, however, the unmistakable accent of the Habsburg petition was that this candidate for the Uniate bishopric had to be chosen. This direct intervention of Emperor Charles built upon two years of similar but preliminary briefs by officials at all levels. These letters detailed the government's and church's growing anxiety over the "backward" Romanians' purportedly facile tendency to revert to heresy. Most notable even at stations far below those of Vienna or the Transylvanian Chancellery was the awareness of the critical importance of rite and Pataki's attitude towards. it.[67] This remained the issue, throughout his prelacy and into his legacy of Jesuit-Roman influences, that would haunt the Uniates. His contemporaries, laying down a foundation that would be built upon by the later nationalists, described him as "*having been* [emphasis supplied] of the Romanian people." The implied question always present in their minds was the extent to which he might possess a genuine ethnic allegiance given his training and transparent preference for the Latin Rite. His protestations that he "would leave behind the customs of the papists [*sic*] and return to those of the Greek Church" sounded all too expedient and cosmetic. The fact that he was "slightly educated and knew some Romanian" did not cast the same weight among the people he would eventually preside over as it did in Habsburg and Latin Rite circles. The congregation that Atanasie had left behind, as well as the important Orthodox community still present in the province., would continue to be far more solicitous over their cultural and liturgical heritage's stamina than swayed by the curriculum vitae of a Jesuit trained prelate.[68]

Even with both Frantz and Szunyogh removed from consideration by 1715 it would still be 1721 before Pataki would be named Uniate bishop and 1723 before it he was installed in his diocese. In the meantime adversaries who would become characteristic of the eighteenth and later centuries' antagonisms towards the Uniate movement made themselves ever more visible. The Orthodox monks, in the eyes' of their enemies the foci of an incipient "nationalism" and "of the inferior culture of these peoples," helped lead a tradition-based resistance to Pataki as the symbol of an unwanted metamorphosis. They and the opposition they represented would, of course, persist in manifesting a heartfelt ethnic contention that these cultural and religious mores displayed essential properties of the Romanian populace and were intimately, indeed inextricably, intertwined with that community's fundamental conception of itself.[69] Complicating this often unspoken clash of cultures were the continuing facts of a Transylvanian desire for autonomy and the fierce ethnic exclusivity of the Magyars (whether of religious or secular prominence). This extraordinary pride, with what would later be termed an exceptional brittle nationalistic edge, entered into the equation of the provincial balance of power not only in resistance to Vienna's goals of centralization cum Germanization, but also where the Romanian Union's survival emerged as a factor. It offered yet another rationale for condescending to the Eastern Rite.[70]

The continuing struggle to obtain the appointment of Ioan Giurgiu Pataki as Uniate bishop of Transylvania became, then, a model in miniature of the plight of the Romanians throughout the eighteenth century. Regardless of whatever ethnic and spiritual goals they might have, they were caught in a far larger contest. Habsburg and Latin Rite establishments had their own uses for the vastly increased power basis represented by the Uniates. On the other hand the happy possessors of current economic and partisan advantage (whether Catholic or Protestant) were determined to relegate the Romanians (Orthodox and Uniate) to the status of a permanent underclass. The Romanians were left scrambling to salvage what they could, an enervating as well as provocative process that had a morphotic impact on the Union.[71] In the meantime, during the years from 1716 until 1721, those parties with a vested interest in the success of Pataki's suit did what they could for him and their not too hidden agenda. Writing in 1716 Vice-Chancellor Kászoni both sought the backing of Cardinal Saxonia for Pataki and, somewhat needlessly one must think, alerted the Primate of Hungary to the dangers threatening the Union. Most significantly, perhaps, this Habsburg official went out of his way to emphasize the ever present influence, indeed menace, of the Orthodox Church in the nearby Ottoman controlled Danubian Principalities. Reciting once more the pertinent population statistics to stress the importance of maintaining a hold on the Romanians, Kászoni ventured the view that the situation would not tolerate any further delay in filling this vacancy and confirming Pataki as Uniate prelate. He went so far as to insist that the "salvation" of the entire Eastern Rite Roman Catholic community depended on this happening immediately. Oddly enough from the modern perspective, but profoundly indicative of the establishment's obliqueness of analysis that would plague the Uniates for the entire century, this proxy of Vienna and Rome then urged that Pataki be authorized to participate in the liturgies of both

Eastern and Latin rites "in order to avoid scandalizing the [Romanian] people." The depth of the Uniates' commitment to the cultural expression of their faith and of their suspicions regarding Pataki's guilelessness as a faithful protector of their ethnic values had still not registered. The fact that such vacillation would merely reinforce the belief that Pataki's true allegiance resided now in Rome for ritual as well as doctrinal matters, that he would be even more likely to be viewed as "*having been* of the [Romanian] people" rather than currently actively espousing their inbred concerns, does not seem to have penetrated this rather opaque mentality. Charles VI also wrote in 1716 to the Pope soliciting Pataki's early confirmation, though this did not change the general tone of the campaign or bring it to the desired rapid fruition. There remained another five years in which native leadership would be lacking to the Uniates before the Church of Rome would finally speak definitively on the matter.[72]

In the final period leading up to Pataki's formal anointing in 1721 the Habsburg administration persevered in its balance between the Romanian clergy's adamant desire to safeguard the liturgy and the laity's (especially the small number of gentry) equal determination to have a bishop who would effectively represent an increasingly militant ethnic awareness. This latter group placed more emphasis on the prelate's use of their native tongue than on the ritual affiliation of that cleric, whoever he might turn out to be. Caught between these two factions, but learning an important political lesson that would later dramatically shape the Society of Jesus' relationship with the Uniate Church, stood the "Theologian." As seen in the careers of the first two "Theologians" who received a quick education, and in Ujházi's case a dramatically abrupt one, there was a major cost in siding with their charges against the prevailing political and religious regimes. The Habsburg administration for its part pledged again in 1718 substantial financial support not only for Pataki as bishop, but also for the Uniate Church. Unfortunately, in that same year and on the eve of the accord that would lead to Pataki's acceptance as bishop by Roman and Viennese authorities yet another disagreement in the arena of the rites issue arose. This time, rather than featuring the liturgy and the preservation of Romanian ecclesiastical culture, the controversy focused on the more arid but bitter point of ecclesiastical jurisdiction.[73]

In the fall of 1718 the Latin Rite bishop of Transylvania, Georgius Mártonffi, wrote in a self-proclaimedly "indignant" manner to Joesephus Cardinal Sacripantes regarding his prerogatives as Latin Rite bishop of Transylvania. Sacripantes' importance in this dispute resulted not only from his position as the official champion of the Greek College in Rome but also from his role as the Curia member with whom all matters relating to the Eastern Rite had to begin. Referring to Pataki somewhat superciliously as "the newly settled upon bishop," Mártonffi vigorously opposed an independent diocese for the prospective Uniate leader. To create such would have been, in the Latin prelate's mind, to undermine his authority, violate Canon Law, and contravene tradition. He most certainly did not wish to share Alba-Iulia, the seat of the Latin Rite episcopate, with the Uniates. Mártonffi, then, went on to insist upon his exclusive jurisdiction over all Roman Catholics in Transylvania, both Greek and Latin rite adherents. He announced that to have an independent Uniate bishopric in his province would produce the ecclesiastical equivalent of "bigamy." The only acceptable Uniate prelate, therefore, would be one who was subordinate to Mártonffi and at some distance removed from the locus of Latin Rite predominance. This squabble over jurisdictional lines would become in the course of the eighteenth century, along with the issues of the "Theologian" and the more general question of the Eastern Rite's cultural integrity, one that would exercise Romanian rancor to the extreme. It would also help concentrate the later nationalist's ire, purportedly evidencing a Latin Rite institutional bent, rampant even if regional, towards "Latinization" and hauteur where the Uniates were concerned.[74]

Growing out of this dispute was an attempt by church and secular officials to satisfy both rites. In 1715 part of the support settled upon the Uniate bishopric centered on holdings in Făgăraş in the extreme southern part of Transylvania. The following year a ministerial decision evolved that would result in the demarcation of the Uniate bishopric to correspond with the foundation in Făgăraş. With little or no chance of compromise or reconciliation on the jurisdictional issue, the administration decided that the simpler course was to remove the Uniate prelate from Alba-Iulia. This direct action would leave Mártonffi in sole control of a diocese that had been Roman Catholic prior to 1556 and the depredations of the Reformation. The new Uniate hierarch in turn would obtain a domain exclusively his and one almost entirely Romanian in its composition.[75] Not unexpectedly, the Society of Jesus in the persons of Gabriel Hevenesi and Laislaus Baranyi had stepped forward to promote the independent diocese in Făgăraş for their protégé. Their decades long concern for the Eastern Rite Romanians and the imagination they brought to bear upon their task now laid the basis for the desired jurisdictional solution. When finally installed, Pataki would be canonically separated from Mártonffi whose jurisdiction was proclaimed to have not been diminished.[76]

Though a thoroughly astute exercise in Jesuit *Realpolitik* which gave the Latin Rite bishop most of what he wanted, the transfer to Făgăraş amounted to something less than half a loaf to the Romanians. True, their bishop would not be termed or treated as a mere vicar of Mártonffi. But, as custodian of the Uniate Church and its patrimony, Pataki would not possess the hallowed church in Alba-Iulia in which Teofil, Atanasie, and their pre-Union predecessors had officiated. Furthermore, in removing the Uniate bishop to this area, the Habsburg and Roman Catholic powers likewise preempted the property of the Orthodox of the Făgăraş region.[77] The Orthodox of the area, already quite aggrieved by the very fact of the Union with Rome and the fiction that their sect no longer existed in Transylvania, now lost a major portion of the physical evidence of their presence. The church building taken from them had been a present from the Prince of Wallachia, Constantin Brâncoveanu, at the end of the seventeenth century. This confiscation, along with the obvious doctrinal difference and the omnipresent loathing of "Latinization," would make of Făgăraş a center of hostility to the Uniates. It along with Braşov (Kronstadt) farther to the east would become the flashpoints for some of the most embittered attacks upon the Eastern Rite Roman Catholics. Făgăraş had al ready demonstrated considerable religious independence as well as a marked aversion to the regime established by the Uniates under Atanasie. Its candidates for the priesthood had journeyed not to Alba-Iulia, but rather across the Carpathian Mountains to Muslim Ottoman occupied Muntenia for ordination. The conflict for the residents of these two Orthodox enclaves became, therefore, more than resistance to Uniate spoils taking or a matter of a pious conscience. They saw it as a struggle for their ancestral heritage and their uniqueness. The proximity of their co-religionists in the Danubian Principalities added to their determination. The influence of Bucharest, stimulated by general hostility and specific grievances such as the

Western reluctance to recognize Orthodox ordinations, contributed to the unfavorable reception that Pataki would receive from many in the region. This maneuver of the Jesuits would temporarily, then, solve the jurisdictional row between Latin and Eastern Rite hierarchy. But it would also help guarantee the long-lived and acrimonious nature of the Orthodox Romanians' repudiation of and assaults upon everything associated with the Latin influences infiltrating into their culture.[78]

The penultimate stage of this overdrawn process finally began in November 1720, when the Congregation for the Propagation of the Faith determined to resolve the jurisdictional conflict by creating a "new" diocese in Făgăraş for the Uniates. Although Pataki would in fact be situated in an existing bishopric, this fiction allowed some degree of maneuverability in dealing with both rites' criteria for administrative autonomy. With the death of Pope Clement XI in early 1721, this decision and the instrument of episcopal installation would be issued by his successor Innocent XIII. In that bull (i.e., "*Rationi congruit*"; May 15, 1721) erecting Pataki's bishopric, the new Pope once and for all discharged the Uniate prelate from any jurisdiction exercised by the Latin Rite bishop of Transylvania. Though not what in canonical terms amounted to an "exempt" diocese, the Uniate clergy and laity were separated from any supervisory authority wielded by either Mártonffi or his heirs in the Latin rite episcopal see. Instead, the Uniate diocese of Făgăraş would be immediately subordinate to the Archbishop of Strigon (i.e., the Primate of Hungary). Finally, this official instrument raising Pataki to the episcopal dignity required of him his definitive transfer to the "Greek Rite" as an inescapable precondition for assuming leadership within the Uniate Church.[79] With all the canonical niceties out of the way by the summer of 1721, Pataki would still remain in Vienna for another two years before his formal installation in the Făgăraş diocese. Other than the habitude engendered by his residence in the Habsburg capitol since 1717, there does not seem to have been a clearly established rationale for this dilatory assumption of his hard won responsibilities as Uniate hierarch. Possibly he experienced some jaundice precipitated by the disparity between the financial support provided to the Latin Rite bishop of Alba-Iulia and his own. Being already displeased by Mártonffi's grab for dominance and the loss of the traditional Romanian see in Alba-Iulia, Pataki could not have relished receiving less than a quarter of the funds his competitor did (13,000 Gulden for the Latin Rite bishop as compared with 3,000 for the Uniate). In any case, whatever the motive, the Uniate clergy and church remained without native leadership for another twenty-six months. This additional and avoidable hiatus in Romanian control also further entrenched the position of the "Theologian/Director" with all that would mean for later tensions between Jesuit and Uniate.[80]

Though Pataki did not take physical possession of his bishopric until 1723, the year 1721 saw him become officially the head of the Romanian Union with Rome. By then both Vienna, through its promise of financial support, and Pataki, by his commitment as a Basilian monk and "permanent" transfer to the Greek Rite, had satisfied Rome's qualms. To understand the storm that was building, however, another look into the depth of the new bishop's cultural convictions is necessary. He had as early as 1717 pledged to accept all the specifications emanating from the Vatican, most specifically that relating to embracing the Eastern Rite. Yet three years after this solemn declaration (i.e., in 1720) and after having taken his vows as a member of the Order of St. Basil, on the very eve of his canonical commission as Uniate prelate, he wrote once again to the Congregation for the Propagation of the Faith in Rome asking to be allowed to celebrate the Latin Rite Mass. Once it had checked to ascertain that he had indeed completed the abbreviated Basilian novitiate required of him (i.e., three months), Rome replied that Pataki's request "no longer made any sense." For by the date of the Vatican's reply in 1721 it had already been determined that he would be invested as the Eastern Rite bishop. Pataki would have to live with his choice.[81] The environment in which he had made his ambivalent decision was one in which the Western cleric did denigrate the culture and liturgy of those influenced by Orthodoxy. Moreover, it remained throughout the eighteenth century a milieu where it was presumed that only the stanch barriers, cultural and doctrinal, of the Latin Rite would prevent relapses into schism. Perhaps, to obtain not only a greater insight into this issue, but also its profound emotional overtones, one can do no better than look to a empathetic Western observer of the twentieth century. Though publishing through the Vatican just after World War II this knowledgeable commentator, in assessing both the Latin Rite's abhorrence of things Eastern and the Greek Rite's sense of affronted dignity in perceiving that attitude, maintained that

> The bishops and archpriests [in accepting the Union with Rome] had stipulated that their 'discipline, church ritual, liturgy, fasts, and customs remain unchanged, if not, neither do our seals bind us.'...To many Latins at this time a change of rite was considered comparable to embracing the Mosaic law in order to convert Jews![82]

Bishop Pataki's obviously Western bent and his lamely disguised hedging on his loyalty to his new rite foretold the cultural antagonism not only of his own period, but just as vividly of the modern world as well.

Almost a decade after Atanasie's death, in August of 1723, Bishop Ioan Giurgiu Pataki finally arrived in Făgăraş to assume his duties as head of the Uniate Church in Transylvania. Although his on-site reign would be an all too brief four years before the return of the Jesuit "Director," Pataki was welcomed into his diocese "with great pomp." The highlights of the day were speeches by himself and by "Theologian" (and former "Director"), Georgius Regai. Belying the tensions that would shortly emerge between the two most important figures in the Uniate Church, the Jesuit's speech was highly laudatory of Pataki. The Uniate bishop, in his turn, replied in a similarly congratulatory fashion. But, then, Pataki went on to make comments that seemed to sum up much of what has been analyzed thus far and which reduced his audience to silence. On this occasion of such importance to the Eastern Rite Catholic Church and to the tone of the incipient administration, Pataki ended his inaugural address to his congregation by praising his Latin Rite education. While this gratitude to the Society of Jesus and to his Western mentors in general was certainly understandable, it did not indicate a deft public relations touch. Sensitivities over the particulars of the liturgy and the sacrosanct nature of the folkloric content of the Byzantine Rite in general would have been yet more exacerbated by this tribute to Roman ways. Even more jolting given the celebratory nature of the event and the obviously favorably inclined crowd, the new bishop went on to conclude his remarks with what sounded like an outright challenge to the outward forms of the faith, if not to the tenets, espoused by the Uniates. Pataki proclaimed that "He had not come to be the bishop of heretics and schismatics."[83]

On the issue of Pataki's education even contemporaries were quite admiring of what he had achieved, certainly when compared with the average Romanian cleric's level of instruction. Later historians, even the nationalists, have seen this introduction of Romanians to Western schools as the foundation of their Transylvanian intelligentsia and nationalism. By the time of Pataki's installation these schools, run by the Jesuits and heavily influenced by the "Theologian" Regai, were well established and flourishing. In the interest of "the formation of youth...and the confirmation of the Union" Romanian boys were educated not only in religion and the arts, but also in the "customs" of their instructors and their non-Romanian fellow students.[84] Here again, then, the obstacle of "Latinization" would materialize despite the acknowledged benefits of exposure to the ideas of the Enlightenment. Looking at Pataki, and in a more general sense the overall impact of Latin Rite schools, some leading Romanian intellectuals would later charge that this type of instruction directly influenced deprecation of the Eastern Rite and occasionally subsequent transference of ecclesiastical and cultural loyalties to the Latin Rite. Taken in this light Pataki's commentaries on his education as well as on not wanting to be the bishop of "heretics and schismatics" can well be understood to have left the residents of the Făgăraş region wondering how they were expected to respond. Was the Western educated Uniate bishop speaking of doctrinal matters or of the liturgy he so wanted to avoid using? In the eyes of the nineteenth, twentieth, and twenty-first century ethnically minded nationalists, these criticisms of Pataki seemed to portend something even more sinister in terms of distortion of native folkways. One went so far as to explain the Western impact and the tenor of this original address with the implication that Pataki had not merely the advantage of a superior Jesuit education but had secretly taken vows joining his mentors. This conjecture has received some support from Jesuit scholarship of the same period.[85]

Despite all these problems and despite being labeled a "renegade" by the more belligerent of modern nationalistic historians, Ioan Giurgiu Pataki's short reign (1723-1727) had only the minor administrative tensions that might be expected. The seeds sown by his training and attitudes, coupled with the long standing structural problems of the Union with Rome, would produce their major disruptions only after he had left the scene. True to both his Roman training and the age's reawakened consciousness of sectarian differences, Pataki began an process of reorganizing his diocese. In this brief interval of relative tranquility for the Uniate hierarchy, he enjoyed the luxury of not merely arranging bureaucratic factors to his taste, but also of testing the extent of his jurisdiction's reach, perhaps to add fringe areas to his diocese. He also brought to these tasks the bearing and sense of élan of a "Prince Bishop," an innovation for the head of the Uniate church in Transylvania. Though this comportment may have alienated some among his fold, it undoubtedly enabled him to deal on more even terms with the economic and political masters of the Romanians' fate. Such flair allowed for far more effective protests and negotiations for concessions where the long sought after privileges promised the Uniates were concerned.[86]

Bishop Pataki, then, stood out in the succession of Uniate hierarchs as the guide who forged the broad lines for future ecclesiastical organization. Aimed initially at areas where the claims of various sects overlapped, this fresh corporate impetus by the Uniates would eventually extend to those districts where the reins of Teofil and Atanasie had been recognized unclearly if at all. It would likewise penetrate into the highly sensitive region of liturgical reform. As will be seen when the hostility of the Saxons to the Union is discussed, the liturgy became a matter not merely of cultural interest to the Western oriented Pataki, but most importantly one infringing on the economic status quo as well. For the number of Uniate priests and fasts days required by the Eastern Rite could, if permitted, drastically affect the wealth of those telling and politically active Lutheran counterweights, the Saxons. Unfortunately, however impressive the organizational genius and drive of Pataki, nothing within his administrative control could undo the two major blows to his position. During Atanasie's time the Uniate bishop had lost the largely honorary, but still culturally quite important, rank of "Metropolitan." With his see's transfer out of Alba-Iulia, Pataki also had to accept the loss of the title of "Bishop of the Romanian nation." In its place he now received the honorific of "Bishop of the Greek Rite." With all that the constitutionally term "nation" implied in Transylvania, this shift of phraseology seemed to portend not merely a greater accuracy in jurisdictional limits but more significantly an insuperable limitation on the political/economic claims the Uniates might make under the various imperial diplomas granted them. Since the issue of the unfulfilled Leopoldine prerequisites would loom so large in the disturbances and apostasies of the eighteenth century, this administrative vulnerability traceable to the altered ecclesiastical grade seriously impeded Pataki's goals.[87]

By the time of the Synod of 1725 Bishop Pataki was complaining on all these points. Not only had he and his church encountered an ongoing Orthodox presence, one still heavily laden with Calvinist ritual as well as doctrine, but also a reinvigorated sense of resistance. The Romanians of his diocese continued to encounter heresy laced books and anomalous celebrations of the Eucharist. His ability to confront these challenges was limited by a number of factors beyond the lack of education endemic in the region and the prevalent lack of interest in Latin Rite mores. Obviously the lessened status of his office made a considerable difference. Of even greater import throughout Pataki's reign and for the rest of the eighteenth century was the fact that the Union with Rome had made little practical difference in the standard of living for the Uniate priests.[88] Though other important factors such as the growing resentment against the control exercised by the Jesuit "Theologian" and the concomitant fear of "Latinization" would generate apostasies, the single greatest source of such radical discontent for the rest of the century would be this failure of both the Habsburg secular authorities and the officials of the Latin Rite to live up to their portion of the bargain establishing the Union. By the year of Pataki's death (1727) the scope of this disgruntlement and the magnitude of defections from the Byzantine Rite Catholic Church had reached the point that the state had to intervene. Though a tactic of questionable success in the long run, the Habsburg civil authorities by that time determined to inhibit apostasy by punishing anyone who attempted to return to Orthodoxy. The Transylvanian Chancellery also pledged, but in a manner that had no real impact and certainly did not satisfy Romanian economic/political aspirations grounded in the Leopoldine diplomas, "to protect those who remained in the Catholic faith from their persecutors."[89]

The most determined of those opponents, adversaries having the inestimable constitutional advantage of already having possessed for centuries the privileges and categorization of "nation" ("*natio*") so coveted by the Romanians, were the Lutheran Saxons. Virtually from the moment he was first considered for the post of bishop down to his installation, Pataki wrote to the Emperor detailing the entrenched opposition of the Transylvanian landed interests. In doing so, he carefully outlined the economic and political bases for this hostility. But he also highlighted the way these impinged on the liturgy and feast days of the Eastern Rite, obviously warning that an already volatile situation could easily be made worse by the Saxons. What the Lutherans clearly perceived was that to implement fully the promises made during the negotiations for the Union with Rome would mean more than an increased Roman Catholic power base in Transylvania. More immediately and far closer to home, given the Uniate diocese so close to their own population concentrations, it foretold an economic and social upheaval of massive proportions.[90] As this battle was joined at the start of Pataki's governance, the Saxons maintained that the Romanians in their region "had continued to confess the old Greek religion and had in no way united [with Rome]." Though in part the same type of fanciful use of statistics for political ends that had led the Latin Rite Catholics to announce the total disappearance of Orthodoxy in Transylvania, this Saxon claim was founded in actual events. They could easily point to the increased hostility in Braşov towards the Union since Pataki's appointment and subsequent experiments with liturgical reform. These, of course, built upon a long standing animosity produced by Latin denial of Orthodox orders as well as the firmly established Western sense of cultural superiority. In Făgăraş the Saxon case received yet more blatant confirmation, since the Romanians there wrote to the Chancellery in 1724 complaining of the harm done their religion and unyieldingly pressing for the restitution of the church building taken by the Uniates. The real intent of the Saxon case and the depth of their concern emerged in another, less dramatically put, portion of their brief. They were already quite alarmed about the "superfluous number of priests" in the Romanian villages, a sum that could not but grow if the attraction of the promised Uniate privileges did indeed eventuate. To have even the current number of Romanian clerics, let alone a vastly larger amount, excused from the traditional payments to Saxon landowners simply could not be allowed. The Lutheran Saxons, no more than the Latin Rite Catholics, had little or no appreciation for the manpower demands of the Romanian community and Eastern Rite liturgy. But should they have had, the practical consideration of the exemptions to be granted to Uniate priests and the loss of revenues would still have prevailed.[91]

Almost from the moment Pataki received his commission as bishop, the Saxons were complaining bitterly and at great length about Uniate pretensions and supposed abuses. With constant references to their traditionally privileged status as well as to specific provisions in the hoary constitution of the province, they objected to the "excessive number of priests," the moral failings of the Uniate clergy, and liturgical irregularities. Despite being Protestant and as such outside the pale where such matters were concerned, the Lutheran Saxons felt no compunction in bringing them to the attention of the "Theologian" Regai or even of invoking the name of "the Lord Bishop Atanasie of blessed memory" when leveling their criticisms. The focus of their grievances, as laid down in detail as early as 1722, revolved around economic matters and how their vested interests might be compromised by the Union with Rome. Despite the Jesuit's entreaties that they honor the privileges guaranteed to the Uniates by Emperor Leopold's various diplomas (supposedly also the law of the land), the Saxons retorted that the Romanians' reproaches clearly had no merit. For the aspirations evidenced in the Uniates' querulous complaints went against long understood and accepted Saxon rights. The fundamental factor, therefore, whenever these questions arose would be that the Transylvanian constitution sided with the Lutheran interpretation of the Uniates' status. As a final rejoinder, the Saxons even threw up to Regai the informal regulation of the number of Eastern Rite parish priests launched in 1712 by the then "Theologian" Franz Szunyogh. Thus, there would no accommodation by the Saxons without, and perhaps even with, conspicuous political pressures from outside.[92] For the Habsburgs did attempt such. Throughout the mid-1720s the Roman Catholic hierarchy in Transylvania, along with adamant support from Charles VI reminiscent of the fervor of Emperor Leopold I, set out to further curtail Protestant power. The Governor of Transylvania, Count Sigismund Kornis did his part in this process by trying to compel compliance with the Uniates' rights. In strong, even righteous, language he brought to Saxons' attention that the Uniates enjoyed certain immunities and privileges under law based on Imperial diplomas. He went on to enjoin the lack of respect shown by them for this legal framework for the Eastern Rite Roman Catholic Church and to order a cessation to any inhibitory activities on their part. Kornis felt obligated to go to the exceptional length of endeavoring to obtain the compliance of Andreas Teutsch, spokesman for the Saxons and a counselor to the Transylvanian Chancellery. In this letter on the eve of Pataki's return to his homeland as the Uniate hierarch, Kornis sought to impress upon the Saxon leader the necessity under law and for the common good to observe the privileges granted to the Eastern Rite

Catholics. Unfortunately, for the beginning of Pataki's stewardship and the long term vitality of the Union, the governor met with no success.[93]

During the four years of Pataki's administration of the diocese of Făgăraş he would conduct a similar correspondence with the Saxons, one not only paralleling that of the Habsburg authorities but likewise equally barren. He, like Governor Kornis, wrote in 1724 directly to Andreas Teutsch to object to the numerous locales within Saxon jurisdiction where the Uniate clergy were economically exploited. However, the Saxon establishment's rhetoric in this regard never changed. Both before and after the personal interventions of Kornis and Pataki their consistent platform declared the Uniates' statements were completely unfounded. The Saxons rejected all intercession on behalf of the Uniates where their affairs were concerned as not based on "genuine information." They proceed to maintain that "in no way had the Romanian priests experienced the least unfairness" at their hands. If Teutsch was being lobbied by Kornis and Pataki, he was under even greater pressure from local Saxon councils. These groups wrote him too making the same arguments. They were right on the scene with better intelligence into local affairs and that the Romanians had nothing to complain about. In an aside for his eyes only, they also emphasized for their spokesman the real issue; namely, the superfluity of Romanians priests and the economic damage this entailed.[94] By the 1724-1725 period the most that the Saxon councils or Teutsch would concede was that, if Uniate privileges did exist based on the Leopoldine diplomas, then they still had to be exercised within the bounds of the traditional constitutional order of Transylvania. In 1725 Teutsch wrote directly to Pataki presenting the Saxons' ultimate legal defense from which neither he nor they would back down; namely, that "according to the ancient constitutions of our fatherland" there were limits on the number of Uniates that could be accorded the sought after privileges, no matter what the basis for them in imperials edicts. While adhering resolutely to this fundamentum, Teutsch did adopt a slightly more public relations conscious modus operandi from this point on. In 1726 he advised the local Saxons leaders "to leave the Romanian priests in their status quo, for the time being, so as not to irritate the Lord Bishop Pataki any further." The local municipal authorities in Saxon areas did not have to change their basic stance on Uniate prerogatives. Teutsch simply urged them to do as he himself intended to act by not causing any additional public show of their resistance. Being in the dominant position and already being the "happy possessors" of all that the Uniates envied, the Saxons could prevail by passive resistance and silence.[95]

Giving pause to the Habsburgs through this period and scope to Saxon intractability was Charles VI's pursuit of recognition for the Pragmatic Sanction. Formally accepted by the Transylvanian Diet in March of 1722 and by that of Hungary proper in June of the same year, this compact legalized the female line of succession and the *Hausmacht* of the Habsburgs. It also removed once and for all the right of the province to elect its prince. However depleted Transylvania's ability to resist further Habsburg encroachments, the landed estates managed exactly that through the recalcitrance they demonstrated for the rest of the century where taxes were concerned. While protecting the inheritance of the future Empress Maria Theresa, as of 1722 the Pragmatic Sanction had achieved merely internal acceptance by the various lands making up the empire. Charles VI would have to continue to bargain, and to look over his shoulder fearing further domestic disturbances in regions like Transylvania, until September of 1725. Only then did the other Great Powers (i.e., Great Britain, Prussia, and France) sign the treaty. Up until that time the position of a group such as the Saxons, with a purely if urgent local agenda, gained some tangential reinforcement from these higher level negotiations. For the Saxons could forcefully demonstrate that, whatever the 1722 Transylvanian acquiescence in the Pragmatic Sanction gave Vienna, it also reinforced the legal basis of their constitutionally protected position and rights. However provincial administrators, religious or secular, might importune them on the issue of Uniate privileges, the Saxons knew their political capital had increased and that they could have their way if their remained circumspect in their partisan rhetoric.[96]

If the vested self-interest of the Saxons and other defenders of the status quo in Transylvania constituted the great external challenge to the Uniate bishop, the major internal restraint for Pataki and his successors became the entrenched position of the Jesuits. Whether their influence was exercised in the form of the institutions of "Director" and "Theologian" or simply as the dominant Roman Catholic religious order of the region, the impact on the Uniates varied little. A report to the Congregation for the Propagation of the Faith in 1716 sketched out the general outline for these tensions as seen both by enemies of the Society of Jesus and, for the rest of the eighteenth century, by an ever increasing portion of the Uniate hierarchy: "The Theologian...had arrogated to himself the authority of the [Uniate] Bishop, disposing in all matters according to his own pleasure...." These words of the "Theologian" Regai, in a letter to the Romanians of Braşov also in 1716, gave ample support to this sharply critical evaluation forwarded to Rome. For in that year he categorically stated that "until the bishop arrives...you must give respect and obedience to our orders."[97] By the time Pataki finally arrived in Transylvania in 1723 the resentment of the "Theologian" and the Uniate perception of an aggravated institutional, if not personal, animosity between their bishop and the Jesuits involved had become quite widespread. Even a year after the imperial appointment of Pataki to the diocese of Făgăraş, the Jesuit superior in Sibiu (Hermannstadt) continued publicly to equate the statures of "the Lord Bishop and the Father Theologian." He specially reminded the Romanians of Transylvania that they were bound by the orders of "the Bishop and 'Theologian'" where their religious lives and duties were concerned. If it had been possible to make the argument in the times of Teofil and Atanasie that such tutelage was called for by the general level of ecclesiastical culture, that excuse certainly no longer existed with the appearance of Bishop Pataki. Yet the attempts at control and, from the Romanian perspective both then and in later times, at intervention in purely Uniate matters continued. Adding a more acrimonious edge to the presence within the Uniate bishop's court of this "symbol of the humiliation and subjugation of the Romanian Church" was the charge that the "Director"/"Theologian" Regai had done more than simply usurp Pataki's powers. According to this ethnically oriented charge, he had "used the bishop's revenues for purposes foreign to the interests of the Romanian church." But, if as Regai had proclaimed, he ran the show until Pataki took physical possession of the diocese, then such actions are understandable if no less objectionable to the in-coming prelate.[98] Although the more perturbing issues of "Latinization" and denial of the imperial privileges would continue as the major points galling the Uniates, the central nature of the "Theologian's" control over their church came ever more to the forefront after Pataki's bishopric. By the time of his death in 1727, with the inception of another five years of completely Jesuit administration of the Uniate diocese, the office of the "Theologian" became a major factor in both the resistance to the Union by the remaining Orthodox of Transylvania and in the significant number of apostasies that occurred. From the perspectives of both the Habsburgs with their political agenda and of the Latin Rite Catholics a frightening number of Romanians found this combination of irritants too much to tolerate any longer. After a generation of Western education through the medium of the Jesuits, the opponents of the Union asked why a Romanian vicar could not be found to administer the diocese until the selection of the next bishop. Certainly the accomplishments of a Pataki proved that the Jesuit schools could produce a qualified Romanian candidate for vicar as well as for bishop. With such an individual there would be no question that both the ethnic and the Eastern Rite devotee need not feel so alienated as with the revived position of "Director." Furthermore, during the reign of Charles VI this educational enterprise among the Romanians had expanded further, presenting yet more hope that it would not be necessary to resort once again to a foreign Jesuit.[99]

In 1727, with the Union in this state of structural and participatory agitation, Bishop Pataki died on October 29 at the relative young age of forty-six. The shock registered among the Uniates as well as their patrons centered not merely on the unexpected and untimely nature of the bishop's passing, but likewise on the exceptionally short tenure he had enjoyed in that role. After a decade of seeking to fill the post Pataki's four years in Făgăraş were all too brief. Even if the two years spent in Vienna after his consecration as the Uniates' leader are included, six years hardly prepared the Eastern Rite community for either another provocative episcopal search or another half decade of Jesuit supervision. Neither was welcome. Both helped heighten existing tensions.[100] With the demise of Bishop Pataki and yet another hiatus in native leadership of the Uniate Church, Georgius Regai became "Director" once again, exercising the same powers that had been his from 1716-1723. Though he would function as "Theologian" until 1738 (with a respite in 1731), this term as "Director" would be quite brief. In remarking on the return to Jesuit administration of the Uniate Church, the Transylvanian Chancellery reported to Charles VI in 1728 that the Society of Jesus continued to enjoy the confidence of the Romanian clergy and people. In particular it was noted that Regai presided over the Eastern Rite Catholic Church in a manner that bore "no little fruit." Despite Regai's longevity as a overseer to the Uniates, without a doubt the Jesuit of the moment and the one having the greatest lasting impact was Adamus Fitter, the rector of the Society's college in Cluj (Klausenburg), who succeeded Regai and labored as the "Theologian" until 1729. A Magyar of noble birth, Fitter brought great ability and the proverbial Jesuit skills of organization to his task of governing the Uniate Church.[101] To gauge Fitter's stature, certainly in the eyes of his peers in the Society of Jesus if not always quite so positively by Romanian nationalists, one has only to read the panegyric offered to his memory. In that Latin poem it was noted that not only had he employed the powers and dignity of the Uniate bishopric wisely and well, but that had he wished he could have been the bishop. Fitter's task, then, was to bring to bear "the discipline of the Fathers of the Society of Jesus for the improvement of morals and education." He was to do this in an atmosphere wracked by protests against a Union now more frequently afflicted by apostasy. Increasingly Fitter and those who followed him would find that even their best efforts as religious inspector generals could not prevent outbreaks of these "latent discontents."[102]

In the words of a contemporary if not friendly Calvinist observer, Fitter faced a situation in which "the Union was held in contempt" by large numbers. His term as "Director" also saw a considerable number of Romanian priests flee to Ottoman Moslem held lands where they recanted their allegiance to Rome. No amount of personal sympathy with Fitter or admiration for his efforts by Union loyalists would be sufficient to dampen such hostility or inhibit the religiously motivated emigrations that would become characteristic of the eighteenth century Romanian community. Indeed the major, contemporary Romanian chronicler of the period, himself a Uniate as well as a product of the Latin Rite schools in Rome and Vienna, saw the root causes of these problems in the very structure of his church. The seemingly perennial administrative control of the Society of Jesus and the concomitant native fear of "Latinization" of necessity produced both the furious resistance becoming more common now and the growing problem of "apostates" returning to the Orthodox Church.[103] These five years (1727-1732) with no Uniate bishop became difficult ones for all those in favor of the Union with Rome. Multiplying that arduousness was the perception, prevalent among both Uniates and Orthodox, that the new "Theologian" had little or no realization of the depth of Romanian commitment to their existing ecclesiastical culture. This intense love of and dedication to the Eastern Rite ran directly counter to what the Romanians believed to be Fitter's

"Catholicizing [i.e., Latinizing] tendency." To their lights it seemed that Fitter had set course on a program that had to lead to the complete, if gradual, eradication of the Easter Rite's cultural and liturgical heritage.[104]

Jesuit scholars writing from a contemporary vantage point have noted the lack of wisdom in Pataki's attempts to "reform" (that is, to make more like the Latin Rite) the liturgy of the Byzantine Rite to which he had supposedly committed himself unconditionally. This modern Jesuit analysis goes on to insist that to substitute for the native bishop a member of the Society of Jesus of Fitter's mentality, even given his remarkable ability and astuteness, could only have been like "putting oil on a fire." Interestingly, given the previously noted caveat offered by the Jesuit Kapi on the issue of Eastern Rite integrity and respect, these criticisms of the "Latinizing" proclivities of Pataki and Fitter were not limited to the hindsight of the modern historian. Some among the Latin Rite leadership of Transylvania saw the risk involved in this, if not the affront and onslaught offered to a different cultural tradition. Writing on behalf of the government Vice-Chancellor Kaszoni had pointed out even before Pataki's installation the seductive qualities of the schismatic Orthodox population's immemorial churchly grace. He also emphasized that the Eastern Rite Romanian Catholics were "not yet sufficiently firm in their commitment to the Holy Union, and might easily slide back." Endeavoring to alter substantively, even if over a protracted period, the most "seductive" of the Romanian cultural attributes, the Eastern Rite with its treasured ceremonials, seemed a guaranteed course to spark controversy and sectarian mutiny. So it turned out to be.[105]

Though this revolt of religious conscience only reached its crest in Fitter's last year as "Director" (i.e., 1729), the foundation for its birth and flowering went back to the origins of the Union. Its acerbic qualities in the late 1720s and its urgency dated, however, from the innovations of the late bishop and his Jesuit successor, nominally only the "Director." If the Uniates were deeply troubled about the invasion of Latin ways, the surviving Orthodox became ever more irate in their desire to protect their "law" (i.e., "*lege*"). They, as well as their Uniate compatriots whom they influenced and often now welcomed back into the ancestral church, demonstrated an increasing impatience with even a hint of "Latinization." They labeled as "foreign" anything that might alter, and thus taint, this complex of rite, liturgy and accustomed folkloric usages which they found so comfortable in their services. In the ethnic voice of the first half of the eighteenth century they pledged "to worship...only in the orthodox Greek law of the East...[and] to remain in the orthodox law of our forefathers...." By the time Fitter left his post as "Director" at the end of the decade of the 1720s, the weakness of a Union built upon an offer of preferential treatment, which the Habsburg could not deliver due to entrenched constitutional opposition, became obvious to even the most parochial of view. For within less than a generation the Transylvanian Union with Rome found itself in what was probably an unavoidable crisis precipitated by an agitated amalgam of ritual, political, and economic considerations, one centered in the very heart of the Uniate diocese.[106] Unfortunately, for relations between adherents of the Eastern and Latin rites ever since this time, Roman Catholic commentators then and now have vastly underestimated the importance of culture and rite in determining Romanian loyalties. In the eighteenth century the emphasis was, of course, on the doctrinal truth of Rome's position and the difficulties of adjusting the provincial power equation to allow for Romanian participation. Building on that basis, the twentieth century contributed to the further growth of misunderstanding. An otherwise balanced Jesuit analysis of the revolts after Pataki's death first claimed that the average Romanian continued "indifferent" to most religious matters, including the preservation of the Eastern Rite. It then proceeded to proclaim that in this period in order to conceal their real intentions the Romanians often resorted to "lies and silence, the Orthodox populace recognizing in such cases no obligation to tell the truth." The gulf between these two mentalities has hardly narrowed over the generations.[107]

The eighteenth century Romanian opposition's attitude, particularly in the preeminent center of such resistance in Braşov, displayed "a profound disapproval of this abandonment of the orthodox religion." Since the arrival of Bishop Pataki in southern Transylvania in his role as Uniate prelate, the Orthodox community in Braşov had led, in rhetoric and practice, the defiance to all that he represented. Speaking for this vast inarticulate refusal to embrace either the Union or more especially the efforts to alter the traditions of their rite, their spokesmen proclaimed that "We [are] true sons of the holy, apostolic church of the East." Worried as they were about the pressures to "Latinize" and Pataki's aggressive stance, they asked simply to be left alone as Atanasie had done. The "peace" they sought applied most specifically to their "law" (i.e., rite and traditions). In definitively throwing down the gauntlet to Pataki and the Uniates, the Orthodox of southern Transylvania insisted that they would not mention, as required for the peace they desired, Pataki in their liturgy but would rather "cling to the old Greek law (rite)" as they understood it.[108] This determined stand by the Orthodox of Braşov and Făgăraş, along with the alluring rhetoric concerning protection of the Eastern Rite, did more than harden resistance to the Union. By 1719 and continuing through the rest of the hiatus before the appointment of a new Uniate bishop, the number of defections increased steadily, often manifested in a tangible fashion by the number of priests journeying to Bucharest to register their formal abjuring of the Union. Their loss was compounded by the fact that the only way for young men to be ordained, lacking a Uniate bishop for Făgăraş, was to approach an Orthodox prelate, thus from the viewpoint of Rome becoming priests in a valid manner but at the hands of a schismatic.[109]

In assessing the different views of the problems after Pataki's demise and before the arrival of the new Uniate bishop, it is interesting to note that both eighteenth century Latin Rite contemporaries of these events and present-day commentators on them persisted in overlooking the impact of rite. Though mentioned, this basic concern of the Romanians, Orthodox and Uniates, did not receive the politically and religiously sensitive attention it deserved. There was, of course, no doubt in these observers minds, then or now, that the failure to raise the Romanian priesthood to the economic and constitutional level of their peers in other sects had had a profoundly detrimental effect. But, granted that the disturbances of this period as well as later in the century had social and "national" (i.e., anti-Habsburgs) elements, the force and staying power remained the fundamental attachment to the Eastern Rite. The eighteenth century official found himself in the position of having to use force, or at least the intimidating authority of the state, to shore up the Union among the Romanians. The modern Latin Rite historian occasionally feels compelled to justify this reliance upon the machinery of governance with the rationalization that the times and local conditions required it.[110] Whatever, the rationale offered, after three bishops and several Jesuit stewards in the guise of the "Director" the Uniates still found themselves in a situation where they were denied their imperial privileges by the combined action of both Protestant and Roman Catholic vested interests. The clumsiness of handling the position of these "official priests" added to an already difficult situation. On the other hand the Orthodox opposition responded to Western condescension by proclaiming that the Uniates were not merely wrong and the betrayers of their heritage, but that their sacraments were "invalid." These failures of the Union and its patrons, after what seemed so long a time in the minds of those dwelling on the promises of the Leopoldine diplomas, to produce the expected yield would now find a more active critic. The next Uniate bishop, Ioan Inocențiu Klein, would prove himself equally adamant where the integrity of his people's ecclesiastical mores came into play as well as on the more obvious "national" issues. He would, in short, emerge as an ethnic and religious leader. In doing so, he would become, in modern nationalistic historiography, a precursor of many of the nation's complaints against the Habsburgs and the use to which they put the Union with Rome.[111]

IV
Conclusion: Birth of National Awareness

The process that would bring about the reign of the next Uniate bishop and frame the tumult of this critical juncture in the development of his church began in 1728. In that year Charles VI ordered the submission of the names of three candidates to fill Pataki's role. To ensure that the proper caliber of nominees was considered and, perhaps, to preclude a repetition of the extraordinarily long hiatus in Uniate leadership before Pataki's installation, the Emperor also insisted on more extensive Latin Rite supervision this time. Both the Latin Rite Bishop of Transylvania, Baron Joannes Antalffi, and select members of the Society of Jesus were to oversee the expeditious and perhaps peaceful election of the new Romanian prelate. Once again the "Director" and Rector of the Society's residence in Cluj, Adamus Fitter, played the pivotal position for the Jesuits. As did Emperor Charles, Fitter displayed great concern for the continued "tranquility" of both the Eastern Rite Catholic church and of the province as a whole. For these reasons he was determined to have a Jesuit-educated Romanian, one who had been formed "under the discipline of the Fathers of the Society of Jesus," for the next bishop. The framework for Fitter's profile for his candidate for the episcopal post can be found in the Uniate Synod of 1728 which he called and presided over. At this pivotal clerical meeting, and due to the escalating seriousness of the Orthodox challenge to the Uniates' position, the "Director" called for increased reliance on the powers of the state to deal with "schismatic" opponents. The Jesuit likewise sought assets to establish a seminary exclusively for Greek Rite candidates for the priesthood so that they would no longer make use of Orthodox educational resources. Although concerned with the persistent denial of the privileges owed to his charges, Fitter as "Director" questioned the sincerity of those Romanians fixated on this problem.[1]

Ioan Inocențiu Klein stood forth arrestingly, then, as the most apt choice in 1728 to help the "Director" accomplish his various objectives. Honored with the German version of his surname [Micu in the

Romanian] as a sign of his ennoblement, this "client of the Jesuits" had not only spent a year in his patrons' novitiate, but after leaving that strict training ground had continued his education in the Society's college in Tîrnavia. A relatively young man at the time he received Fitter's endorsement (born in 1692), Klein had yet another year of study for the priesthood under the terms of the foundation set up by Cardinal Kollonich for Greek Rite Catholic seminarians. Despite his youth and inexperience, he would become for every subsequent generation of Romanians "an apostle" protecting the Union and the Greek Rite.[2] Granted the fact that Klein met his mentors' specifications for background influences and education, it would appear that, perhaps, too much stock was placed on his apparent impressionability. Based on his formation to this point he seems to have presented to a man of Fitter's constitution the suggestion of greater pliancy to Jesuit and Latin Rite authority than would prove to be the case. Despite having never functioned in any official capacity in his church before his consecration by the Uniate bishop of Munkács, Klein would demonstrate both ability and industry in his first and only post as a prelate. Besides, those responsible in both Rome and Vienna counted on his awe of and friendship with the Jesuits to render him susceptible to their guidance in all matters of import. In any case, the very constitution of the Uniate Church provided for the important safeguard of the Jesuit "Theologian's" presence at his shoulder "for advice in the governance" of his diocese. Unfortunately, while the Latin Rite authorities guessed quite correctly that his education and native talents would compensate for his inexperience in bureaucratic matters, they would encounter in Klein an unexpected independence of spirit. He would become not merely "an apostle" where factors of liturgical and spiritual significance emerged, but likewise in those pertaining specifically to the unique ethnic interests of the Romanians. Indeed, there would later be some chagrin in having presumed that the Uniate bishop's molding by the Jesuit educational system had not precluded a feistiness that bordered on the politically reckless in seeking Romanian "national" goals.[3]

With Klein's nomination and subsequent appointment to the Uniate episcopacy there began, then, a complex "political, religious, cultural, and social movement" that not only dominated eighteenth century Romanian life in Transylvania, but which in many ways has transmitted a clamorous legacy down to the present century. For the prospective

Uniate prelate and his people the mid-eighteenth century would continue the pattern of the early Union. They would still face the determined and formidable resistance of the established orders. Latin Rite Roman Catholics as well as the Protestants, whenever it appeared that the pursuit of the Romanians' corporate improvement and political identity would diminish the preponderant controls of such vested interests, resisted the Uniates' ambitions.[4] In challenging this glacis of entrenched privilege Klein would become "the most preeminent figure produced by the Uniate hierarchy" according to the historiographical canon of prevailing Romanian nationalism. For his goals would very quickly develop far beyond the stage achieved by his three predecessors. No longer would the Romanian bishop in Făgăraş be content simply to seek the perquisites promised by the various imperial diplomas. Klein, slightly naively and somewhat impetuously, ran head-on into the hidden agenda of the Union's sponsors as well as its enemies. For, in the view of the modern Romanian nationalist, he

> promoted an extraordinary program for the good of the church, for the elimination of the abysmal ignorance in which the clergy and people groped their way, and for the emancipation of the Romanian nation from the political slavery to which the centuries had delivered them.[5]

Even if somewhat colorfully put, this observation certainly captured not only the animus of the stylish nationalist, but also that of the eighteenth century ethnic who would during and after Klein's episcopacy demonstrate ever more stridently for a guaranteed position among the elite of the province.

In the spring of 1729, then, Emperor Charles VI nominated for the Uniate episcopacy the man who would not only found the Uniate educational and monastic center in Blaj, but who became in the eyes of his contemporaries and subsequent nationalistic spokesmen the author of the Transylvanian Romanians' political program for the rest of the century. Important to remember in this regard is the fact that Charles made this selection in the context of increasing unrest among the Romanians of this sensitive political frontier. His governor for the province, Sigismund Kornis, would in the course of that year comment in his official capacity on the "latent tensions" between the "true Uniate priests" and those who merely presented a facade of such commitment. He very clearly communicated the judgment that the "the bad intentions and work of the schismatics" were not merely growing, but had spread to such a large extent as to necessitate vigorous underwriting by the state of the Uniate movement. Klein's appointment, and of course his role as a lever for Habsburg intentions, assumed even greater importance in this situation.[6] The Emperor's formal nomination of Klein reflected all of these concerns and goals. Though nominated for the Uniate bishopric Klein's ascendancy would not be without conditions or condescension. As might be expected the appointment was made in the context of Emperor Leopold's various diplomas and specifically on the condition of the continued presence of the Jesuit "Theologian" alongside Klein. Perhaps also to be anticipated, but something of an affront in its baldness, was the stricture that he was challenged to preserve even among the Romanians the "uncontaminated" quality of the Roman Catholic Church "in every chapter and point." The rigor of the brief nominating him obviously divined the opposition that would arise in the course of the ecclesiastical scrutiny that Klein would enjoy. Even with the Emperor's backing and the indispensable support of the Society of Jesus he could rather accurately be portrayed as too young, relatively uneducated, and most importantly totally without the experience normally qualifying a candidate for the trust of the episcopacy.[7]

When finally extended, therefore, Pope Clement XII's confirmation of Ioan Inocențiu Klein as Uniate bishop specified that, due to the candidate's lack of theological training, he must accept "the continual assistance of the Roman Catholic theologian." Until actually installed as Uniate prelate in Făgăraş (i.e., 1732), Klein's diocese would be administered by the Jesuit "Theologians" Georgius Regai and Emericus Görgei. Later, during his difficulties with the Society of Jesus over the nature of the "Theologian's" office, Klein may well have reread this edict of Clement XII's sensing a different, more disturbing undertone behind the traditional formalities of this papal testimonial. For that "continual assistance" to be rendered by the "Theologian" to his clerical charge could just as easily, and perhaps more aptly, be translated as "perpetual shepherding." However circumscribing to Romanian pride and ambitions the Emperor's decree nominating Klein in 1729 may have been, it set the stage for the first of many acts demonstrating the future bishop's vision and initiative. In order to more closely approximate both the promises made by Emperor Leopold and the status of the established religions of Transylvania, Klein asked for both a patent of nobility and for a place in the provincial diet.[8]

In eliciting the first favor from Charles he employed the telling comparison of the Uniate bishop's present humble status with that of the Latin Rite bishop of Transylvania's possession of the title of baron. This elevation to the aristocracy represented far more for Klein and his people than a significant honorific, as flattering as such might be. The improvement in status of the Uniate hierarch would become both a symbol of community enhancement and the aspiration of the entire clerical leadership. For

> Only social distinctions, titles of different sorts conferred the right to tax exemptions, to favors, to jobs, to property, to a public life. Not to pursue ennoblement meant to renounce any and all role in the public sector. A title of nobility represented as much a necessity for entry into contemporary public life as did a scholastic diploma.[9]

Shadowing the second request Klein pointed out that the dominant religions and their corresponding ethnic enclaves all found a voice in the diet. Only the Eastern Rite Roman Catholic Romanians were left out of this important political arena. For whatever reasons, perhaps to solidify the position of this prospective prelate given the large number of apostasies during the recent hiatus in Uniate hierarchical development, Charles VI approved both petitions. By the fall of 1729 the Romanians' ecclesiastical candidate was christened Baron Ioan Inocențiu Klein with all the appropriate panoply of such a distinction. At the end of 1732 he received the coveted appointment to the Transylvanian diet, actually taking his seat the following year as the first Romanian bishop to attain this level of prominence and to advocate openly the peculiarly ethnic goals of his church.[10]

Having completed his final year of theological studies and the required monastic initiation as a novice of the Order of St. Basil, Klein was consecrated Uniate bishop in Munkács in 1730. With the Jesuit "Theologian" administering his new episcopate for him, the Uniate prelate did not enter Făgăraş until 1732. There on September 28 he was finally installed as Pataki's successor and Eastern Rite leader in what would prove to be a critical and tumultuous period for Romanian development at the mid-point of the eighteenth century. Having been duly honored by the presence of various notables, his clergy, and the ever attendant Jesuit "Theologian" (Georgius Regai at this time), Bishop Klein hurried to meet the many challenges awaiting him. Besides the reorganization of his court and diocesan administration considered in the General Synod accompanying his enthronement, he turned to the types of issues so crucial to Romanian advancement and sectarian integrity. Such particulars would, of course, shortly bring him into less than harmonious contact with the prevailing political order of Transylvania.[11] As had happened so many times since Baranyi first approached Teofil concerning the Union with Rome, the necessities of the Eastern Rite liturgy and the conflicting constraints imposed by the landholding classes demanded the attention of the Uniate prelate during this General Synod of 1732. In the spring of that year Klein had already complained to Charles VI regarding non-fulfillment of the privileges promised his flock. Most particularly he represented to the Emperor the indignation of Eastern Rite Roman Catholics forced to pay duties to Protestants, especially to the Saxon Lutherans. During the General Synod that fall Klein brought up the other side of that same coin of inferior status and the landed element's refusal to deal fairly with the Uniates. Since it meant more Romanians off the rolls and a diminution of their economic power, estate owners had vigorously resisted permitting the full number of priests and deacons required for the Eastern Rite service. The new bishop now specified publicly before his assembled clergy that four clerics constituted the minimum norm for the traditional Romanian solemnities. Then he besought the Emperor's assistance in this matter so essential to his people's rite and political well being.[12]

In December 1732, only three months after having been formally installed as the Uniate bishop, Klein received a seemingly marked boost from Charles VI. In his various complaints to the Emperor he had detailed the Uniates' unhappiness with their opponents' rigidity where legitimate Romanian petitions were concerned. Charles VI now responded with a "*Mandatum*" to the Transylvanian diet which certainly provided a sop to the Romanians' pride and aspirations, if not a functional remedy to the harsh economic and political realities of the province's power structure. In this injunction the Habsburg monarch ordered the observance of all Uniate economic, political, and social privileges, including exemption from the hated payments to Protestant ministers. The Romanian Uniates, Charles declared, were indeed "sons of the fatherland" in every legal sense. He even danced delicately around the issue of the number of participants required for the Eastern Rite liturgy, appearing to give the Uniates much of what they wanted without dramatically or of necessity categorically interfering with the self-interest of the landed estates. In reading this directive, so comprehensive and decisive on the surface, one has the distinct impression that the Habsburg was still more concerned with having the Uniates "added to the Transylvanian Catholic ranks" (i.e., to the population statistics essential to Vienna's political base) than with having them truly "computed" as citizens. As a memo the "*Mandatum*" served as a useful bureaucratic ploy, but without consistent enforcement would not radically change the existing conditions of Uniate life. What did provide some hope and an outlet for Romanian dissatisfaction was the establishment by Charles VI of a commission to hear all complaints regarding violations of the specifics of the Leopoldine diplomas. Headed by a Royal Commissioner Plenipotentiary, Count Francisc Paul de Wallis, this committee would investigate such abuses and how they affected the fundamentals of the Eastern Rite. Wallis had the obvious advantage in this matter not only of significant political stature, but just as importantly of being the Imperial commander of the troops in the Hermannstadt area of southern Transylvania. He would, then, be in a position to render both administrative and, if necessary, physical support to Klein and the Uniates.[13]

Indicative of Charles VI's intent and the seriousness of the situation were the quality of the other participants on the Wallis commission. Besides the general, both Roman Catholic bishops of Transylvania (representing the Eastern and Latin rites respectively), and Baron Samuil Francisc de Rebentisch (a Court Counselor and Legal Director of the Transylvanian Chamber). These dignitaries had the delicate task of sifting through the complaints of the Uniates to discover which had basis against the background of the documents promulgated by Leopold I establishing the Union. Perhaps, just as awkward a political agenda revolved around their obligation to determine the status (in fact as opposed to the legalistic veneer) of the Romanian Uniates. While the urgency from Klein's standpoint devolved from the unacceptable conditions of his charges, that of the Habsburg regime emerged from its concern that the hemorrhage of apostasies be stemmed and not grow to the extent reached by defections after Atanasie's death. The Transylvanian administration also had to tread warily lest it provoke a repetition of the regional backlash to Viennese bureaucratic incursions typified earlier in the century by Rákóczi's rebellion.[14] The dual purposes that this commission would serve and the conflicting, if not irreconcilable, pressures it was subject to can be seen in the career of Wallis on the eve of his appointment to this important committee. This high government official, entrusted with the task of discerning the legitimacy of Uniate grievances and protecting their rights, had the year before (1731) seen fit to place a limit on the number of Romanian priests in a village. Though aware of the liturgical arguments against doing so, Wallis felt this action necessary lest too many Romanian clerics be exempted from the usual financial levies of the province. What must have been most disturbing to Bishop Klein, and a foreshadowing of what might be expected from the commission, was the fact that in imposing this limitation Baron de Wallis made no distinction between Uniate and Orthodox (i.e., "schismatic") priests, counting both towards the total of Romanians allowed for the village's religious services. The fact that the two groups' ceremonies were separate and distinct did not seem to matter. What from the Romanian Uniate view seemed calloused and imperceptive of their spiritual integrity was simply part of a larger framework of obliviousness to differentiations of rite and privilege (e.g., in the nearby frontier regiments even non-Uniates had recently been obligated to honor Latin Rite Roman Catholic feast days).[15]

The "virtual war of religion" that modern Romanian historians have seen erupting in the mid-eighteenth century took at this juncture and under Klein's leadership a marked, perhaps even pinched, "constitutional" tack. Indeed, the bishop's emphasis upon legalisms and the text of the various Leopoldine diplomas would approach the level of biblical exegesis, unaware or perhaps heedless of the force of the political realities at play. Only gradually would it become apparent to Bishop Klein and his clergy that the rights and privileges they sought through the force of these documents would not be forthcoming simply on the basis of rational debate. However well documented their argument might be, the shift in regional power it portended counted for far more.[16] In this simulated concern for political niceties the Wallis commission played its part. "In order to be better informed about the state of the entire Romanian church," Wallis and his commission cooperated with the Uniate prelate in conducting a census of the Transylvanian Uniate diocese. Besides acknowledging the Habsburg administration's dual purpose in dealing with Klein (i.e., to keep the Uniates somewhat content, but to avoid significant change in the province's basic structure lest there be another outbreak of rebellion), this census would project questionable data for a variety of other reasons. As with so much of the material collected during the first hundred years of the Habsburg re-occupation of Transylvania, the census of 1733 would not compare with modern efforts in terms of statistical accuracy or scientific rigor. But, then, none of the parties participating in it for their own overt as well as hidden agenda demonstrated even the pretense of the modern sociologist's disinterestedness.[17]

In asking the Wallis Commission to conduct the 1733 census Klein obviously sought hard evidence to support his contention that the problems, indeed the decay, of the Romanians' Union with Rome stemmed from the Habsburgs' failure to implement fully the perquisites promised by Emperor Leopold. The difficulties of assembling census figures under the conditions prevalent at this time, the complete omission of some locales, and the unrepentant ethnic as well as confessional character of the process likewise limited its reliability for the social scientist if not for the modern national advocate. In line with his suggestions of 1730 for actions to be taken against non-Uniates, Klein's approach to the census process was equally combative and oriented towards the goal of enhancing the lot of his church. With a single member of his flock living there a Transylvanian village became officially "mixed" in its ethnic character as well as homogeneously Uniate where any and all Romanians were concerned.[18] The Uniate bishop's contentiousness where the census was concerned was heightened by the foundation laid in the very year of his nomination to the episcopal throne (1729) for the restoration of the Orthodox hierarchy. The implications for Uniate political aspirations, should this reemergence of a Orthodox hierarch eventuate, were sweeping. Such a rival for Habsburg attention and Romanian loyalties would obviously befoul any claim to a unified ethnic campaign for constitutional rights. Conducted rapidly, then, the intent behind this survey of the Romanian population clearly betrayed a major plank in the platform Klein would build to advance his case for claiming *natio* status (i.e., political privilege and economic well-being) for his people. Furthermore it was not simply the number of Uniates that mattered to him. Rather his thesis would come to emphasize the fact that "the Romanians are not only the most numerous people of the province," but also pay the most taxes of any ethnic group in the area. Finally, the census also allowed Bishop Klein a more factual seeming context in which to insinuate what would become the basis for Romanian "Latinism;" namely, the historiographically and politically potent avowal that the Romanians were "the most ancient segment of all the inhabitants for Transylvania."[19]

Given the mixed agenda present in 1733 for both the Transylvanian administration and the Uniate hierarchy, there must then be added the lack of awareness on the part of the largely peasant population being questioned (especially the Orthodox) as to the catalysts at play. Directed by an imperial edict to answer a puzzling set of questions, those opposing Klein and his link with Rome would be at something of a loss to fathom the motives behind such a varied array of inquiries as:

> 1. Are they Uniates or schismatics? 2. Where were they ordained? 3. How many wives have they had? 4. How many horses do they have? 5. How many cows? 6. How many sheep? 7. How many beehives? 8. How many pigs?[20]

The concatenation of such disparate queries would have alarmed not only the hostile "schismatic" but even a loyal Uniate concerned about his tax burden or family life. Question number three certainly contained enough emotional charge to frighten any cleric. For this question involved self-indictment on the charge of being guilty of bigamy; namely, any Romanian priest who married again after the death of his first wife was declared *bigamus*. Not knowing the reasoning behind such probing and not aware of the true intent of the survey, almost any one interviewed would have been on the defensive. But, however flawed in impetus and scientific rigor, this first catalog focusing exclusively on the Transylvanian Romanians raised their statistical presence to a new level of political importance. Indeed, the 1733 census probably contained no more defects or skewing of focus for political purposes than other gatherings of data designed for the levying of taxes during the eighteenth century's period of Jesuit control of the Uniate Church (namely, in 1703, 1718, 1721, 1754, 761, 1766, and 1771).[21]

Interestingly, the debate over the controversial character of Klein's 1733 census of the Transylvanian Uniates assumed a markedly different tone and axis for those closest to him chronologically than for the more modern critic. All too often the modern researcher, both Romanian and Western, has riveted his readers' attention on the obvious lapses from sound "scientific" methodology to be found in the 1773 document. The core interest becomes, then, the disingenuousness of Klein and Vienna in "pretending" that all Transylvanian Romanians became Uniates in 1701. These historians have had great success in demonstrating the existence of villages and regions where as much as two-thirds of the population continued in the Orthodox faith.[22] However, such emphasis, besides being anachronistic, would have been wide of the mark for Klein's eighteenth century competitors for pride of place and political dominance. His counterparts focused on the sheer number of Romanians and their significance in the province for reasons of financial as well as administrative stability. Rather than being surprised by the slanted nature or untidiness of the census procedures, the eighteenth century mentality – more or less presuming these – highlighted "the overarching demand" of Bishop Klein for equating the Uniates with the three constitutionally recognized Transylvanian "nations." Though aware of the questionable quality of the 1733 statistics and of the earnestness of some purported Uniates, the Habsburg administrator of Klein's time found himself more engaged by the ultimate goal of the prelate than the means employed to arrive at that politically sensitive destination.[23]

As Bishop Klein began his charge to alter the feudal status of his flock, his opponents came to see him as something far more dangerous than an inexact demographer. Indeed, his allegations that the weakness of the Union sprang directly from the failure of the Habsburgs to live up to the Leopoldine diplomas earned him a wide range of more caustic epithets than the carelessness and disingenuousness later attributed to him. In attempting to compel recognition of the Romanians as a "nation" he was knowingly undermining the feudal political sanctuaries of his adversaries, both Protestant and Roman Catholic. For them such a transformation encompassed an economic, juridical, and political upheaval transcending an academic preoccupation with precise designations of community. Thus, for his contemporaries hostile to the Uniate cause he became at the very least a "restless" clerical malcontent trying to intrude upon their privileges. For all too many, especially for the Imperial administration in Vienna, he took on the guise of a "determinedly impetuous fanatic" who saw every obstacle as the result of conspiracy against the Romanian nation. In the long run this intemperance would earn Klein the reputation of leading the Uniates in an "anti-government" crusade. Perhaps even more importantly for the abbreviated nature of his episcopal career, the Romanian bishop projected the image of one willing to debase, even drastically weaken, the foundations of the Uniate Church in order to achieve his radical national goals. He assumed, then, the burden of being perceived as the "author and conductor" of a movement more subversive and factional in intent than religious.[24]

By this point, then, Klein was attempting far more than an occasional, stopgap improvement in the Romanians' practical or political situations. This overweening enterprise on his part constituted the most pressing fact recognized by the Habsburgs as well as by his enemies. In the voguish idiom this "...apostle, imbued with a fanatic love and energy...attained a moral victory that was determinative in our [the Romanians'] later national struggle." However, unsuccessful in the mundane terms of taxes and privileges, the Uniate Bishop did establish the fundamental goals and orientation of Romanian ethnic activity in Transylvania. He wanted his people's and church's improved situation to be rooted in the bedrock of constitutional change, not in the transient goodwill of Vienna. Klein understood, then, and proceeded to base his actions on the realization that without a "radical improvement," one based securely in law, any supposed changes in the Romanian situation would remain paper palliatives. With an almost modern emphasis, one centered on the "Romanian question" as described by a twentieth century commentator, Klein embraced the concept of "*natio*" and the resultant improved constitutional status for his people. This alone would ensure a basic alteration in that ethnic group's position in the province and guarantee participation in all aspects of public life.[25]

Once this political objective had been accentuated, Klein's tenure became insecure at best. After a sojourn in Vienna he fled to Rome in 1744, only to be dismissed from his episcopal see in 1752. The root cause of this fall from grace was the charge that he had become "a revolutionary and danger to the public order." Dying in 1768, Klein had achieved both for his contemporaries and many later patriots the distinction of being "a martyr for the Romanian national cause."[26] Though the Jesuits would continue in their determinative role vis-à-vis the Uniate Church until the suppression of the Society of Jesus in the latter part of the eighteenth century, the advent of Bishop Klein had precipitated a basic alteration in their status as well. Before his installation virtually all sources dwelt on the good relations between Uniates and the Jesuit "Theologian." Afterwards even Roman Catholic commentators noted a fundamental hostility towards such Latin Rite tutelage. This rejection of Jesuit control, of a vassalage that would not be reconstituted even after the order's rebirth in the first quarter of the nineteenth century, centered on the figure of Klein "as a precursor of modern national consciousness...[who] almost always used 'nation' in the broader, modern sense to designate a community united by common origins and customs." At the end of the twentieth century one Orthodox critic called the Jesuit dominated essay in union a "failure" as envisioned and manipulated by the "Theologian." As so many over the generations this observer saw the eighteenth century Romanians as minimally interested in theological matters and riveted on the preservation of their liturgical heritage.[27]

Since the fall of Communism in Eastern Europe in 1989, these old antagonisms and ambivalences – political as well as religious – have sprung to the fore again. The "Official Bulletin of the Romanian Patriarchate" proclaimed almost immediately that the Union with Rome had been a forced melding of disparate religious cultures. Indeed this journal charged that the Jesuits had centered their thrust into Transylvania on the task of imposing a "political authority" on the Romanians, one that would "plant a Latin mission in the Orthodox landscape." In back of this lament stands the obvious question of intent. If Cardinal Kollonich thought the Romanians so "*rudis*" (that is, so rough and uncultivated in their Christianity) as not to be trusted and to need the enlightenment of Latin schooling immediately, what other than political considerations had prompted the Union with Rome. Another spokesman for the modern Orthodox Church in Romania announced that the Union with Rome was an "injury to our people; an act of treason towards the faith and people for a golden image."[28]

Those familiar with the historiography of Romanian nationalism and religious development will find nothing extraordinary in such screeds. The preeminent Romanian historian of the twentieth century, Nicolae Iorga, believed that the "[Orthodox] Church and nation formed a single body." Although he recognized Bishop Klein's transcendent importance and the political significance of the Union, this historian believed that the Orthodox Church of Transylvania was "persecuted," especially by the Society of Jesus.[29] One perspective that brings such equivocalness into focus is that of the composer Ralph Vaughan Williams. Though writing about art and music, the tenor of his observation can be applied directly to the complex of views generated by the mix of religion, politics, and culture in eighteenth century Transylvania:

> Every composer cannot expect to have a worldwide message, but he may reasonably expect to have a special message for his own people and many young composers make the mistake of imagining they can be universal without at first having been local.... The moral of this, namely, that if the roots of your art are firmly planted in your own soil and that soil has anything individual to give you, you may gain the whole world and not lose your own souls.[30]

Bishop Klein, that "precursor of modern national consciousness," therefore embodied a particular image of modern nationalism, one that "is a political movement depending on a feeling of collective grievance against foreigners." In this instance, a Latin religious alien with his own policymaking agenda and cultural goal of westernization stood front and center in the person of the episcopal court's resident Jesuit. One of the twentieth century's foremost theoreticians on the nature of nationalism saw this phenomenon as having three phases. For peoples such as the Transylvanian Romanians of the eighteenth century:

> The first stage may be loosely labelled [*sic*] *stirrings*. This is the period in which the nation becomes aware of itself as a nation suffering oppression. Frequently it is a period of revulsion against foreign ideas and foreign ways of doing things. It is a time of casting around for a cultural identity. It is a likely, for example, that a religion which was abandoned in the first flush of enthusiasm for foreign ideas will be revived.[31]

To fashion a summary of the political/religious impact on Romanian ethnicity of the Union with Rome one can turn to the period between the world wars. In that context the amalgam of enthusiasms for and rejections of the Jesuits' mission assumed a modern form, "Romanianism." This concept was defined as "an alliance of Latinity of race with an adhesion to Orthodoxy.... Theology then is not only a field of study reserved to the specialist, but a cultural discipline...." In this compound of religion, politics and ethnicity Orthodoxy "incarnated" a Romanian version of Latinity different from that of Western Europe. It became "an axis of national identification, a bastion of resistance against all influences portending denationalization...."[32] The admixture of faith and culture had become so much "a major pole for the expression of national identity" that the United States embassy in Bucharest stressed its impact on the political scene. In 1926 that diplomatic outpost reported to the Secretary of State that "the whole power of the Greek Orthodox Church was thrown against the selection of [Iuliu] Maniu as Prime Minister on the ground that he is a member of the 'Uniat' [*sic*] Church...."[33]

In the tradition of the entire Uniate political/religious process, however, the Romanian head of state during World War II, Marshall Ion Antonescu, attempted the same sort of bargain that began the Uniate movement. In July 1943 the American representative in Bern informed the Secretary of State that Antonescu, one of Hitler's staunchest allies, had had a private audience with Pope Pius XII. This diplomat *understood* [emphasis added] that "the conversation turned largely on [the] problem of unification of Orthodox and Roman Catholic churches in Rumania. While it would appear that some progress [was] made the problem nevertheless is far from being solved." He went on to observe that "...(probably more realistically) that Antonescu came to Italy to explore the possibilities of drawing away from Germany...." The Vatican, in the twentieth as well as the eighteenth century, became a focal point for Romanian political ambitions and negotiations. In an explanatory follow-up to the previous day's telegram to the Secretary of State, the same diplomat reviewed Antonescu's bargaining with the Pope:

> According to a sincere but untested religious source, [the] purpose of [the] visit to [the] Pope, reported n Paragraph one of my 4027, July 8, was [the] desire of Antonescu to sound out [the] possibility of obtaining [the] Pope's assistance [in the] requisition [of] entire Transylvania in return for unification [of] Orthodox and Uniate churches throughout Rumania. [34]

Bishop Klein would have understood Antonescu's motivations and approved. The survival and prosperity of the national community assumed paramount importance. He would also have agreed with the philosopher of nationalism quoted above that

> the concept of the nation is almost entirely empty of content until a content is – arbitrarily – supplied from local circumstances. This is the reason why there is so much difficulty in trying to define a nation. This can only be done within a particular context.[35]

But once that context is identified, then it must be pursued with vigor. Unfortunately for the fastidious of mind, when dealing with nationalism the "Reality is much less tidy [than the theory]. ...These ideas are chameleons that take on the colour of the locality around them...." And, of course, they take on the necessities of the political landscape, however that is focused through the prism of culture and religion.[36]

Notes

Chapter I:
Introduction: Politics and Religion

1. George Popoviciu, *Uniunea românilor din Transilvania cu biserica romano-catolică sub împĕratul Leopold I* (Logoj: Tipariul Tipografiei Diec. din Caransebeş, 1901), 24; Hugo Hantsch, *Die Geschichte Österreichs*, III (Graz-Wien-Köln: Verlag Styria, 1962); 26, 38, 73.

2. Otto Brunner, "Oesterreich und die Walachei während des Turkenkrieges von 1683-1699," *Mitteilungen des Österreichischen Instituts für Geschichtsforschung,* 44 (Innsbruck: Universitäts-Verlag Wagner, 1930), 303.

3. Hantsch, *Die Geschichte Österreichs,* 28; N. Iorga, *Histoire des Roumains de Transylvanie et de Hongrie*, II (Bucarest: Joseph Göbl, 1915), 5-6; *Istoria Romîniei*, III (Bucureşti: Editura Academiei Republicii Populare Romîne, 1964), 225.

4. Johann Christof Bartenstein, *Kurzer Bericht von der Beschaffenheit der zerstreuten zahlreichen Illyrischen Nation in kaiserl. loenigl. Erblanden* (Frankfurt und Leipzig: 1802), 54; Augustin Bunea, "Istoria autonomiei bisericesci," *Discursuri Autonomia bisericescă, Diverse* (Blaş: Tipografia Seminariului Archidiecesan, 1903), 310; Johannes Crisian, *Beitrag zur Geschichte der kirchlichen Union der Rumänen in Siebenbürgen unter Leopold I* (Hermannstadt: Archidiöcesan-Druckerei, 1882), 22.

5. Georgie Bariţiu, *Părţi alese din istoria Transilvaniei pre două sute de ani din urmă*, I (Sibiu: W. Krafft, 1889), 9.

6. Onisifor Ghibu, *Universitatea Daciei Superioare* (Bucureşti: "Cultura Naţională," 1929), 4; Crisian, *Beitrag zur Geschichte der kirchlichen Union*, 11; Silviu Dragomir, *Istoria Desrobirei Religioase a Românilor din Ardeal în secolul XVIII*, I (Sibiu: Editura şi tiparul Tipografiei arhidiecezane, 1920), 1.

7. Eudoxiu Freiherrn von Hurmuzaki, *Fragmente zur Geschichte der Rumänen.* II. (Bucuresci: Socecŭ, Sander & Teclu, 1881), 19-22, 43; Dragomir, *Istoria Desrobirei Religioase*, 2-3.

8. Crisian, *Beitrage zur Geschichte*, 23; Iorga, *Histoire des Roumains de Transylvanie et de Hongrie*, II, 366-7; Hantsch, *Die Geschichte Österreichs*, II, 39-40, 67-8.

9. Mathias Bernath, *Habsburg und die Anfänge der Rumänischen Nationsbildung* (Leiden: E. J. Brill, 1972), 34; *Din Istoria Transilvaniei*, I (Bucureşti: Editura Academiei Republicii Populare Romîne, 1961), 227.

10. *Istoria Romîniei*, III, 229, 232; Joseph Fiedler, "Die Union der Walachen in Siebenbürgen unter K. Leopold I," *Sitzungsberichte der kaiserlichen Akademie der Wissenschaften*, Philosophisch-Historische Classe. XXVII (1858), 354.

11. Libloy, Friedrich Schuler von, *Materialen zur siebenbürgischen Rechtsgeschichte*, III (Hermannstadt: Th. Steinhaussen, 1861), 79.

12. Libloy, Fridrich Schuler von, *Siebenbürgische Rechtsgeschichte*, I (Hermannstadt: Buchdruckerei der v. Closius'schen Erbin, 1868), 341-2.

13. Bariţiu, *Părţi alese din istoria Transilvaniei*, 88 -9, 127, 154-5.

14. I. Lupas, "Desbinarea bisericească a Românilor ardeleni, în lumina documentelor din I-a jumătate a veacului al XVIII-lea," *Studii, conferinţe şi comunicări istorice*, I (1927), 233-4; I. Lupas, "Sfârşitul suzeranităţii otomane şi începutul regimului habsburgic în Tran-

silvania," *Analele Academiei Române, Memoriile Secţiunii Istorice*, Seria III, XXV (1943), 829-32.

15. Bernath, *Habsburg und die Anfänge der Rumänischen Nationsbildung*, 37-8; Alexandru Pop, *Desbindarea în Biserica Românilor din Ardél şi Ungaria, 1697-1701.* (Bucureşti: Wiegand, C. Savociu & C-nie, 1892), 17.

16. Hurmuzaki, *Fragmente zur Geschichte der Rumänen*, 24-5; John Spielman, *Leopold I of Austria* (New Brunswick: Rutgers University Press, 1977), 47, 121, 161-5.

17. Iacob Marza, *Scoala şi natiune* (Cluj-Napoca: Editura Dacia, 1987), 55; Fiedler, "Die Union der Walachen," 354; Keith Hitchins, "The Sacred Cult of Nationality: Rumanian Intellectuals and the Church in Transylvania, 1834-69," *Intellectual and Social Developments in the Habsburg Empire from Maria Theresa to World War I.* Stanley B. Winters and Joseph Held, eds. (New York: East European Monographs, distributed by Columbia University Press, 1975), 133.

18. Wilhelm de Vries, *Rom und die Patriarchate des Ostens* (Freiburg/Munchen: Verlay Karl Alber, 1963), 133-4; Samuil Micu, *Scurta cunostinta a istorii rominilor.* Introduced and edited by Cornel Cimpepanu. (Bucuresti: Editura Stiintifica, 1963), v-vi.

19. Baritiu, *Parti alese*, 155, 160;

20. Libloy, *Materialen zur siebenburgischen Rechtsgeschichte*, III, 88-90; Spielman, *Leopold I*, 161-5; Bernath, *Habsburg und die Anfange*, 37, 41-2.

21. Dragomir, *Istoria Desrobirei Religioase*, I, 3; Gheorghie Sincai, *Chronica Romanilor*, III, 2nd ed. (Bucuresci: Tipografia Academiei Romane, 1886), 275-6; Sandor Szilagyi, *Monumenta Comitialia Regni Transylvaniae*, XXI (Budapest: A M. Tud. Akademia Konyvkiado-Hivatala, 1898), 139, 144.

22. *Konferenzen und Vertrage*, Teil II, Band 3. Zweite Auflage. Helmuth K. G. Ronnefarth, ed. (Wurzburg: A. G. Ploetz, 1958), 116-19; Bernath, *Habsburg und die Anfange*, 34.

23. Nicolae Albu, *Istoria invatamantului romanesc din Transilvania pana la 1800* (Blaj: Tipografia "Lumina," Miron Rosu, 1944), 88-9; Bunea, "Istoria autonomiei bisericesci," 355; Onisifor Ghibu, *Catolicismul unguresc inn Transilvania şi politica religioasa a statului roman* (Cluj: Institut de Arte Grafice "Ardealul," 1924), 41.

24. Baritiu, *Parti alese*, 7-8, 85-6, 88, 127-8.

25. Franz von Krones, "Zur Geschichte des Jesuitenordens in Ungarn seit dem Linzer Frieden bis zum Ergebnisse der ungarischen Magnatenverschworung 1645-1671," *Archiv für österreichische Geschichte*, Bd. 79 (1893), 303; Stephano Katona, *Historia Critica Regum Hungariae, Stirpis Austriacae*, 16 (Budae: Typis et Sumpstis Regiae Universitatis Pestanae, 1804), 715.

26. Sincai, *Chronica Romanilor*, III, 275-6;

27. Vries, *Rom und die Patriarchate des Ostens*, 151-2; Lucian Blaga, *Gindirea romanesca in Transilvania in secolul al XVIII-lea.* George Ivascu, ed. (Bucuresti: Editura Stiintifica, 1966), 25-6; Hurmuzaki, *Fragmente*, 25-6.

28. Martinus Szent-Ivany, S.J. *De Ortu, Progressu, ac Diminutione Schismatis Graeci* (Tyrnavia: Typis Academicis, 1703) [pagination by page and number, but incomplete].

29. Bernath, *Habsburg und die Anfange*, 61-2; Adolf Armbruster, *La romanite des Roumains, Histoire d'une idee*, Bibliotheca Historica Romaniae, Monographies XVII (Bucuresti: Editura Academiei Republicii Socialiste Romania, 1977), 248; Octavian Barlea, *Ostkirchliche Tradition und westlicher Katholizismus, Die Rumanische Unierte Kirche zwischen 1713-1727* (Monachii: Societatea Academica Romana, 1966), 88-9.

30. Bernath, *Habsburg und die Anfange*, 54; Krones, "Zur Geschichte des Jesuitenorderns," 304; Joseph Fiedler, "Beitrage zur Geschichte der Union der Ruthenen in Nordungern und der Immunitat des Klerus derselben," *Sitzungsberichte der Kaiserlichen Akademie der Wissenschaften*, Philosophisch-Historische Classe. XXXIX, Heft 3 & 4 (1862), 485-6, 491-3.

31. A. Perbal, O.M.I., "Projets, Fondation et Debuts de la Sacree Congregation de la Propagande," *Histoire Universelle des Missions Catholiques*, II. S. Delacroix, ed. (Paris: Librairie Grund, 1957), 116-8; Anton Pieper, "Romische Archive," *Romische Quartalscrift für Christliche Altertumskunde und für Kirchengeschichte*, I (1887), 85-6.

32. Athanasius G. Welykyj, OSBM, *Documenta Pontificum Romanorum Historiam Ucrainae Illustrantia*, I (1075-1700). (Romae: Sumptibus Ucrainorum apud Exteros Degentium, 1953), 113-15.

33. Fiedler, "Beitrage zur Geschichte der Union der Ruthenen," 493.

34. Welykyj, *Documenta Pontificum Romanorum*, I, 115.

35. Augustin Bunea, *Episcopul Ioan Inocentiu Klein (1728-1751)*. (Blaş: Tipografia Seminariului Archidiecesan gr.-cat., 1900), 119.

36. Augustin Bunea, *Episcopii Petru Paul Aron şi Dionisiu Novacovici, sau istoria Romanilor transilvanei de la 1751 pana la 1764* (Blaş: Tipografia Seminariului Archidiecesan, 1902), 96; *Istoria Rominiei*, III, 237, 423-4.

37. Samuelis Klein, "Historia Daco-Romanorum sive Valachorum," A. Treb. Laurianu, ed., *Instructiunea Publica*, 1861, 89-90; C. I. Gulian, ed., *Istoria gindirii sociale şi filozofice in Rominia* (Bucuresti: Editura Academiei Republicii Populare Romine, 1964), 85; Stefan Lupsa, *Biserica ardeleana şi "unirea" in anii 1697-1701* (Bucuresti: Editura Institutului Biblic şi de Misiune al Bisericii Ortodoxe Romane, 1948), 12.

38. *Istoria Rominiei*, III, 239, 426; D. Prodan, "La lutte de Inochentie Micu pour le relevement politique des Roumains de Transylvanie," *Revue Roumiane D'Histoire*, IV (1965), nr. 3, 478.

39. Keith Hitchins, *Orthodoxy and Nationality, Andreiu Saguna and the Rumanians of Transylvania, 1846-1873* (Cambridge: Harvard University Press, 1977), 29; Bernath, *Habsburg und die Anfage*, 39-41, 50-1, 73.

40. Pop, *Desbindarea in Biserica Romanilor*, 17-8; Stefan Metes, *Relatiile bisericii romanesti ortodoxe din Ardeal cu Principatele Romane in veacul al XVIII-lea* (Sibiu: Tiparul Tipografiei Arhidiecezane, 1928), 1; Lupas, "Desbindarea bisericeasca a Romanilor ardeleni," 233.

41. Silviu Dragomir, *Rominii din Transilvania şi Unirea cu Biserica Romei. Documente apocrife privtoae la inceputurile unirii cu catolicismul roman (1697-1701)*. (Bucuresti: Editura Institutului Biblic şi de Misiune Ortodoxa, 1963), 22, 26-8; Friedrich Schuler von Libloy, *Siebenburgische Rechtsgeschichte*, I (Hermannstadt: Buchdruckerei der v. Closius'schen Erbin, 1868), 339-40; Iorga, *Histoire des Roumains de Transylvanie*, II, 11.

42. Robert A. Kann, *A History of the Habsburg Empire, 1526-1918* (Berkley: University of California Press, 1974), 74; Baritiu, *Parti alese*, 14-5; Bunea, "Istoria autonomiei bisericesci," 354-5.

43. Bunea, "Istoria autonomiei bisericesci," 310-2, 339.

44. Georgiu Baritiu, *Catechismulu calvinescu impusu clerului şi poporuli romanescu sub domni'a principiloru Georgiu Rakoczy I. şi II.* Sibiu: W. Krafft, 1879), 101-2; Alesandru Grama, *Institutiunile calvinesci in biserica romanesca din Ardelu* (Blasiu: Tipografia Seminariului archidiecesanu, 1895), 2-5.

45. Georgiu Baritiu, *Catechismulu calvinescu,* 102, 109, 115.

46. G. Baritiu, "Din cronic'a lui Michailu Cserei. 1661-1711 (Continuare)," *Transilvani'a*, II (1869), nr. 15, 169; Georgiu Baritiu, *Catechismulu calvinescu*, 114; Baritiu, *Parti alese*, 5.

47. *Ibid.*, 125, 155, 163; Bunea, *Episcopul Ioan Inocentiu Klein*, 144.

48. Imre Revesz, "La Reforme et les Roumains de Transylvanie," *Archivum Europae Centro-Orientalis*, III (1937), 282-3, 285; Crisian, *Beitrag zur Geschichte*, 11.

49. Bunea, "Istoria autonomiei bisericesci," 354; Revesz, "La Reforme," 282-3.

50. Stefan Metes, *Istoria Bisericii şi a vietii religioase a Romanilor din Transilvania şi Ungaria*, I, Editia II (Sibiu: Editura Librariei Arhidiecdzane, 1935), 485.

51. St. Lupsa, *Istoria Bisericeasca a Romanilor Bihoreni* (Oradea: [Estras din Monografia-Almanah a Bihorului], 1935), 14; Stephen Metes, "Viata bisericeasca a Romanilor din Tara Oltului, Note istorice," *Transilvania*, 60 (1929), nr. 1, 22-3.

52. Zenove Paclisan, "Biserica romaneasca şi Calvinismul dela moartea lui Gavrila Bethlen pana la Unirea cu Roma," *Cultura Crestina*, II (1912), Part II, nr. 9, 263-5.

53. Ion Mateiu, *Preotimea romaneasca-ardeleana in veacul al XVII-lea* (Sibiu: Tiparul Tipografiei Arhidiecezane, 1911), 21-4, 27-8; Metes, *Istoria Bisericii şi a vietii religioase*, 464, 476.

54. Vries, *Rom und die Patriarchate des Ostens*, 135-7.

55. Mateiu, *Preotimea romaneasca-ardeleana*, 16; Bunea, "Istoria autonomiei bisericesci," 346; Ghibu, *Universitatea Daciei Susperioare*, 4.

56. Baritiu, *Parti alese*, 7,123-4, 151, 156-7.

57. Tim. Capariu, ed., *Acte şi fragmente latine romanesci pentru istori'a beserecei romane mai alesu unite* (Blasiu: Cu tipariulu Semin. diecesanu, 1855), xvi, 67-8, 71; Dragomir, *Rominii din Transilvania şi Unirea*, 4.

58. Grama, *Institutiunile calvinesci*, 19, 22-3; Johann Hintz, *Geschichte der griechisch=nichtunirten Glaubensgenossen in Siebenburgen* (Hermannstadt: Vereins für siebenburgische Landeskunde, 1850), 32-3.

59. Grama, *Institutiunile calvinesci*, 39, 53, 76.

60. *Ibid*, 269; Micu, *Scurta cunostinta a istorii rominilor*, 102-3; J. M. Moldovanu, *Spicuire in istor'a baserecesca a Romaniloru* (Blasiu: V. Krafft, 1873), 16-7.

61. Grama, *Institutiunile calvinesci*, 76, 269-70.

62. *Ibid.*, 265-7; Alesandru Gram'a, *Istori'a Basericei Romanesci unite cu Rom'a* (Blasiu: Tipariulu Seminariului Archideicesanu, 1884), 76.

63. Etienne Metes, "La vie menee par les Roumains en Transylvanie du XVI-e au XVIII-e," *La Transylvanie* (Bucuresti: Imprimeria Nationala, 1938), 286; Baritiu, *Parti alese*, 210-3.

64. Gram'a, *Istori'a Basericei Romanesci unite cu Rom'a*, 78-9; Crisian, *Beitrag zur Geschichte*, 13-4, 17.

65. Lupsa, *Biserica ardeleana şi "unirea,"* 7.

66. Mateiu, *Preotimea romaneasca-ardelelana*, 24, 58.

67. Wilhelm de Vries, S.J., "Der christliche Osten in Geschichte und Gegenwart," *Das ostliche Christentum*, Heft 12 (1951), 108; Revesz, "La Reforme," 302.

68. Paclisan, "Biserica romaneasca şi Calvinismul," 262-3; Nicolao Nilles, S.J., *Symbolae ad illustrandam historiam ecclesiae orientalis in terris coronae S. Stephani*, I (Oeniponte: Typis et Sumptibus Feliciani Rauch, 1885), 146, 151-2.

69. N. Iorga, *Histoire des Roumains de Transylvanie*, II, 13-4; I. Ursu, "Un manifest romanesc tiparit cu litere latine al Imparatului Leopold I din anul 1701," *Analele Academiei Romane, Memoriile Sectiunii Istorice*. Seria II, XXXIV (1911-2), 1051.

70. Grama, *Institutiunile calvinesci*, 275-6.

71. Hurmuzaki, *Fragmente zur Geschichte*, 14; Episcopulu Mellchisedec, *Biserica ortodoxa in lupta cu protestantismulu in specialu cu clavinismulu in veaculu XVII-lea*, Extract from *Analele Academiei Romane, Memoriile Sectiunei Istorice*, Seria II, Tom. XII (Bucuresci: Carol Gobl, 1890), 61.

72. Bunea, "Istoria autonomiei bisericesci," 344-7.

73. Hurmuzaki, *Fragmente zur Geschichte*, 6, 8-10, 17.

74. Lupsa, *Biserica ardeleana şi "unirea,"* 10; Mateiu, *Preotimea romaneasca-ardelelana*, 30-1, 58.

75. Andre Ivanka, "The Romanian Greek-Catholic Church," *The Eastern Churches Quarterly*, VIII (1949), nr. 3, 156.

76. Aloisie Tautu *et al.*, *Biserica Romana Unita. Doua sute cinci zeci de ani de istorie* (Madrid: Rivadeneyra, 1952), 44, 46-7.

77. Revesz, "La Reforme," 301; Ursu, "Un manifest romanesc," 1050.

78. Revesz, "La Reforme," 302-3, 307.

79. Grama, *Institutiunile calvinesci*, 336; Revesz, "La Reforme," 312, 314.

80. Augustin Bunea, *Vechile episcopii romanesci a Vadului, Geoagiului, Silvasului şi Belgradului* (Blaş: Tipografia Seminariului Archidiecesan, 1902), 148-51; Dragomir, *Istoria Desrobirei Religioase*, I, 4.

81. Bunea, *Vechile episcopii romanesci*, 142;

82. Pop, *Desbindarea in Biserica Romanilor*, 16; Grama, *Institutiunile calvinesci*, 460.

83. Metes, *Istoria Bisericii şi vietii religioase*, 446, 451; Metes, "La vie menee par les Roumains," 285.

84. *Istoria Literaturii Romine*, I (Bucuresti: Editura Academiei Republicii Populare Romine, 1964), 335, 519; Baritiu, *Parti alese*, 431.

85. Bernath, *Habsburg und die Anfange*, 58.

86. Vries, *Rom und die Patriarchate des Ostens*, 134-5.

87. Ferdinand von Zieglauer, *Die politische Reformbewegung in Siebenburgen in de Zeit Joseph's II. und Leopold's II.* (Wien: Wilhelm Braumuller, 1881), 481; Josephus Benko, *Transsilvania*, II (Claudiopoli: Typis Lycei Regii, 1833), 135.

88. Josephus Benko, *Transsilvania*, I, 2nd ed. (Claudiopoli: Typis Lycei Regii, 1834), 471-2.

89. Benko, *Transsilvania*, II, 229; Petrus Bod, *Historia Hungarorum Ecclesiastica*, II (Leiden: E. J. Brill, 1890), 347

90. Fiedler, "Die Union der Walachen," 351-2.

91. Libloy, *Siebenburgische Rechtsgeschichte*, I, 332-3; Libloy, *Materialen zur siebenburgischen Rechtsgeschichte*, III, 48.

92. Libloy, *Materialen zur siebenburgischen Rechtsgeschichte*, III, 52.

93. Hantsch, *Die Geschichte Österreichs*, II, 81.

94. N. Iorga, *Sate şi Preoti din Ardeal* (Bucuresti: Inst. de Arte Grafice "Carol Gobl," 1902), 89-90, 92, 168.

95. Albu, *Istoria invatamantului romanesc din Transilvania*, 113.

96. Baritiu, *Parti alese*, 384, 386-7.

97. N. Iorga, *Histoire des Roumains de Transylvanie et de Hongrie*, I (Bucarest: Joseph Gobl, 1915), 367-8.

98. *Ibid.*, 390-1.

99. *Ibid.*, 395-8, 402.

100. Lupsa, *Biserica ardeleana şi "unirea,"* 7-8.

101. Mateiu, *Preotimea romaneasca-ardelelana*, 21-2, 38-9; Baritiu, *Parti alese*, 135.

102. Ivanka, "The Romanian Greek-Catholic Church," 155-6, 470; Libloy, *Siebenburgische Rechtsgeschichte*, I, 345-6.

103. Baritiu, *Parti alese*, 9, 121.

104. Lupsa, *Biserica ardeleana şi "unirea,"* 11-2, 14.

105. Hintz, *Geschichte der griechisch=nichtunirten Glaubensgenossen*, 30-1; Nicolao Nilles, "Die Rumanen unter der Herschaft der protestantischen Fursten siebenburgens," *Zeitschrift für katholische Theologie*, IV (1880), 189.

106. Krones, "Zur Geschichte des Jesuitendorderns," 303; Baritiu, "Din cronic'a lui Michailu Cserei," 169.

107. G. Baritiu, "Din cronic'a lui Michailu Cserei. 1661-1711, (Continuare), (Despre unire)," *Transilvani'a*, II (1869), nr. 16, 183; Baritiu, *Parti alese*, 85, 161, 252.

108. Rudolphus Bzenski, "Historica relatio de initio et progressu missiosnis Coronensis Societatis Iesu in Transilvania. (1688-1720)," *Quellen zur Geschichte der Stadt Brasso*, VI. O. Netoliczka, ed. (Brasso: Br. Schneider & Feminger, 1915), 326-7; Friedrich Schuyler von Libloy, *Kurzer Ueberblick der Literaturgeschichte Siebenburgens, von der altesten Zeit bis zu Ende des vorigen Jahrhunderts* (Hermannstadt: Georg v. Closius, 1857), 10.

109. Vries, *Rom und die Patriarchate des Ostens*, 138; Bernath, *Habsburg und die Anfange*, 65.

110. Antal Hodindka, *A munkacsi gor. szert. puspokseg okmanytara*, I (1458-1715). (Ungvar: Nyomatott az "Unio Konyvnyomda R.T." Konyvnyomdajaban, 1911), 390-3;

111. Bernath, *Habsburg und die Anfange*, 57, 104-5.; Hurmuzaki, *Fragmente*, II, 25.

112. Baritiu, *Parti alese*, 20; Silviu Dragomir, *Rominii din Transilvania şi Unirea cu Biserica Romei. Documente apocrife privitoare la inceputurile unirii cu catolicismul roman (1697-1701).* (Bucuresti: Editura Institutului Biblic şi de Misiune Ortodoxa, 1963), 4-5, 76.

113. Crisian, *Beitrag zur Geschichte der kirchlichen Union*, 25; Blaga, *Gindirea romanesca*, 42.

114. Hurmuzaki, *Fragmente*, II, 19-20, 25-6, Ovid Densusianu, *Literatura Romina Moderna*, I, 3rd ed. (Bucuresti: Edit. Libr. "Universala" Alcalay & Co., 1929),

115. Szent-Ivany, *De Ortu, Progressu, ac Diminutione Schismatis Graeci*, [no page number, Caput IV].

116. N. Iorga, "Doua scrisori ale lui Atanase Anghel," *Memoriile Sectiunii Istorice* (Academia Romana), Seria III, XIII (1932), 131, 136; Ferdinand von Zieglauer, *Hartenech, Graf der sachsischen Nation, und die siebenburgischen Parteikampfe seiner Zeit. 1691-1703* (Hermannstadt: Th. Steinhaussen, 1869), 64-5.

117. Hitchins, *Orthodoxy and Nationality*, 207; Fr. Teutsch, *Die Kirchlichen Verhaltnisse Siebenburgens* (Halle a.S.: Eugen Strien, 1906), 57.

118. D. Popovici, *La Litterature Roumaine a l'Epoque des Lumieres* (Sibiu: Centrul de Studii şi Cercetari privitoare la Transilvania, 1945), 83-4; Pop, *Desbindarea in Biserica Romanilor*, 107.

119. Gabriel Patacsi, S.J., "Die unionsfeindlichen Bewegungen der orthodoxen Rumanen Siebenburgens in den Jahren 1726-1729," *Orientalia Christiana Periodica*, XXVI (1960), nr. 2, 359-60; Baritiu, *Parti alese*, 164.

120. Dragomir, *Istoria Desrobirei Religioase*, I, 4, 6, 72, 77-8.

121. Grama, *Institutiunile calvinesci*, 4-5; Gram'a, *Istori'a Basericei Romanesci unite cu Rom'a*, 79-83.

122. Baritiu, *Parti alese*, 153; Stefan Haragus, *Preotimea romana in veacul al XVIII-lea* (Sibiu: Tiparul Tipografiei Arhidiecezane, 1907), 6.

123. Lajos Kelemen, *Ujabb adattar a vargyasi Daniel csalad tortenetehez* (Kolozsvar: Nyomatott Ajtai K. Albert Konyvnyomdajaban, 1913), 181.

124. Libloy, *Siebenburgische Rechtsgeschichte*, I, 204; Metes, *Istoria Bisericii şi vietii religioase*, 470.

125. Vries, "Der christliche Osten," 107-8.

126. Bartenstein, *Kurzer Bericht von der Beschaffenheit*, 55-6; Mihail Dan, "In jurul unirii cu Roma, cu deobsebita privire asupra rolului iezuitului Carol Neurautter," *Mitropolia Banatului*, VIII (1958), nr. 7/8/9, 326.

127. Blaga, *Gindirea romanesca*, 39-40; Cluj. Academia Romania, Filiala Biblioteca. Manuscrise Latine 29. "Brevis Valachorum Transylvaniam incolentium Historia" [by Petrus Bod, 1764], 267.

128. Bunea, *Episcopii*, 101; A. Bunea, *Cestiuni din dreptulu şi istoria bisericei romanesci unite*, II (Blasiu: Tipografia Seminariului gr.-cat., 1893), 311-2; Bunea, "Istoria autonomiei bisericesci," 354.

129. Lupsa, *Biserica ardeleana şi "unirea,"* 10; N. Iorga, *Istoria Literaturii Romanesti*, II, 2nd ed. (Bucuresti: Editura Liberariei Pavel Suru, 1926), 18.

130. Ivanka, "The Romanian Greek-Catholic Church," 158-9.

131. *Ibid.*, 159; Hurmuzaki, *Fragmente*, II, 18.

Chapter II: Rome and Ethnic Schism

1. Nicolao Nilles, S.J., "Weitere Inedita zur Geschichte der kirchlichen Wiedervereinigung der Rumanen," *Zeitschrift für katholische Theologie*, IV (1880), 577-8.

2. Wilhelm de Vries, *Rom und die Patriarchate des Ostens* (Freiburg/Munchen: Verlag Karl Alber, 1963), 138; Mathias Bernath, *Habsburg und die Anfange der Rumanischen Nationsbildung* (Leiden: E. J. Brill, 1972), 57-8.

3. Leopold's reacquisition of Transylvania for the Habsburg dynasty was negotiated by a French Jesuit, Antidvis Dunod, S.J. See John P. Spielman, *Leopold I of Austria* (New Brunswick: Rutgers University Press, 1977), 121; Georgie Baritiu, *Parti alese din istoria Transilvaniei pre doua sute de ani din urma*, I (Sibiu: W. Krafft, 1889), 35, 37, 63-4, 159-61.

4. Franciscus Fasching, S.J., *Nova Dacia*, I (Claludiopoli: Typ. Acad. S.J., 1743), 22; Joseph Fiedler, "Die Union der Walachen in Siebenburgen unter K. Leopold I," *Sitzungsberichte der kaiserlichen Akademie der Wissenschaften*, Philosophisch-Historische Klasse, XXVII (1858), Heft 3, 355-6.

5. Vries, *Rom und die Patriarchate des Ostens*, 138-40; Zenovie Paclisanu, "Din istoria bisericeasca a Romanilor ardeleni. 'Teologul' vladicilor uniti," *Memoriil Sectiunii Istorice* (Academia Romana), Seria III, I (1923), 151.

6. Tim Cipapriu, *Acte şi fragmente latine romanesci pentru istori'a beserecei romane mai alesu unite* (Blasiu: Cu tipariulu Semin. diecesanu, 1855), x; Baritiu, *Parti alese*, 176, 228.

7. Baritiu, *Parti alese*, 157; Augustin Bunea, *Vechile episcopii romanesci a Vadului, Geoagiului, Silvasului şi Belgradului* (Blas: Tipografia Seminariului Archidiecesan, 1902), 141-2, 151.

8. N. Iorga, *Histoire des Roumains de Transylvanie et de Hongrie*, I (Bucharest: Joseph Gobl, 1915), 365-6; Cipapriu, *Acte şi fragmente*, xi; Bunea, *Vechile episcopii*

romanesci, 148; Eudoxiu Freiherrn von Hurmuzaki, *Fragmente zur Geschichte der Rumanen*, II (Bucuresti: Socecu, Sander & Teclu, 1881), 17.

9. I. Ursu, "Un manifest romanesc tiparit cu litere latine al Imparatului Leopold I din anul 1701," *Analele Academiei Romane. Memoriil Sectiunii Istorice*, Seria II, XXXIV (1911-12), 1053; *Condica Santa*, I (Bucuresti: Tipo-Litografia Cartilor Bisericesci, 1886), 69.

10. Zenove Paclisan, "Biserica romaneasca şi Calvinismul dela moartea lui Gavrila Bethlen pana la Unirea cu Roma," *Cultura Crestina*, II (1912), Part II, nr. 9, 263; Augustin Bunea, "Istoria autonomiei bisericesci," *Discursuri, Autonomia bisericesca, Diverse* (Blas: Tipografia Seminariului Archidiecesan, 1903), 352-4.

11. Collectio Hevenesiana, Tom. 24, Eötvös Loránd Tudományegyetem Központi Könyvtára, 43-8; Johann Hintz, *Geschichte der griechisch=nichtunirten Glabuensgenossen in Siebenburgen* (Hermannstadt: Vereins für siebenburgische Landeskunde, 1850), 83-9.

12. Baritiu, *Parti alese*, 156; Stefan Metes, *Istoria Bisericii şi vietii religioase a Romanilor din Transilvania şi Ungaria*, I. Editia II. (Sibiu: Editura Librariei Arhidiecezane, 1935), 319, 328.

13. Bernath, *Habsburg und die Anfange*, 70-1.

14. Archdale A. King, *The Rites of Eastern Christendom*, II (Rome: Tipografia Poliglotta Vaticana, 1948), 39; Hurmuzaki, *Fragmente zur Geschichte*, II, 28-9.

15. Andreas Illia, S.J., *Ortus et progressus variarum in Dacia gentium ac religionum cum principibus ejusdem* (Claudiopoli: Typis Academicis Societatis Jesu, 1764), 7-10; George Popviciu, *Uniunea romanilor din Transilvania cu biserica romano-catholica sub imperatul Leopold I* (Lugoj: Tipariul Tipografiei Diec. din Caransebes, 1901), 61.

16. Cluj. Academia Romania, Filiala Biblioteca. Manuscrise Latine 29. "Brevis Valachorum Transylvaniam incolentium Historia" [by Petrus Bod, 1764], 171, 178-82.

17. Gheorghie Sincai, *Chonica Romanilor*, III, 2nd ed. (Bucuresti: Tipografia Academiei Romane, 1886), 275-6, 382-3.

18. Bunea, "Istoria autonomiei bisericesci," 354; Octavian Barlea, *Ostkirchliche Tradition und westlicher Katholizismus, Die Rumanische Unierte Kirche zwischen 1713-1727* (Monachii: Societatea Academica Romana, 1966), 13-4.

19. Alisie Tautu et al., *Biserica Romana Unita. Doua sute cinci zeci de ani de istorie* (Madrid: Rivadeneyra, 1952), 48; Silviu Dragomir, *Rominii din Transilvania şi Unirea cu Biserica Romei. Documente apocrife privitoare la inceputurile unirii cu catolicismul roman (1697-1701)*. (Bucuresti: Editura Institutului Biblic şi de Misiune Ortodoxa, 1963), 4-5.

20. Nicolao Nilles, S.J., *Symbolae ad illustrandam historiam eccclesiae orientalis in terris coronae S. Stephani*, I (Oeniponte: Typis et Sumptibus Feliciani Rauch, 1885), 162-3.

21. Fiedler, "Die Union der Walachen in Siebenburgen," 356.

22. Nilles, *Symbolae ad illustrandam historiam*, I, 165-8.

23. *Ibid.*, 168-70.

24. N. Iorga, *Histoire des Roumains de Transylvanie et de Hongrie*, II (Bucharest: Joseph Gobl, 1916), 17-8; *Condica Santa*, I, 69-72.

25. Nilles, *Symbolae ad illustrandam historiam*, I, 170; *Condica Santa*, I, 72-3.

26. G. Hofmann, S.J., *Documenta Concilii Florentini de Unione Orientalium, I. De Unione Graecorum. 6 Iulio 1439*. Series Theologica, 18 (Romae: Pontifica Universitas Gregoriana, 1935), 5, 12-7.

27. George Popoviciu, *Uniunea romanilor din Transilvania cu biserica romano-catholica sub imperatul Leopold I* (Logoj: Tipografiei Diec. din Caransebes, 1901), 26; Fiedler, "Die Union der Walachen in Siebenburgen," 354-5.

28. Hurmuzaki, *Fragmente zur Geschichte*, II, 25-6; Wilhelm de Vries, S.J., *Der christliche Osten in Geschichte und Gegenwart* (Wurzburg: Augustinus Verlag, 1951), 108.

29. Endre Ivanka, "The Rumanian Greek-Catholic Church," *The Eastern Churches Quarterly*, VIII (1949), nr. 3, 159; Stefan Lupsa, *Biserica ardeleana şi "unirea" in anii 1697-1701* (Bucuresti: Editura Institutului Biblic şi de Misiune al Bisericii Ortodoxa Romane, 1948), 39.

30. Samuil Micu, *Scurta cunostinta a istorii rominilor*. Cornel Cimpeanu, ed. (Bucuresti: Editura Stiintifica, 1963), 104-5; Samuelis Klein, "Historia Daco-Romanorum sive Valachorum," *Instructiunea Publica*, (March/April 1961), 89-93.

31. Vries, *Rom und die Patriarchate des Ostens*, 412.

32. Nilles, *Symbolae ad illustrandam historiam*, I, 163, 170.

33. Collectio Hevenesiana, Tom. 24, 53-4.

34. "Brevis Valachorum Transylvaniam incolentium Historia," 170; Petrus Bod, *Historia Hungarorum Ecclesiastica*, II (Leiden: E. J. Brill, 1890), 210.

35. Vries, *Rom und die Patriarchate des Ostens*, 144, 146; Jacob Radu, *Istoria vicariatului greco-catolic al Hategului* (Lugoj: Tipografia "Gutenberg," 1913), 104-5.

36. Lucian Predescu, *Enciclopedia Cugetarea* (Bucuresti: Georgescu Delafras, 1940), 844; King, *The Rites of Eastern Christendom*, II, 39.

37. Nilles, *Symbolae ad illustrandam historiam*, I,180; Francisus Fasching, S.J., *Nova Dacia*, I (Claudiopoli: Typ. Acad. S.J., 1744), 21.

38. S. Dragomir, "Rominii din Transilvania şi Uniarea cu Biserica Romei," *Studii şi Materiale de Istorie Medie*, III (Bucuresti: Editura Academiei Republicii Populare Romine, 1959), 327; N. Iorga, "Doua scrisori ale lui Atanase Anghel," *Memoriile Sectiunii Istorice*, Seria III (Academia Romana), XIII (1932), 131-2; Nic. Densusianu, *Cercetari istorice in archivele şi bibliotecele Ungariei şi ale Transilvaniei* (Bucuresti: Tipografia Academiei Romane, 1880), 101.

39. Etienne Metes, "La vie menee par les Roumains den Transylvanie du XVI-e siecle," *La Transylvanie* (Bucuresti: Imprimeria Nationala, 1938), 286; Metes, *Istoria Bisericii,* 445; Joane M. Moldovanu, *Acte sinodali ale baserecei romane de Alb'a Julia şi Fagarasiu*, I (Blasiu: S. Filltsch, 1869), 168, 171-3.

40. Nilles, *Symbolae ad illustrandam historiam*, I, 192-4; Vries, *Rom und die Patriarchate des Ostens*, 151-2.

41. Nilles, *Symbolae ad illustrandam historiam*, I, 269-0.

42. Ursu, "Un manifest romanesc," 1054; Bernath, *Habsburg und die Anfange*, 85-7.

43. Popoviciu, *Uniunea romanilor din Transilvania*, 26-7; Alesandru V. Gram'a, *Istoria Basericei Romanesci unite cu Rom'a* (Blasiu: tipariulu Seminariului Archidiecesanu, 1884), 80-1.

44. Hurmuzaki, *Fragmente zur Geschichte*, II, 30-1; Collectio Hevenesiana, Tom. 24, 91-2.

45. Collectio Hevenesiana, Tom. 24, 65-6.

46. George Michael Gottleib v. Herrmann, *Das Alte und Neue Kronstadt*, I (Hermannstadt. Franz Michaelis, 1883), 52.

47. Klein, "Historia Daco-Romanorum sive Valachorum," 94; Stephano Katona, *Historia Critica Regum Hungariae, Stirpis Austriacae*, 17 (Budae: Typis & Sumptis Regiae Universitatis Pestanae, 1805), 63-7.

48. Collectio Hevenesiana, Tom. 24, 72-5.

49. Nilles, *Symbolae ad illustrandam historiam*, I, 204, 207.

50. *Ibid.*, 212, 215, 218-20.

51. B. Barbat, S.J., "L'institution de l'office du 'theologien' dans l'Eglise Roumaine Unie," *Orientalia Christiana Periodica*, XXX (1963), nr. 1, 155; Bunea, "Istoria autonomiei bisericesci," 358; G. Baritiu, "Din cronic'a lui Michailu Cserei. 1661-1711, (Continuare), (Despre unire)," *Transilvani'a*, II (1869), nr. 16, 182.

52. Cluj. Academia Romania, Filiala Biblioteca. Manuscrise Franciscane. "Syllogimaeorum Transylvaniae Ecclesiae" [by Rudolphus Bzenszky, S.J.; 1699-1700], 87; Bernath, *Habsburg und die Anfange*, 97, 99-100; A. Grama, *Cestiuni din dreptulu şi istoria bisericei romanesca unite*, I (Blasiu: Tipografia Seminariului gr.-cat., 1893), 7-8, 10-11.

53. Vries, *Rom und die Patriarchate des Ostens*, 147-8; Nilles, *Symbolae ad illustrandam historiam*, I, 1031-2.

54. Bernath, *Habsburg und die Anfange*, 103-5; Popoviciu, *Uniunea romanilor din Transilvania*, 63, 101.

55. Vries, *Rom und die Patriarchate des Ostens*, 144-6, 152-5.

56. *Ibid.*, 170-4; Dragomir, *Rominii din Transilvania şi Unirea cu Biserica Romei,* 78.

57. Hurmuzaki, *Fragmente zur Geschichte*, II, 27; Vries, *Rom und die Patriarchate des Ostens*, 157-8.

58. Martinus Szent-Ivani, *Opusculorum Polemicorum*, II (Tyrnaviae: Academicae Tyranviensis Tyupographiae, 1730), 176-9; Fiedler, "Die Union der Walachen in Siebenburgen," 373; Michael Lacko, S.J., *Synodus episcoporum ritus byzantini catholicorum ex antinqua Hungaria Vindobonae a. 1773 celebrata* (Roma: Pontificium Institutum Orientalium Studidorum, 1975), 85-8.

59. Kurt Wessely, "A doua Diploma Leipoldina," *Memoriile Sectiunii Istorice*, Academia Romana, Seria III, XX (1938), 271; Collectio Hevenesiana, Tom. 24, 92-6.

60. F. Krones, "Zur Geschichte Ungarns in Zeitalter Franz Rakoczi's II. Historische Studie nach gedruckten und ungedrucktken Quellen," Erste Abtheilung. *Archiv für österreichische Geschichte*, 42 (1870), 268; Sandor Szilagyi, *Monumenta Comitalia Regni Transylvaniae*, XXI (Budapest: A. M. Tud. Akademia Konyvkiado-Hivatala, 1898), 434-5; Collectio Hevenesiana, Tom. 24, 123-4.

61. Baritiu, *Parti alese*, 1-2, 182, 185; Bela Obal, *Die Religionspolitik in Ungarn dem Westfalischen Frieden wahrend der Regierung Leopold I* (Halle a.S.: Wischan & Burkhardt, 1910), 10.

62. Dragomir, *Rominii din Transilvania şi Unirea cu Biserica Romei,* 60-2, 64.

63. Bernath, *Habsburg und die Anfange*, 49-50.

64. Eudoxiu de Hurmuzaki, *Documente privitore la Istoria Romanilor*, V (I) (1650-1699). (Bucuresti: Socecu & Teclu, 1885), 540.

65. *Ibid.*, 541; N. Iorga, *Istoria Literaturii Romanesti*, III, 2nd ed. (Bucuresti: Editura Fundatiei "Regele Ferdinand," 1933), 12.

66. Fiedler, "Die Union der Walachen in Siebenburgen," 275-6, 359; Hurmuzaki, *Fragmente zur Geschichte*, II, 41, 46-7; Collectio Hevenesiana, Tom. 24, 27.

67. I. Lupas, *Documente istorice transilvane*, I (1599-1699). (Cluj: Tipografia "Cartea Romaneasca," 1940), 478-81; Barlea, *Ostkirchliche Tradition und westlicher Katholizismus*, 35; Hurmuzaki, *Documente privitore la Istoria Romanilor*, V (I), 537-8.

68. Vries, *Rom und die Patriarchate des Ostens*, 150-1, 164-5; Barlea, *Ostkirchliche Tradition und westlicher Katholizismus,* 9.

69. Barbat, "L'institution de l'office du 'theologien'," 160; Baritiu, *Parti alese*, 180, 212-3; Josephus Trausch, *Chronicon Fuchsio-Lupino-Oltar-dinum*, II (Coronae: Johannes Gott, 1848), 278-80, 284.

70. Johannes Crisian, *Beitrag zur Geschichte der kirchlichen Union der Rumanen in Siebenburgen unter Leopold I* (Hermannstadt: Archidiocesan-Druckekrei, 1882), 56, 59; Dragomir, *Rominii din Transilvania şi Unirea cu Biserica Romei,* 97.

71. Nicolau Pope'a, *Vechi'a metropolia ortodosa romana a Transilvaniei, suprimerea şi restaurarea ei* (Sabiniu: S. Filtsch, 1870), 126; Dragomir, "Rominii din Transilvania şi Uniarea cu Biserica Romei," 334-5.

72. Barlea, *Ostkirchliche Tradition und westlicher Katholizismus*, 34-5.

73. Barbat, "L'institution de l'office du 'theologien'," 164; Baritiu, *Parti alese*, 182.

74. Baritiu, *Parti alese*, 151-2,163-4, 171, 209; Zenovie Paclisanu, "Contributii istorice privitoare la situatia materiala a preotimii romane din Ardeal şi Ungaria," *Cultura Crestina*, VI (1916), nr. 6, 164; D. Prodan, *Supplex Libellus Valachorum* (Cluj: Editura Universitatii "Victor Babes," 1948), 126.

75. Constantin C. Giurescu, *Istoria Romanilor*, III (Part 1). (Bucuresti: Fundatia Regala pentru Literatura şi Arta, 1942), 197, 394; Ioan Lupas, *Istoria bisericeasca a Romanilor ardeleni* (Sibiu: Editura şi tiparul tipografiei arhidiecezane, 1918), 109-10.

76. Silviu Dragomir, "Contributii privitoare la relaltile Bisericii romanesti cu Rusia in veacul XVII," *Memoriile Sectiunii Istorice*, (Academia Romana), Seria II, XXXIV (1912), 1135-6, 1222, 1226-7.

77. Gabriel Patacsi, S.J., "Die unionsfeindlichen Bewegungen der orthodoxen Rumanen Siebenburgens in den Jahren 1726-1729," *Orientalia Christiana Periodica*, XXX (1960), nr. 2, 370-1; Dragomir, "Rominii din Transilvania şi Uniarea cu Biserica Romei," 326; Silviu Dragomir, *Istoria Desrobirei Religioase a Romanilor din Ardeal in secolul XVIII*, I (Sibiu: Editura şi tiparul Tipografiei arhidiecezane, 1920), 36-7.

78. Hurmuzaki, *Fragmente zur Geschichte*, II, 18; Fiedler, "Die Union der Walachen in Siebenburgen," 360; Alexandru Pop, *Desbindarea in Biserica Romanilor din Ardeal şi Ungaria, 1697-1701* (Bucuresti: Wiegand, C. Savocu & C-nie, 1892), 17-8.

79. Martinus Szentivany, S.J., *Dissertatio Paralipomenonica rerum Memorabilium Hungariae* (Tyrnaviae: Typis Academ., 1699), 234;

80. Augsutin Bunea, *Episcopii Petru Paul Aron şi Dionisiu Novacovici, sau istoria Romanilor transilvanei de la 1751 pana la 1764* (Blas: Tipografia Seminariului Archidiecesan, 1902), 42-3.

81. Crisian, *Beitrag zur Geschichte,* 36; "Brevis Valachorum Transylvaniam incolentium Historia," 267; Dragomir, "Rominii din Transilvania şi Uniarea cu Biserica Romei," 62, 77-8.

82. Lupas, *Istoria bisericeasca a Romanilor ardeleni*, 116; I. Lupas, "O incercare de reunie a bisericilor romane din Transilvania la 1798," *Studii, conferinte şi comunicari*, I (Bucuresti: Editura Casei Scoalelor, 1928), 389.

83. Vries, *Rom und die Patriarchate des Ostens*, 134-5; Friedrich Schuler von Libloy, *Kurzer Ueberblick der Literaturgeschichte Siebenburgens, von der altesten Zeit bis zu Ende des vorigen Jahrhunderts* (Hermannstadt: Georg v. Closius, 1857), 2.

84. I. Nistor, "Emigrarile de peste munti," *Analele Academiei Romane. Memorile Sectiunii Istorice.* Seria II, XXXVII (1914-15), 844; Johannes Hochsmann, "Sstudien zur Geschichte Siebenburgens aus dem 18. Jahrhundert. II," *Archiv des Vereines für siebenburgische Landeskunde*, 16 (1880), Heft 16, 111-13.

85. Dragomir, *Rominii din Transilvania şi Unirea cu Biserica Romei*, 58, 60, 76-8.

86. Stefan Metes, *Manastirile romanesti din Transilvania şi Ungaria* (Sibiu: Tiparul Tipografiei Archidiecezane, 1936), I, XXI-XXIII; Stefan Metes, *Pastori ardeleni in principatele romane* (Arad: Tiparul Tipografiei Diecezane, 1925), 164.

87. Prodan, *Supplex Libellus Valachorum*, 125-6; H. Schlandt, "Ausgang aus Cserei Mihaly Hisitoriaja. 1661-1704," *Quellen zur Geschichte der Stadt Brasso*, VI (Brasso: Br. Schneider & Feminger, 1915), 267.

88. Gram'a, *Istoria Basericei Romanesci unite cu Rom'a*, 95; A. Bunea, *Cestiuni din dreptulu şi istoria bisericei romanesca unite*, II, 311-12.

89. Vries, *Rom und die Patriarchate des Ostens*, 144, 146.

90. Micu, *Scurta cunostinta a istorii rominilor*, 108-9; Klein, "Historia Daco-Romanorum sive Valachorum," 98-9.

91. Nilles, *Symbolae ad illustrandam historiam*, I, 192; Onisifor Ghibu, *Catolicismul unguresc in Transilvania şi politica religioasa a statului roman* (Cluj: Institut de Arte Grafice "Ardealul," 1924), 201.

92. Micu, *Scurta cunostinta a istorii rominilor*, 107-8; Metes, *Istoria Bisericii şi vietii religioase a Romanilor,* 457-60; Patacsi, "Die unionsfeindlichen Bewegnungen der orthodoxen Rumanen Siebenburgens," 361-2.

93. Collectio Hevenesiana, Tom. 24, 79-82; Dragomir, *Istoria Desrobirei Religioase*, I, 65.

94. Joane M. Moldovanu, *Acte sinodali ale baserecei romane de Alb'a Julia şi Fagarasiu*, II (Blasiu: Tipografi'a Seminariale, 1872), 115-19, 122.

95. Vries, *Rom und die Patriarchate des Ostens*, 165-7; Collectio Hevenesiana, Tom. 24, 103-4.

96. Dragomir, "Rominii din Transilvania şi Uniarea cu Biserica Romei," 324; Collectio Hevenesiana, Tom. 24, 263-5, 267-72.

97. Sterie Stinghe, *Documente privitoare la trecutul Rominilor din Schei*, I (1700-1783). (Braşov: Tipografia Ciurcu & Comp., 1901), 5-8, 11-3, 22-3, 25-9.

98. A. Papiu Ilarianu, *Istori'a Romaniloru din Daci'a Superiore* (Vienna: C. Gerold sis Fiiu, 1851), 67; Virginia Vasiliu, "Constantino Brancoveanu e il Cattolicismo, Alcune notizie nuove intorno alla sua politica religioasa," *Ephemeris Dacoromana*, III (1925), 115, 118, 124-5.

99. Barbat, "L'institution de l'office du 'theologien'," 161-4.

100. *Ibid.*, 164-5; Dragomir, *Rominii din Transilvania şi Unirea cu Biserica Romei*, 89.

101. Vries, *Rom und die Patriarchate des Ostens*, 180; Dragomir, *Rominii din Transilvania şi Unirea cu Biserica Romei*, 93-4.

102. Vries, *Rom und die Patriarchate des Ostens*, 167-8, 419-20, 422-3.;

103. *Ibid.*, 168, 176.

104. Collectio Hevenesiana, Tom. 24, 247-53.

105. Nilles, *Symbolae ad illustrandam historiam*, I, 99, 282; Vries, *Rom und die Patriarchate des Ostens*, 172-4, 406-7, 412-15.

106. Nilles, *Symbolae ad illustrandam historiam*, I, 283-6.

107. Vries, *Rom und die Patriarchate des Ostens*, 170, 174.

108. Collectio Hevenesiana, Tom. 24, 255-7; Iosif Fessler, "Relatio historica de Daco-Romanis in Transilvania et Hungaria cum Ecclesia Romana unitis vel uniendis," *Analele Academiei Romane. Memoriile Sectiunii Istorice*, Seria III, XXIV (1942), 651.

109. Nilles, *Symbolae ad illustrandam historiam*, I, 280; Bunea, *Episcopii Petru Paul Aron şi Dionisiu Novacovici,* 362.

110. "Brevis Valachorum Transylvaniam incolentium Historia" [Petrus Bod], 196-8.

111. Barlea, *Ostkirchliche Tradition und westlicher Katholizismus*, 15.

112. Joseph Maurer, *Cardinal Leopold Graf Kollonitsch, Primas von Ungarn* (Innsbruck: Fel. Rauch, 1887), 369.

113. Collectio Hevenesiana, Tom. 24, 51-2, 219-21.

114. *Ibid.*, 219-21.

115. *Ibid.*; Bunea, *Episcopii Petru Paul Aron şi Dionisiu Novacovici,* 362.

116. Nilles, *Symbolae ad illustrandam historiam*, I, 287, 304, 307-8; Collectio Hevenesiana, Tom. 24, 34-6.

117. Kurt Wessely, "A doua Diploma Leopoldina," 271-2; Iorga, *Histoire des Roumains de Transylvanie et de Hongrie*, II, 33-4.

118. Hurmuzaki, *Fragmente zur Geschichte*, II, 55-6.

119. *Ibid.*, 62; Dragomir, *Rominii din Transilvania şi Unirea cu Biserica Romei*, 91.

120. Nilles, *Symbolae ad illustrandam historiam*, I, 126; Ferdinand v. Zieglauer, Harteneck, *Graf der sächsischen Nation, und die siebenbürgischen Parteikämpfe seiner Zeit, 1691-1703* (Hermannstadt: Th. Steinhaussen, 1869), 64-5.

121. Collectio Hevenesiana, Tom. 24, 28-33; Fiedler, "Die Union der Walachen in Siebenburgen," 360-3, 376-80.

122. *Ibid.*

Chapter III:
Jesuits and an Ethnic Hierarchy

1. G. Baritiu, "Din cronic'a lui Michailu Cserei. 1661-1711. (Continuare), (Despre unire)," *Transilvani'a*, II (1869), nr. 16, 182; Collectio Hevenesiana, Tom. 24, Eötvös Loránd Tudományegyetem Központi Könyvtára, 179-81.

2. Nicolae Nilles, S.J., *Symbolae ad illustrandam historiam eccclesiae orientalis in terris coronae S. Stephani*, I (Oeniponte: Typis et Sumptibus Feliciani Rauch, 1885), 188-91; Samuil Micu, *Scurta cunostinta a istorii rominilor*, Cornel Cimpeanu, ed. (Bucuresti: Editura Stiintifica, 1963),112-3.

3. Augustin Bunea, "Istoria autonomiei bisericesci," *Discursuri, Autonomia bisericesca, Diverse* (Blas: Tipografia Seminariului Archidiecesan, 1903), 358-362; Silviu Dragomir, *Rominii din Transilvania şi Unirea cu Biserica Romei. Documente apocrife privitoare la inceputurile unirii cu catolicismul roman (1697-1701)* (Bucuresti: Editura Institutului Biblic şi de Misiune Ortodoxa, 1963), 92-3.

4. Wilhelm de Vries, *Rom und die Patriarchate des Ostens* (Freiburg/München: Verlag Karl Alber, 1963), 177; Georgie Baritiu, *Parti alese din istoria Transilvaniei pre doua sute de ani din urma*, I (Sibiu: W. Krafft, 1889), 207.

5. Octavian Barlea, *Ostkirchliche Tradition und westlicher Katholizismus, Die Rumanische Unierte Kirche zwischen 1713-1727* (Monachii: societatea Academica Romana, 1966), 84-5; Augustin Bunea, *Cestiuni din dreptulu şi istoria bisericei romanesci unite*, II (Blasiu: Tipografia Seminariului gr.-cat., 1893), 63-5.

6. Eudoxiu Freiherrn von Hurmuzaki, *Fragmente zur Geschichte der Rumänen*, II (Bucuresti: Socecu, Sander & Teclu, 1881), 98-9; Z. Paclisanu, "In jurul 'Diplomei a doua Leopoldine,'" *Cultura Crestina*, XVIII (1938), nr. 8-9, 469-70.

7. Fr. Teutsch, *Die Kirchlichen Verhaltnisse Siebenbürgens* (Halle a.S.: Eugen Strien, 1906), 57; Lucian Blaga, *Gindirea romaneasca in Transilvania in secolul al XVIII-lea*, George Ivascu, ed. (Bucuresti: Editura Stiintifica, 1966), 44.

8. Nilles, *Symbolae ad illustrandam historiam,* I, 269; Collectio Hevenesiana, Tom. 24, 51-2.

9. Ferdinand von Zieglauer, *Die politische Reformbewegung in Siebenbürgen in der Zeit Joseph's II. und Leopold's II.* (Wien: Wilhelm Braumüller, 1881), 527-8; Keith Hitchins, *The Idea of Nation. The Romanians of Transylvania, 1691-1849* (Bucharest: Editura Stiintifica şi Enciclopedica, 1985), 25-6.

10. *Istoria Rominiei*, III (Bucuresti: Editura Academiei Republicii Populare Romine, 1964), 239, 243, 355; Alexandru Pop, *Desbindarea in Biserica Romanilor din Ardeal şi Ungaria, 1697-1701* (Bucuresti: Wiegand, C. Savocu & C-nie, 1892), 101.

11. Ioan Lupas, *Istoria bisericeasca a Romanilor ardeleni* (Sibiu: Editura şi Tiparul tipografiei arhidiecezane, 1918), 113.

12. Silviu Dragomir, *Istoria Desrobirei Religioase a Romanilor din Ardeal in secolul XVIII*, I (Sibiu: Editura şi stiparul Tipografiei arhidiecezane, 1920), Anexe: 5-9, 13; Collectio Hevenesiana, Tom. 24, 187-97.

13. Mihail Dan, "In jurul unirii cu Roma, cu deosebita privire asupra rolului iezuitului Carol Neurautter," *Mitropolia Banatului*, VIII, 1958), nrs. 7/8/9, 318; Collectio Hevenesiana, Tom. 24, 243-6.

14. Nilles, *Symbolae ad illustrandam historiam eccclesiae orientalis*, I, 343-52; Collectio Hevenesiana, Tom. 24, 267-72; Sterie Stinghe, *Documente privitoare la trecutul Rominilor din Schei*, I (1700-1783) (Brasov: Tipografia Ciurcu & Comp., 1901), 34-7.

15. I. Mateiu, *Contributiuni la istoria dreptuluii bisericesc*, I (Bucuresti: Tipografia Cartilor Bisericesti, 1922), 68, 78; Joane M. Moldovanu, *Acte sinodali ale baserecei romane de Alb'a Julia şi Fagarasi*, I (Blasiu: S. Filtsch, 1869), 180-2.

16. Nicolau Pope'a, *Vechi'a metropolia ortodoxa romana a Transilvaniei, suprimerea şi restaurarea ei* (Sabiniu: S. Filtsch, 1870), 136; Nicolae Nilles, S.J., *Symbolae ad illustrandam historiam ecclesiae orientalis in terris coronae S. Stephani*, II (Oeniponte: Typis et Sumsptibus Feliciani Rauch, 1885), 960.

17. Nilles, *Symbolae ad illustrandam historiam ecclesiae orientalis,* II, 512.

18. *Istoria Rominiei*, III, 243; Vries, *Rom und die Patriarchate des Ostens*, 416-7.

19. Collectio Hevenesiana, Tom. 24, 243-6.

20. Nilles, *Symbolae ad illustrandam historiam eccclesiae orientalis*, I, 323, 326;

21. *Ibid.*, 308, 360; Joseph Maurer, *Cardinal Leopold Graf Kollonitsch, Primas von Ungarn* (Innsbruck: Fel. Rauch, 1887), 374; Stephen Pop, "In jurul hirotonirii a doua alui Atanasie Anghel," *Cultura Crestina*, III (1915), nr. 15, 464.

22. Nilles, *Symbolae ad illustrandam historiam eccclesiae orientalis*, I, 351-2.

23. Johann Hintz, *Geschichte der griechisch=nichtunirten Glaubensgenossen in Siebenburgen* (Hermannstadt: Vereins für siebenburgische Landeskunde, 1850), 32-3; Joesph Fiedler, "Die Union der Walachen in Siebenburgen unter K. Leopold I," *Sitzungsberichte der kaiserlichen Akademie der Wissenschaften*, XXVII (1858), Heft 3, 381-2; Stephano Katona, *Historia Critica regum Hungariae, Stirpis Austriacae*, 17 (Budae: Typis et Sumptis regiae Universitatis Pestanae, 1805), 203-3.

24. Eudoxiu de Hurmuzaki, *Documente privitoare la Istoria Romanilor*, VI (1700-1750). (Bucuresti: Socecu, Sander, & Teclu, 1878), 19; S. Dragomir, "Rominii din Transilvania şi Unirea cu Biserica Romei," *Studii şi Materiale de Istorie Medie*, III (Bucuresti: Editura Academiei Republicii Populare Romine, 1959), 326.

25. Mathias Bernath, *Habsburg und die Anfänge der Rumänischen Nationsbildung* (Leiden: E. J. Brill, 1972), 43.

26. Hurmuzaki, *Fragmente zur Geschichte der Rumänen*, II, 71-2.

27. *Ibid.*, 69, 79.

28. Bernath, *Habsburg und die Anfänge*, 43; Hurmuzaki, *Fragmente*, II, 79, 81-3.

29. Bernath, *Habsburg und die Anfänge*, 43; Baritiu, *Parti alese din istoria Transilvaniei*, 235-6; Hugo Hantsch, *Die Geschichte Österreichs*, II (Graz-Wien-Köln: Verlag Styria, 1962), 87, 90-2, 103.

30. Bernath, *Habsburg und die Anfänge*, 42; Hurmuzaki, *Fragmente*, II, 78, 80, 86-7.

31. Baritiu, *Parti alese*, 128, 226-8; Dragomir, *Istoria Desrobirei Religioase*, I, 74.

32. I. Lupas, "Contributiuni documentare la istoria satelor transilvane," *Studii, conferinte şi comunicari istorice*, IV (Sibiu: Institutul de Arte Grafice "Dacia Traiana," 1943), 201; George Popviciu, *Uniunea romanilor din Transilvania cu biserica romano-catolica sub imperatul Leopold I.* (Logoj: Tipariul Tipografiei Diec. din Caransebes, 1901), 183, 220.

33. Imre Révész, "Esquisse de l'histoire de la politique religieuse hongroise entre 1705 et 1860," *Studia Historica*, #26 (Budapest: Academiae Scientiarum Hungaricae, 1960), 6, 9, 13; Aloisie Tăutu et al. *Biserica Română Unită. Două sute cinci zeci de ani de istorie* (Madrid: Rivadeneyra, 1952), 61.

34. Béla K. Király, *Hungary in the Late Eighteenth Century, The Decline of Enlightened Despotism* (New York: Columbia University Press, 1969), 46*n*; Bernath, *Habsburg und die Anfänge*, 45.

35. Bunea, "Istoria autonomiei bisericesci," 362; Baritiu, *Parti alese*, 237.

36. Silviu Dragomir, *Istoria Desrobirei Religioase a Romanilor din Ardeal in secolul XVIII*, II (Sibiu: Editura şi tiparul Tipografiei arhidiecezane, 1930), 203; Dragomir, *Istoria Desrobirei Religioase*, I, 75-6; Hurmuzaki, *Documente privitoare la Istoria Romanilor*, VI, 52-4.

37. Baritiu, *Parti alese*, 269, 271-2; Nilles, *Symbolae ad illustrandam historiam eccclesiae orientalis*, I, 372-3.

38. Kilály, *Hungary in the Late Eighteenth Century*, 5; Baritiu, *Parti alese*, 226-7.

39. Dragomir, *Istoria Desrobirei Religioase*, I, 75-6; Nilles, *Symbolae ad illustrandam historiam eccclesiae orientalis*, I, 386-7, 289-90.

40. I. Mateiu, *Vacantele Mitropoliei ortodoxe din Ardeal in veacul XVIII-lea* (Cluj: Tipografia Dr. S. Bornemisa, 1922), 8-9; Barlea, *Ostkirchliche Tradition und westlicher Katholizismus*, 16-7.

41. Franz von Krones, "Zur Geschichte Ungarns im Zeitalter Franz Rákóczi's II. Historische Studie nach gedruckten und ungedruckten Quellen," Zweite Abteilung. *Archiv für österreichische Geschichte*, 43 (1870), 6; Hantsch, *Die Geschichte Österreichs*, II, 103, 106-7.

42. Eudoxiu de Hurmuzaki, *Documente privitoare la Istoria Romanilor*, XV (II) (1601-1825), N. Iorga, ed. (Bucuresti: Socec & Comp., 1913), 1550-2; Dragomir, *Rominii din Transilvania şi Unirea cu Biserica Romei*, 92-3.

43. Dragomir, "Rominii din Transilvania şi Unirea cu Biserica Romei," 326.

44. Radu Tempea, *Istoria sfintei besereci a Scheilor Brasovului*. Edited by Octavian Schiau and Livia Bot. (Cluj: Editura pentru Literatura, 1969), 88; Nilles, *Symbolae ad illustrandam historiam eccclesiae orientalis*, I, 390.

45. Augustin Bunea, *Episcopii Petru Paul Aron şi Dionisiu Novacovici, sau istoria Romanilor transilvanei de la 1751 pana la 1764* (Blas: Tipografia Seminariului Archidiecesan, 1902), 362.

46. Baritiu, *Parti alese*, 436-7.

47. Barlea, *Ostkirchliche Tradition*, 9, 88.

48. *Ibid.*, 13, 17.

49. Nilles, *Symbolae ad illustrandam historiam eccclesiae orientalis*, I, 372, 393; Imre Revesz, "La Reforme et les Roumains de Transylvanie," *Archivum Europae Centro-Orientalis*, III (1937), 307.

50. Nilles, *Symbolae ad illustrandam historiam eccclesiae orientalis*, I, 394-6; Z. Paclisanu, "Discutii Marunte," *Cultura Crestina,* XIX (1939), nr. 1-2, 52.

51. Zenovie Paclisanu, "Alegerea şi denumire episcopului unit Ioan Patachi," *Cultura Crestina*, VI (1916), nr. 2-3, 43; Jacob Radu, *Fostii elevi romani-uniti şi scoalelor din Roma* (Beius: Tiparul Tipografiei "Ateneul," 1929), 8; Georghie Sincai, *Chronica Romanilor*, III, 2nd ed. (Bucuresti: Tipografia Academiei Romane, 1886), 395-6.

52. Paclisanu, "Alegerea şi denumire episcopului unit," 38-9, 41, 70.

53. Alesandru V. Gram'a, *Istoria Basericei Romanesci unite cu Rom'a* (Blasiu: Tipariulu Seminariului Archidiecesanu, 1884), 106-7; Paclisanu, "Discutii Marunte," 52.

54. Nilles, *Symbolae ad illustrandam*, I, 87, 406-7; Dragomir, *Istoria Desrobirei Religioase*, I, Anexe, 18-9.

55. Barlea, *Ostkirchliche Tradition*, 158; Collectio Hevenesiana, Tom. 24, 33, 55-6.

56. Nilles, *Symbolae ad illustrandam*, I, 317; Dragomir, *Istoria Desrobirei Religioase*, I, 91.

57. Baritiu, *Parti alese*, 322; Barlea, *Ostkirchliche Tradition*, 20.

58. Dragomir, *Istoria Desrobirei Religioase*, I, Anexe, 21.

59. Nilles, *Symbolae ad illustrandam*, I, 398.

60. Silviu Dragomir, "Alegera şi numirea episcopului unit Ioan Patachi," *Revista Teologica*, IX (1915), nr. 16-18, 266-9; Mircea Pacurariu, *Istoria Bisericii Ortodoxe Romane*, II (Bucuresti: Editura Institutului Biblic şi de Misiune al Bisericii Ortodoxe Romane, 1981), 320.

61. Z. Paclisanu, "O statistica a Romanilor ardeleni dela inceputul veacului al XVIII-lea," *Societatea de Maine*, IV (1927), nr. 13-14, 183; Dragomir, *Istoria Desrobirei Religioase*, I, Anexe, 18.

62. I Bianu, "Vito Piluzio, Documente inedite din Archivulu Popagandei," *Columna lui Traianu*, IV (1883), 272; Dragomir, *Istoria Desrobirei Religioase*, I, Anexe, 21-2.

63. Barlea, *Ostkirchliche Tradition*, 13-4; Dragomir, "Alegera şi numirea episcopului unit," 263, 265.

64. Dragomir, *Istoria Desrobirei Religioase*, I, Anexe, 18; Paclisanu, "Alegerea şi denumire episcopului unit," 70.

65. Bernath, *Habsburg und die Anfänge*, 45; Barlea, *Ostkirchliche Tradition*, 121.

66. Barlea, *Ostkirchliche Tradition*, 27-8.

67. Nilles, *Symbolae ad illustrandam*, I, 87, 403-4, 408-11.

68. Tempea, *Istoria sfintei besereci a Scheilor Brasovului*, 88;

69. Henry Marczali, *Hungary in the Eighteenth Century* (Cambridge: Cambridge University Press, 1910), 286-7; Hurmuzaki, *Fragmente*, II, 90.

70. Franz von Krones, "Zur Geschichte Ungarns im Zeitalter Franz Rákóczi's II. Historische Studie nach gedruckten und ungedruckten Quellen," Erste Abteilung. *Archiv für österreichische Geschichte*, 42 (1870), 268; *Idem*., *Ungarn unter Maria Theresia und Joseph II. 1740-1790* (Graz: Lueschner & Lubensky, 1871), 23-4. This sentiment was, undoubtedly, best put in the generations-old epithet of the Magyar aristocracy: "Extra Hungaricam not est vita, et si est vita – non est ita!" ["Outside of Hungary there is no life, and if there is life – it is not such as it is here!"].

71. Barlea, *Ostkirchliche Tradition*, 90; Constantin C. Giurescu, *Istoria Românilor*, III (Part I). (Bucureşti: Fundaţia Regală pentru Literatură şi Artă, 1942), 394.

72. Nilles, *Symbolae ad illustrandam*, I, 411-15.

73. *Ibid.*, 426; Barlea, *Ostkirchliche Tradition*, 89-90.

74. Hurmuzaki, *Fragmente*, II, 95-6; Nilles, *Symbolae ad illustrandam*, I, 421-2.

75. Bunea, "Istoria autonomiei bisericesci," 263; Dragomir, "Alegera şi numirea episcopului unit," 275.

76. Max Heimbucher, *Die Orden und Kongregationen der katholischen Kirche*, II (Paderborn: Verlag Ferdinand Schöning, 1934), 183-4; Michael Lacko, S.J., *Synodus episcoporum ritus byzantini catholicorum ex antiqua Hungaria Vindobonae a. 1773 celebrata* (Roma: Pontificium Institutum Orientalium Studiorum, 1975), 307.

77. Barlea, *Ostkirchliche Tradition*, 9, 33-4, 37, 47-8, 90; Gabriel Patacsi, S.J., "Die unionsfeindlichen Bewegungen der orthodoxen Rumänen Siebenbürgens in den Jahren 1726-1729," *Orientalia Christiana Periodica*, XXVI (1960), nr. 2, 374-5.

78. Barlea, *Ostkirchliche Tradition*, 62- 4, 66, 76; Stinghe, *Documente privitoare la trecutul Rominilor din Schei*, I, III-IV; Tempea, *Istoria sfintei besereci a Scheilor Brasovului*, 88.

79. Nilles, *Symbolae ad illustrandam*, I, 89, 430-2, 436-8, 442; Barlea, *Ostkirchliche Tradition*, 9; Paclisanu, "Alegerea şi denumire episcopului unit," 74-5.

80. Barlea, *Ostkirchliche Tradition*, 41, 54.

81. *Ibid.*, 39-40, 53, 115, 119-20; Paclisanu, "Alegerea şi denumire episcopului unit," 75.

82. Archdale A. King, *The Rites of Eastern Christendom*, II (Rome: Tipografia Poliglotta Vaticana, 1948), 40-1; Nilles, *Symbolae ad illustrandam*, I, 454.

83. Tempea, *Istoria sfintei besereci a Scheilor Brasovului*, 102-3; Tim. Cipariu, ed., *Acte şi fragmente latine romanesci pentru istori'a beserecei romane mai alesu unite* (Blasiu: Cu tipariulu Semin. diecesanu, 1855), 141.

84. Nilles, *Symbolae ad illustrandam*, I, 404-6, 455; Antnal Hodinka, *A munkácsi gör. szert. püspökség okmánytára*, I (1458-1715). (Ungvár: Nzomatott az "Unio Könyvnyomda R.T." Könyvnyamdájaban, 1911), 524.

85. Sincai, *Chronica Romanilor*, III, 395-6; Gram'a, *Istoria Basericei Romanesci unite*, 107; Nicolao Nilles, "Ueber das Wirken der Jesuiten unter den katholischen Rumänen," *Zeitschrift für katholische Theologie*, III (1879), 805.

86. Mircea Pacuariu, *Istoria Bisericii Ortodoxe Române*, II (Bucureşti: Editura Institutului Biblic şi de Misiune al Bisericii Ortodoxe Române, 1981), 318; Barlea, *Ostkirchliche Tradition*, 34-5, 59, 77-8, 91-2.

87. Aloisie Tăutu et al., *Biserica Română Unită. Două sute cinci zeci de ani de istorie* (Madrid: Rivadeneyra, 1952), 128; Vries, *Rom und die Patriarchate des Ostens*, 423.

88. Nilles, *Symbolae ad illustrandam*, I, 463-4, 466-75; Zenovie Paclisanu, "Contributi istorice privitoare la situatia materiala a preotimii romane din Ardeal şi Ungaria," *Cultura Crestina*, VI (1916), nr. 6, 166, 168.

89. *Istoria Rominiei*, III, 423; Barlea, *Ostkirchliche Tradition*, 81-2.

90. Z. Paclisanu, "Contributiuni la biografia episcopului I. Patachi," *Cultura Crestina*, XVII (1937), nr. 2-3, 130, 132-3, 136; Giurescu, *Istoria Românilor*, III (Part I), 394.

91. Hurmuzaki, *Documente privitoare la Istoria Romanilor*, XV (II), 1601-2; Barlea, *Ostkirchliche Tradition*, 62-3, 77, 176.

92. Hurmuzaki, *Documente privitoare la Istoria Romanilor*, XV (II), 1591-4;

93. Baritiu, *Parti alese*, 284-5; Hurmuzaki, *Documente privitoare la Istoria Romanilor*, XV (II), 1596-8.

94. Hurmuzaki, *Documente privitoare la Istoria Romanilor*, XV (II), 1599, 1602-6.

95. *Ibid.*, 1607-8, 1614-18.

96. Hantsch, *Die Geschichte Österreichs*, II, 100-1; Bernath, *Habsburg und die Anfänge*, 45-6.

97. Barlea, *Ostkirchliche Tradition*, 83-4; Stinghe, *Documente privitoare la trecutul Rominilor din Schei*, I, 55-6.

98. Hurmuzaki, *Documente privitoare la Istoria Romanilor*, XV (II), 1596; Zenovie Paclisanu, "Din istoria bisericeasca a Romanilor ardeleni. 'Teologul' vladicilor uniti," *Memoriile Sectiunii Istorice*, Seria III, I (1923), 153.

99. Augustin Bunea, *Episcopul Ioan Inocentiu Klein (1728-1751)*. (Blas: Tipografia Seminariului archidiecesan gr.-cat., 1900), 5; Gram'a, *Istoria Basericei Romanesci unite*, 109-10; Baritiu, *Parti alese*, 331.

100. Dragomir, *Istoria Desrobirei Religioase*, I, 110.

101. Nilles, *Symbolae ad illustrandam*, I, 443, 478-9, 481-4; Mircea Pacurariu, *Istoria Ortodoxe Romane*, II (Bucuresti: Editura Institutului Biblic şi Misiune al Bisericii Ortodoxe Romane, 1981), 320, 323-4.

102. Nilles, *Symbolae ad illustrandam historiam ecclesiae orientalis,* II, 499-501, 1019-20; Hurmuzaki, *Documente privitoare la Istoria Romanilor*, XV (II), 1627-8.

103. Cluj. Academia Romania, Filiala Biblioteca. Manuscrise Latine 29. "Brevis Valachorum Transylvaniam incolentium Historia" [by Petrus Bod, 1764], 278-9; Tăutu, *Biserica Română Unită.*, 7.

104. Hurmuzaki, *Fragmente*, II, 90, 100; Sincai, *Chronica Romanilor*, III, 424.

105. Patacsi, "Die unionsfeindlichen Bewegungen," 384-5; Dragomir, *Istoria Desrobirei Religioase*, I, Anexe, 22.

106. Stinghe, *Documente privitoare la trecutul Rominilor din Schei*, I, 61-2, 66-9, 83; Patacsi, "Die unionsfeindlichen Bewegungen," 325-3; 355-6, 362.

107. Patacsi, "Die unionsfeindlichen Bewegungen," 382-3, 392-3.

108. Tempea, *Istoria sfintei besereci a Scheilor Brasovului*, 21, 27-8, 98-9, 103-5.

109. Patacsi, "Die unionsfeindlichen Bewegungen," 385-6, 388-9.

110. *Ibid.*, 393, 395-8, 400.

111. *Ibid.*, 357-60, 363-6, 370.

Chapter IV: Conclusion: Birth of National Awareness

1. Nicolao Nilles, S.J., *Symbolae ad illustrandam historiam ecclesiae orientalis in terris coronae S. Stephani*, II (Oeniponte: Typis et Sumptibus Feliciani Rauch, 1885), 497-501; Joane M. Moldovanu, *Acte sinodali ale baserecei romane de Alb'a Julia şi Fagarasisu*, II (Blasiu: Tipografi'a Seminariale, 1872), 101-2, 106-7.

2. Heinrich Herbert, "Die Gegenreformation in Hermannstadt zur Zeit Karls VI," *Archiv des Vereines für siebenbürgische Landeskunde*, 29 (1899), 56; Gheorghie Şincai, *Chronica Românilor*, III (Bucuresti: Academiei Române, 1886), 423-4; N. Comşa, *Episcopul Ion Inochentie Micu* ((Blaj: Tipografia Seminarului, 1943), 8, 10-1.

3. Augustin Bunea, *Episcopul Ioan Inocenţiu Klein (1728-1751)* (Blaş: Tipografia Seminariului archidiecesan gr.-cat., 1900), 7-8; Joannicius Basilovits, *Brevis notitia fundationis Theodori Koriathovits*, II (Cassoviae: Typographia Ellingeriana, 1799), 175-6.

4. Constantin C. Giurescu, *Istoria Românilor*, III (Part I). (Bucureşti: Fundaţia Regală pentru Literatură şi Artă, 1942), 394; Bunea, *Episcopul Ioan Inocenţiu Klein*, 271.

5. Lucian Blaga, *Gîndirea româneascǎ în Transilvania în secolul al XVIII-lea*. George Ivaşcu, ed. (Bucureşti: Editura Ştiinţicǎ, 1966), 45; Bunea, *Episcopul Ioan Inocenţiu Klein*, 13.

6. N. Comşa, *Episcopul Ion Inochentie Micu* (Blaj: Tipografia Seminarului, 1943), 1-2; Eudoxiu de Hurmuzaki, *Documente privitoare la Istoria Românilor,* XV (Part II)(1601-1825). N. Iorga, ed. (Bucureşti: Socec & Comp. 1913), 1625-8.

7. Nilles, *Symbolae ad illustrandam*, II, 501, 503-4.

8. *Ibid*., 506-7; Bunea, *Episcopul Ioan Inocenţiu Klein*, 9, 11.

9. D. Prodan, *Supplex Libellus Valachorum* (Cluj: Editura Universităţii "Victor Babeş," 1948), 119.

10. Augustin Bunea, "Istoria autonomiei bisericesi," *Discursuri Autonomia bisericéscă, Diverse* (Blaş: Tipografia Seminariului Archidiecesan, 1903), 363-4; Bunea, *Episcopul Ioan Inocenţiu Klein*, 5.

11. Basilovits, *Brevis notitia*, II, 175-6; Nilles, *Symbolae ad illustrandam*, II, 501-2, 506-7, 520-3.

12. Hurmuzaki, *Documente privitoare la Istoria Românilor,* XV (Part II), 1638.

13. Nilles, *Symbolae ad illustrandam*, II, 512-7; Hurmuzaki, *Documente privitoare la Istoria Românilor,* XV (Part II), 1641-2.

14. Nicolau Togan, *Românii din Transilvania la 1733. Conscripţia Episcopului Ioan In. Klein de Sadu* (Sibiu: Tipariul Tipografiei Archidiecesane, 1898), 1-4, 44-5.

15. Eudoxiu de Hurmuzaki, *Documente privitóre la Istoria Românilor*, VI (1700-1750). (Bucuresti: Socecŭ, Sander & Teclu, 1878), 409-10, 495.

16. D. Popovici, *La Littérature Roumaine à l'Epoque des Lumières* (Sibiu: Centrul de Studii şi Cercetări privitoare la Transilvania, 1945), 81, 83, 88.

17. Togan, *Românii din Transilvania la 1733*, 2; E. A. Bielz, *Handbuch der Landeskunde Siebenbürgens* (Hermannstadt: S. Filtsch, 1857), 146-7.

18. George Bogdan-Duică, "Statistica Romînilor din Transilvania în 1733," *Convorbiri literare*, II (1896), No. 12, 629-31; Silviu Dragomir, *Istoria Desrobirei Religioase a Românilor din Ardeal în secolul XVIII*, I, (Sibiu: Editura şi tiparul Tipografiei arhidiecezane, 1920), Anexe 24.

19. Zenovie Pâlişanu, *Corespondenţa din exil a episcopului Inochentie Micu Klein, 1746-1768* (Bucureşti: Cultura Naţională, 1924), 8-9; Gabriel Patacsi, S.J., "Die unionsfeindlichen Bewegungen der orthodoxen Rumänen Siebenbürgens in den Jahren 1726-1729," *Orientalia Christiana Periodica*, XXVI (1960), nr. 2, 393-4.

20. Radu Tempea, *Istoria sfintei besereci a Şcheilor Braşovului*, Octavian Şchiau and Livia Bot, eds. (Cluj: Editura pentru Literatură 1969), 144-5, 149.

21. Bunea, *Episcopul Ioan Inocenţiu Klein*, 303; Bogdan-Duică, "Statistica Romînilor din Transilvania în 1733," 626-8.

22. Keith Hitchins and Ioan Baju, "Conscripţia comitatenză a clerului român din Alba de Jos, anul 1773," *Mitropolia Ardealului*, XXXII (1987), Nr. 4, 81-3; Keith Hitchins and Ioan N. Beju, "Conscripţia a clerului român de pe pămîntul crăiesc. Anul 1733," *Mitropolia Ardealului*, XXXIV (1989), Nr. 3, 103, 107, 111.

23. Johann Christof Bartenstein, *Kurzer Bericht von der Beschaffenheit der zerstreuten zahlreichen Illyrischen Nation in kaiserl. koenigl. Erblanden* (Frankfurt und Leipzig: np, 1802), 22;

24. Blaga, *Gîndirea româneascǎ în Transilvania în secolul al XVIII-lea*, 106-7; George Bogdan-Duică, *Procesupiscopului Ioan Inochentie Clain* (Caransebeş: Tipografia Diecesană, 1896), 6, 9-10, 18, 23.

25. Zenovie Pâlişanu, *Corespondenţa din exil a episcopului Inochentie Micu Klein, 1746-1768* (Bucureşti: Cultura Naţională, 1924), 7-8.

26. Lucian Predescu, *Enciclopedia Cugetarea* (Bucureşti: Georgescu Delafras, 1940), 426.

27. Keith Hitchins, "Religious Tradition and National Consciousness among the Romanians of Transylvania, 1730-1780," *Concepts of Nationhood in Early Modern Eastern Europe*, I. Banac and F. E. Sysyn, eds. Harvard Ukrainian Studies, X. (Cambridge: Ukrainian Research Institute, Harvard University, 1987), 551-2; Violeta Barbu, "Biserica română unită cu Roma în căutarea identităţii: problema ritului şi activitatea misionarilor iezuiţi," *Revista Istorică*, III (1992), nr. 5-6: 531, 544.

28. Ion Bria, "Uniatismul în România: anacronic şi antiecumenic," Biserica Ortodoxă Română, CIX (1991), nr. 1-3: 30; Teodor M. Popescu, "Uniaţia în lumina adevărului istoric. Cauzele ei sociale şi politice," *Biserica Ortodoxă Romană*, CIX (1991), nr. 1-3: 62.

29. Nicolae Iorga, *My American Lectures* (Bucharest: State Printing Office, 1932), 41-2, 61.

30. Ralph Vaughan Williams, *National Music* (London Oxford University Press, 1934), 16, 19.

31. K. R. Minogue, *Nationalism*. (New York: Basic Books, 1967), 25-6.

32. Catherine Durandin, "Orthodoxie et Roumanite, Le debut de l'entre deux guerres," *Rumanian Studies*, Keith Hitchins, ed. (Leiden: E. J. Brill, 1986), 107, 109, 122, 124.

33. *Records of the Department of State Relating to the Internal Affairs of Romania, 1910-1944*. W. S. Culbertson, 31 March 1926, Decimal File 871. Washington: National Archives Microfilm Publications, 1981. Roll 3: No. 167.

34. *Ibid*., Harrison, 8 July 1943, Decimal File 871.404. Roll 40: No. 154 and 9 July 1943, Decimal File 871.404. Roll 40: No. 155.

35. Minogue, *Nationalism*, 154.

36. *Ibid*., 26, 153.

Bibliography

Archival Material

Academia România, Biblioteca Filialei Cluj. Manuscrise latine.
Academia România, Biblioteca Filialei Cluj. Manuscrise romaneşti.
Eötvös Loránd Tudományegyetem Központi Könyvtára. Collectio Hevenesiana.

Primary Sources

Acte, documente şi scrisori din Şcheii Brasovului. Ed. Vasile Oltean. Bucureşti: Editura Minerva, 1980.

Archivu pentru filologia şi istoria. Ed. Tim. Cipariu. Blasiu: 1867-71.

Chronologisch-systematische Sammlung der Berggesetze der Konigreiche, I-XXV, Zweite Abteilung. Ed. Franz Anton Schmidt. Wien: Aus der k.k. Hof-und Staats-Aerarial-Druckerey, 1834-38.

Condificazione Canonica Orientale - Fonti. Testi vari di diritto nuovo (1550-1902). Sacra Congregazione Orientale. Fasc. I (1930) & Fasc. II (1931). Roma: Tipografia Poliglotta Vaticana.

Documenta Concili Florentini de Unione Orientalium. I: *De Unione Graecorum*. Series Theologica, 18. Ed. G. Hofmann, S.J. Romae: Pontifica Universitas Gregoriana, 1935.

Documenta Pontificum Romanorum Historian Ucrainae Illustrantia, I (1953) & II (1954). Ed. Athanasius G. Welykyj, OSBM. Romae: Sumptibus Ucrainorum apud Exteros Degentium.

Documenta Romana Historiae Societatis Iesu in Regnis olim Corona Hungarica Unitis, I (1550-1570). Ed. Ladislaus Lukács, S.I. and Ladislaus Polgár, S.I. Romae: Rotaprint Curia Gener. S.I., 1959.

Documente istorice despre starea politică şi ieratică a Romanilorŭ din Transilvania. Ed. A. T. Laurian. Vienna: J. P. Sollinger, 1850.

Documente istorice transilvane, I (1599-1699). Ed. I. Lupaş. Cluj: Tipografia "Cartea Românească," 1940.

Documente privitoare la trecutul Romînilor din Şchei, I-V. Ed. Sterie Stinghe. Braşov: Tipografia Ciurcu & Comp. 1901-1906.

Documente privitóre la Istoria Românilor. Ed. Eudoxiu de Hurmuzaki. V (1885), VI (1878), VII (1876), & XV (1913).Bucureşti: Socec & Comp.

Documente străine despre români. Ed. Ionel Gal. Bucureşti: Direcţia generală a Arhivelor Statului din Republica Socialistă România, 1979.

Documents pour servir a l'Histoire des Domiciles de la Compagnie de Jésus dans le Monde entier de 1540 à 1773. Ed. Alfred Hamy, S.J. Paris: Alphonse Picard, 1892.

Quellen zur Geschichte der Stadt Brassó. Ed. O. Netoliczka. Brassó: IV (1903), A Gust; V (1909), Ciurcu & Comp.; VI (1915) & VII (1918), Br. Schneider & Feminger, 1915.

Siebenbürger Zeitung (Hermannstadt), 1784.

United States Department of State, *Records Relating to the Internal Affairs of Romania, 1910-1944*. Washington, D.C.: National Archives Microfilm Publications, 1981. Decimal File 871: Rolls 1-44.

Secondary Sources

Adamescu, Gh. *Istoria Literaturii Române*. Bucureşti: Editura Librăriei Leon Alcaly, n.d.

Albu, Nicolae. *Istoria învăţământului românesc din Transilvania până la 1800*. Blaj: Tipografia "Lumina," Miron Roşu, 1944.

Anuarul Liceului de băieţi român unit "Sf. Vasile cel Mare," – Blaj pe anul şcolar 1939/40. Blaj: Tipografia Seminarului, 1940.

Anuichi, Silviu. "Relaţii bisericesti româno-sîrbe din secolul al XVII-lea şi al XVIII-lea," teză de doctorat. *Biserica Ortodoxă Română*, XCVII (1979), nr. 7-8: 869-1054.

Ardeleanu, I. "Documente istorice din Vaticanu, relative le istori'a nóstra, comunicate de profesorulu Ioanu Ardeleanu..., despre românii carii au studiatu in colegiulu de propaganda fide." *Transilvani'a* X (1877), nr. 11: 123-25.

Ardeleanu, Joanu. *Istori'a diecesei romane greco-catolice a Oradei Mari*, I. Gherl'a: Imprimari'a "Auror'a" p. A. Todoranu, 1883; II Blasiu: Tipografi'a Seminariului gr. cat., 1888.

____. "Petru Paulu Aronu de Bistr'a." *Foi'a besericésca şi scolastica* II (1889), nr. 19: 295-6, nr. 22: 343-5, nr. 23: 359-61.

Armbruster, Adolf. *La romanité des Roumanins, Histoire d'une idée*. Bibliotheca Historica Romaniae, Monographies XVII. Bucureşti: Editura Academiei Republicii Socialiste România, 1977.

Balan, Ioannes, ed. *Disciplina Bizantina (Rumeni): Testi di diritto particolare dei Rumeni*. Condificazione Canonica Orientale, Fonti. Vol. 10. Rome: Tipografia Poliglatta Vaticana, 1933.

Bălan, Ioan. "Un sinod diecezan necunoscut, de sub Rednik." *Cultura Creştină* XVI (1936), nr. 5: 283-96.

Bărbat, B., S.I. "L'institution de l'office du 'théologien' dans l'Eglise Roumaine Unie." *Orientalia Christiana Periodica* XXIX (1963), 1: 155-200.

Barbu, Violeta. "Biserica română unită cu Roma în căutarea identităţii: problema ritului şi activitatea misionarilor iezuiţi." *Revista Istorică* III (1992), nr. 5-6: 529-45.

Bariţiu, Georgiu. *Catechismulu calvinescu impusu clerului şi poporului romanescu sub domni'a principiloru Georgiu Rákoczy I şi II*. Sibiu: W. Krafft, 1879.

Bariţiu, Georgiu. "Din cronic'a lui Michailu Cserei. 1661-1711 (Continuare)." *Transilvani'a* II (1869), 15: 169-72.

____. "Din cronic'a lui Michailu Cserei. 1661-1711 (Continuare), (Despre Unire)." *Transilvani'a* II (1869), 16: 181-4.

____. *Istori'a regimentului alu II. romanescu.* Brasiovu: Römer & Kamner, 1874.

____. "Materialu pentru istoria regimentului I. granitiariu din Transilvani'a." *Transilvani'a* XV (1884), 23-24:177-82; XVI (1885), 1-2: 1-5, 3-4: 17-22, 5-6: 33-8, 7-8: 49-54, 9-10: 65-8.

____. *Părţi alese din istoria Transilvaniei pre două sute de ani din urmă*, I. Sibiu: W. Krafft, 1889.

Bârlea, Octavian. *Ostkirchliche Tradition und westlicher Katholizismus, Die Rumänische Unierte Kirche zwischen 1713-1727.* Monachii: Societatea Academica Româna, 1966.

Bartenstein, Johann Christof. *Kurzer Bericht von der Beschaffenheit der zerstreuten zahlreichen Illyrischen Nation in kaiserl. koenigl. Erblanden.* Frankfurt und Leipzig: 1802.

Basilovits, Joannicius. *Brevis notitia fundationis Theodori Koriathovits*, I. Cassoviae: Typographia Ellingeriana, 1799; II. Cassoviae: Typis Joannis Josephi Ellinger, 1805.

Batthyáni, Ignatius Comes de. *Leges Ecclesiasticae Regni Hungariae, et Provinciarum Adiocentium*, I. Albae-Carolinae: Typis Episcopalibus, 1785.

Benkö, Josephus. *Transilvania*, I (2nd ed., 1834) & II (1833). Claudiopoli: Typis Lycei Regii.

Bernath, Mathias. *Habsburg und die Anfänge der Rumänischen Nationalsbildung.* Leiden: E. J. Brill, 1972.

Beza, Marcu. *The Rumanian Church.* London: Society for Promoting Christian Knowledge, 1943.

Bianu, I. "Vito Piluzio, Documente inedite din Archivulu Propagandei." *Columna lui Traianu* IV (1883): 142-64, 257-87.

Bianu, Ioan and G. Nicolaiasa. *Catalogul Manuscriptelor Româneşti.* Biblioteca Academiei Române, III. Craiova: "Scrisul Românesc" S.A., 1931.

Bibliografia Dell'Archivo Vaticano, I (1962) & II (1963). Città del Vaticano: Presso L'Archivio Vaticano.

Bielz, E. A. *Handbuch der Landeskunde Siebenbürgens.* Hermannstadt: S. Filtsch, 1857.

Bitay, A. "Un amănunt recunoscut din viaţa lui Atanasie Anghel (1703)." *Revista Istorică* XXI (1935), 1-3:21-23.

Blaga, Lucian. *Gîndirea românească în Transilvania în secolul al XVIII-lea.* Ed. George Ivaşcu. Bucureşti: Editura Ştiinţifică, 1966.

Bod, Petrus. *Historia Hungarorum Ecclesiastica*, I (1888) & II (1890). Lugduni-Batavorum: E. J. Brill.

Bogdan-Duică, George. *Călugĕrul Visarion Sarai.* Caransebeş: Tipariul Tipografiei Diecesane, 1896.

Bogdan-Duică, George. "Statistica Romînilor din Transilvania în 1733." *Convorbiri literare* XXX, Vol. II (1896), nr. 12: 626-42.

____. *Procesul Episcopului Ioan Inochentie Clain*. Caransebeş: Tipografia Diecesană, 1896.

____. "Grigorie Maior." *Revista Orăştiei* II (1896, nr. 15: 67-8.

Böhm, Constantin E. von. *Die Handschriften des Kaiserlichen und Königlichen Haus-, Hof- und Staats-Archivs*. Wien: Wilhelm Braumüller, 1873.

Bria, Pr. Prof. Ion. "Uniatismul în România: anacronic şi antiecumenic." *Biserica Ortodoxă Română* CIX (1991), nr. 1-3: 29-32.

Brunner, Otto. "Oesterreich und die Walachei während des Türkenkrieges von 1683-1699." *Mitteilungen des Österreichischen Instituts für Geschichtsforschung* 44 (1930): 265-323.

Bunea, Augustin. *Cestiuni din dreptulu şi istoria bisericei românesci unite*, II. Blaşiŭ: Tipografia Seminariului gr.-cat., 1893.

____. *Episcopii Petru Paul Aron şi Dionisiŭ Novacovici, saŭ istoria Românilor transilvănei de la 1751 pănă la 1764*. Blaş: Tipografia Seminariului Archidiecesan, 1902.

____. *Episcopul Ioan Incoenţiu Klein (1728-1751)*. Blaş: Tipografia Seminariului archidiecesan gr.-cat., 1900.

____. "Istoria autonomiei bisericesci." *Discursuri Autonomia bisericéscă, Diverse*. Blaş: Tipografia Seminariului Archidiecesan, 1903.

____. "Istorie scurtă a Bisericei române unite cu Roma." *Şematismul veneratului cler al archidiecesei metropolitane greco-catolice române de Alba-Iulia şi Făgăraş*. Blaş: Tipografia Seminariului Archidiecesan, 1900.

____. "Statistica românilor din Transilvania în anul 1750." *Transilvani'a* XXXII (1901), nr. 9: 237-92.

____. *Vechile episcopii românesci a Vadului, Geoagiului, Silvasului şi Bĕlgradului*. Blaş: Tipografia Seminariului Archidiecesan, 1902.

Buzan, Sever. "Latinitate şi catolicism la români." *Revista Teologică, Revista Oficială a Mitropoliei Ardealului*, Serie Nouă, II (1992), Nr. 1: 33-40.

Căciulă, Olimp. "Cultele în România." *Enciclopedia României*, I. Bucureşti: Imprimeria Naţională, 1936.

Călinescu, G. *Istoria Literaturii Române*. Bucureşti: Fundaţia Regală pentru Literatură şi Artă, 1941.

Catalogus librorum manuscriptorum bibliothecae universitatis r. scientiarum Budapestieensis, I (1889) & II (1894). Budapestini: Typis Typographiae Universitatis Reg. Scientarum.

Chindriş, Ioan. "Petru Maior şi epoca sa." *Anuarul Institutul de Istorie şi Arheologie Cluj-Napoca* XXVII (1985-1986):19-30.

Cicanci, Olga. *Companiile greceşti din Transilvania şi comerţul european în anii 1636-1746*. Bucureşti: Editura Academiei Republicii Socialiste România, 1981.

Ciobanu, Virgil. "Statistica Românilor ardeleni din anii 1760-1762." *Anuarul Institutului de Istorie Naţională* III (1924-5): 616-700.

Cipariu, Tim, ed. *Acte şi fragmente latine romanesci pentru istori'a beserecei romane mai alesu unite*. Blasiu: Cu tipariulu Semin. diecesanu, MDCCCLV.

Comşa, Nicolae. *Episcopul Ion Inochentie Micu*. Blaj: Tipografia Seminarului, 1943.

____. *Manuscrisele Românesti din Biblioteca Centrală dela Blaj*. Blaj: Tipografia "Lumina," Miron Roşu, 1944.

Condica Sântă, I. Bucureşti: Tipo-Litografia Cărţilor Bisericesci, 1886.

Crisian, Johannes. *Beitrag zur Geschichte der kirchlichen Union des Rumänen in Siebenbürgen unter Leopold I*. Hermannstadt: Archideöcesan-Druckerei, 1882.

Daicoviciu, Constantin and Miron Constantinescu, eds. *Brève histoire de la Transylvanie*. Bucharest: Éditions de L'Académie de la République Socialiste de Roumanie, 1965.

Dampier, Margaret G. *History of the Orthodox Church in Austria-Hungary*. London: Rivingtons, 1905.

Dan, Mihail. "In jurul unirii cu Roma, cu deoasebita privire asupra rolului iezuitului Carol Neurautter." *Mitropolia Banatului* VIII (1958), nrs.7-8-9: 296-328.

Daróczi, Georgius, S.J. *Ortus et progressus collegii academici Societatis Jesu Claudiopolitani, ab anno M.D.LXXIX*. Claduiopoli: Typis Acad. Soc. Jesu, M.D.CC.XXXVI.

Densuşianu, Nic. *Cercetari istorice în archivele şi bibliotecele Ungariei şi ale Transilvaniei*. Bucureşti: Tipografia Academiei Române, 1880.

____. *Independenta bisericéscă a mitropoliei române de Alba-Julia*. Braşovŭ: Tipografia Mureşianu, 1893.

Densusianu, Ovid. *Literatura Romîna Modernă*, I, 3rd ed. Bucureşti: Edit. Libr. "Universala" Alcalay & Co., 1929.

Din Istoria Transilvaniei, I. Bucureşti: Editura Academiei Republicii Populare Romîne, 1961.

Doboşi, Al. "Cum descrie stările politice şi economice din Transilvania un nobil ungur la 1744." *Anuarul Institutului de Istorie Naţionala* VII (1936-1938): 674-85.

Dobrescu, Nicolae. *Fragmente privitoare la istoria bisericii române*. Budapesta: Institutul Tipografic "Luceafărul," 1905.

Dragomir, Silviu. "Alegerea şi numirea episcopului unit Ioan Patachi." *Revista Teologică* IX (1915), nr.16-18: 261-76.

____. "Contribuţii privitoare la relaţile Bisericii româneşti cu Rusia în veacul XVII." *Memoriile Secţiunii Istorice*, Seria II, XXXIV (1912): 1065-1247.

____. *Istoria Desrobirei Religioase a Românilor din Ardeal în secolul XVII*, I (1920) & II (1930). Sibiu: Editura şi tiparul Tipografiei arhidiecezane.

____. *Rominii din Transilvania şi Unirea cu Biserica Romei. Documente apocrife privitoare la începuturile unirii cu catoliciusmul roman (1697-1701)*. Bucureşti: Editura Institutului Biblic şi de Misiune Ortodoxă, 1963.

____. "Romînii din Transilvania şi Unirea cu Biserica Romei." *Studii şi Materiale de Istorie Medie* III (1959): 323-39.

Drăgulin, Pr. Prof. Gheorghe I. "Uniaţia ardeleană şi o necesara reintepretare a istoriei ei." *Biserica Ortodoxă Română* CIX (1991), nr. 1-3: 32-9.

Duhr, Bernhard, S.J. *Geschichte der Jesuiten in den Ländern deutscher Zunge*, I (1907), II (1913), III (1921), IV (1928). Freiburg im Breisgau: Herdersche Verlagshandlung.

Durandin, Catherine. "Orthodoxie et Roumanite, Le debut de l'entre deux guerres." *Rumanian Studies*. Ed. Keith Hitchins. Leiden: E. J. Brill, 1986: 104-24.

Duţu, Alexandru. *European Intellectual Movements and Modernization of Romanian Culture*. Bucureşti: Editura Academiei Republicii Socialiste România, 1981.

Eliade, Pompiliu. *De L'Influence Francaise sur L'Esprit Public en Roumanie*. Paris: Ernest Leroux, 1898.

Enăcénu, Ghenadie. "Unaţia séŭ legea a treia." *Biserica Orthodoxă Română* VII (1883), nr. 8: 496-515.

Engel, Johann Christian von. *Geschichte des Urgarischen Reichs*, I-III (1813) & IV-V (1814). Wien: Comesinaschen Buchhandlung.

Fabritius, Karl. "Namen und Verwendung der Jesuiten, welche von 1720-173 in den siebenbürgische Ordensbäuern wirkten." *Archive des Vereines für siebenbürgische Landeskunde* 11 (1873): 167-252.

Fasching, Franciscus, S.J. *Nova Dacia*, I-III (1743), IV-V (1744). Caludiopoli: Typ. Acad. S.J.

Fejér, Georgius. *Historia Academiae Scientiarum Pazmaniae Archi-Episcopalis ac M. Theresianae Regiae Literaria*. Budae: Typis Regiae Scientiarum Universitatis Hungariae, 1835.

Fessler, Iosif. "Relatio historia de Daco-Romanis in Transilvania et Hungaria cum Ecclesia Romana unitis vel uniendis." *Analele Academiei Române. Memoriile Secţiunii Istorice*. Seria III. Vol. XXIV (1942): 627-59.

Fiedler, Joseph. "Beitrage zur Geschichte der Union der Ruthenen in Nordungern und der Immunität des Klerus derselben." *Sitzungsberichte der Kaiserlichen Akademie der Wissenschaften, Philosophisch-Historische Classe* XXXIX (1862), Heft 3-4: 481-524.

____. "Die Union der Walachen in Siebenbürgen unter K. Leopold I." *Sitzungsberichte der Kaiserlichen Akademie der Wissenschaften, Philosophisch-Historische Classe*, XXVII (1858), Heft 3: 350-82.

Florescu, Radu R. "The Uniate Church: Catalyst of Rumanian National Consciousness." *The Slavonic and East European Review* XLV (1967), nr. 105: 324-42.

Furtuna, A. *Preoţimea românească în secolul al XVIII-lea. Starea ei culturală şi material*. Vălenii-de-Munte: "Neamul Romănesc," 1915.

Gáldi, Ladislaus. "Simeon Magyar, ein rumänischer Pionier der josephinischen Schulreform." *Archivum Europae Centro-Orientalis* VII (1941), Fasc. 4: 489-526.

Gáldi, Ladislaus and Ladislaus Makkai. *Geschichte der Rumänen*. Budapest: Sárkány- Buchdruckerei A.G., 1942.

Găzdaru, D. "Contribuţie la relatiile lui Grigore Maior, Gheorghe Şincai şi Petru Maior cu Roma." *Revista Critică* VII (1933), nr. 1: 1-20.

Georgescu, Ioan. *Istoria bisericei creştine universale, cu deosebită privire la istoria bisericei româneşti unite cu Roma.* Blaj: Editura Tipografia Seminarului teologic, 1921.

Ghibu, Onisifor. *Catolicismul unguresc in Transilvania şi politică religioasa a statului român.* Cluj: Institut de Arte Grafice "Ardealul," 1924.

____. *Chemare la judecata istoriei*, I. Bucureşti: Editura Albatros, 1992.

____. *Universitatea Daciei Superiorare.* Bucureşti: "Cultura Naţională, 1924.

Ghişe, Dumitru and Pompiliu Teodor. "Petru Maior: Aufklärung and Nation." *Enlightenment and Romanian Society.* Ed. Pompiliu Teodor. Cluj-Napoca: Editura Dacia, 1980, pp. 260-77.

Giurescu, Constantin C. *Istoria Românilor*, III (Part I, 1942) & (Part II, 1946). Bucureşti: Fundaţia Regală pentru Literatură şi Artă.

Göllner, Carol. *Regimentele grănicereşti din Transilvania, 1764-1851.* Bucureşti: Editura Militară, 1973.

Grama, Alesandru. *Cestiuni din dreptulu şi istoria bisericei românesci unite*, I. Blaşiŭ: Tipografia Seminariului gr.-cat., 1893.

____. *Institutiunile calvinesci în biserica românéscă din Ardélu.* Blaşiu: Tipografia Seminariului archidiecesanu, 1895.

Gram'a, Alesandru V. *Istori'a Basericei Romanesci unite cu Rom'a.* Blasiu: Tipariulu Seminariului Archidiecesanŭ, 1884.

Grellmann, H. M. G. *Statistische Aufklärungen über wichtige Theile und Gegenstände der österreichischen Monarchie*, I. Göttingen: Vandenhock und Ruprecht, 1795.

Guglia, Eugen. *Das Theresianum in Wien, Vergangenheit und Gegenwart.* Wien: Verlag von Anton Schroll, 1912.

Gulian, C. I., ed. *Istoria gîndirii sociale şi filozofice în Romînia.* Bucureşti: Editura Academiei Republicii Populare Romîne, 1964.

Haneş, Petre. *Istoria LIteraturii Românesti*, 3rd ed. Bucureşti: Editura Autorului, n.d.

Hantsch, Hugo. *Die Geschichte Österreichs*, II. Graz-Wien-Köln: Verlag Styria, 1962.

Haragus, Stefan. *Preotimea romana in veacul al XVIII-lea.* Sibiu: Tiparul tipografiei arhidiecezane, 1907.

Heimbucher, Max. *Die Orden und Kongregationen der katholischen Kirche*, II. Paderborn: Verlag Ferdinand Schönigh, 1934.

Herbert, Heinrich. "Die Gegenreformation in Hermannstadt zur Zeit Karls VI." *Archiv des Vereines für siebenbürgische Landeskunde* 29 (1899): 25-113.

Hergenröther, Joseph Cardinal. *Handbuch der allgemeinen Kirchengeschichte*, III, 3rd ed. Freiburg im Breisgau: Herdei'sche Verlagshandlung, 1886.

Herrmann, George Michael Gottlieb v. *Das Alte und Neue Kronstadt*, I (1883) & II (1887). Hermannstadt: Franz Michaelis.

Hintz, Johann. *Geschichte der griechisch=nichtunirten Glaubensgenossen in Siebenbürgen*. Hermannstadt: Vereins für siebenbürgische Landeskunde, 1850.

Hitchins, Keith. "An East European Elite in the Eighteenth Century: The Romanian Uniate Hierarchy." *The Rich, the Well Born, and the Powerful*. Ed. Frederic C. Jaher. Urbana: University of Illinois Press, 1973.

____. *Orthodoxy and Nationality, Andreiu Saguna and the Rumanians of Transylvania, 1846-1873*. Cambridge: Harvard University Press, 1977.

____. "Religious tradition and National Consciousness among the Romanians of Transylvania, 1730-1780." *Concepts of Nationhood in Early Modern Eastern Europe*. Ed. I. Banac and F. E. Sysyn. Harvard Ukrainian Studies, X. Cambridge: Ukrainian Research Institute, Harvard University, 1987.

____. *The Idea of Nation. The Romanians of Transylvania, 1691-1848*. Bucharest: Editura Ştiinţifică şi Enciclopedică, 1985.

____. *The Rumanian National Movement in Transylvania, 1780-1849*. Cambridge: Harvard University Press, 1969.

____. "Samuel Clain and the Romanian Enlightenment in Transylvania." *Enlightenment and Romanian Society*. Ed. Pompiliu Teodor. Cluj-Napoca: Editura Dacia, 1980, pp. 230-44.

____. *Studies on Romanian National Consciousness*. Pelham N.Y.: Nagard Publisher, 1983.

____. "The Sacred Cult of Nationality: Rumanian Intellectuals and the Church in Transylvania, 1834-69." *Intellectual and Social Developments in the Habsburg Empire from Maria Theresa to World War I*. Ed. Stanley B. Winters and Joseph Held. New York: East European Monographs, Columbia University Press, 1975.

Hitchins, Keith and Ioan Beju. "Conscripţia comitatenză a clerului român din Alba de Joş, anul 1733." *Mitropolia Ardealului* XXXII (1987), Nr. 4: 75-90.

____. "Conscripţia scaunală a clerului român de pe pămîntul craiesc. Anul 1733." *Mitropolia Ardealului*, XXXIV (Mai-Iunie 1989), Nr. 3: 99-116.

Höchsmann, Johann. "Studien zur Geschichte Siebenbürgens aus der ersten Hälfte des 18. Jahrhunderts." *Archiv des Vereines für siebenbürgische Landeskunde* 11 (1873): 253- 310.

____. "Studien zur Geschichte Siebenbürgens aus dem 18. Jahrhundert II." *Archiv des Vereines für siebenbürgische Landeskunde* 16 (1880), Heft I:28-157

Hodinka, Antal. *A munkácsi gör. szert. püspökség okmányhtára*, I (1458-1715). Ungvár: Nyomatott oz "Unio Könymyomda R. T." Könyvnyomdájaban, 1911.

Horányi, Alexius. *Nova Memoria Hungarorum et Provincialium*. Pestini: Kilian, 1795.

Hurmuzaki, Eudoxius Freiherrn von. *Fragmente zur Geschichte der Rumänen*, II. Bucureşti: Socecŭ, Sander & Teclu, 1881.

Illia, Andreas, S.J. *Ortus et progressus variarum in Dacia gentium ac religionum cum principibus ejusdem*. Claudiopoli: Typis Academicis Societatis Jesu, 1764.

Iorga, N. "Două scrisori ale lui Atanase Anghel." *Memoriile Secțiunii Istorice*. Seria III. XIII (1932): 131-38.

____. "Francisc Rákóczy al II-lea, invietorul conştiinţi naţionale Ungureşti şi Românii." *Analele Academiei Române*. Memoriile Secțiunii Istorice, Seria II. XXXIII (1910-11): 1-33.

____. *Histoire de l'enseignement en pays roumains*. Bucharest: Casa Şcoalelor, 1933.

____. *Histoire des Roumains de Transylvanie et de Hongrie*, I (1915) & II (1916). Bucharest: Joseph Göbl.

____. *Histoire des Roumains et de la romanité orientale*. VII. Bucureşti: Imprimeria Naţională, 1940.

____. *Istoria bisericii româneşti şi a vieţii religioase a Românilor*, I (1928) & II (1930). Bucureşti: Editura Ministeriului de Culte.

____. *Istoria Literaturii Romănești*, II, 2nd ed. Bucureşti: Editura librăriei Pavel Suru, 1926.

____. *Istoria Literaturii Romănești*, III, 2nd ed. Bucureşti: Editura Fundaţiei "Regele Ferdinand," 1933.

____. *Istoria Românilor,* VI. Bucureşti "Datina Românească, 1938.

____. *My American Lectures*. Bucharest: State Printing Office, 1932.

____. *Sate şi Preoţi din Ardeal*. Bucureşti: Inst. de Arte Grafice "Carol Gobl," 1902.

____. *Studii şi documente cu privire la istoria Romînilor*, IV (1902), X (1905), & XII-XIII (1906). Bucureşti: I. V. Socecu.

Istoria Bisericii Romîne, I (1957) & (1958). Bucureşti: Editura Institutului Biblic şi de Misiune Ortodoxa.

Istoria Literaturii Romîne, I. Bucureşti: Editura Academiei Republicii Populare Romîne, 1964.

Istoria Literaturii Române, II. Bucureşti: Editura Academiei Republicii Socialiste România, 1968.

Istoria Romîniei, III. Bucureşti: Editura Academiei Republicii Populare Romîne, 1964.

Ivánka, Endre. "The Rumanian Greek-Catholic Church." *The Eastern Churches Quarterly* VIII (1949), nr. 3: 154-162.

Janin, Raymond. *Les Eglises orientales et les Rites orientaux*. Paris: Maison de la Bonne Presse, 1926.

"Joanu Inocentiu L. B. Clain de Szád, I." *Foi'a besericésca şi scolastica* I (1888), nr. 11: 181-4.

Kann, Robert A. *A History of the Habsburg Empire, 1526-1918*. Berkeley: University of California Press, 1974.

Kanner, Bénédict. *La Société Littéraire Junimea de Jassy et son Influence sur le Mouvement Intelleectuel en Roumanie*. Paris: Bonvalot-Jouve, 1906.

Katona, Stephano. *Historia Critica Regum Hungariae, Stirpis Austriacae*, vols. 16-22 (1802-1819). Budae: Typis et Sumptis Regiae Universitatis Pestanae.

Kazy, Franciscus. *Historia Universitatis Tyrnaviensis Societatis Jesu*. Tyrnavia: Typis Academicis, 1737.

Kelemen, Lajos. *Újabb adattár a vargyasi Daniel család történetéhez*. Kolozsvár: Nyomatott Ajtai K. Albert Könyvyomdájában, 1913.

King, Archdale A. *The Rites of Eastern Christendom*, I (1947) & II (1948). Rome: Tipografia Poliglotta Vaticana.

Király, Béla K. *Hungary in the Late Eighteenth Century*. New York: Columbia University Press, 1969.

Klein, Sammuelis. "Historia Daco-Romanorum sive Valachorum," *Instructiunea Publică*. Ed. A. Treb. Laurianu. Bucureşti: 1861.

Klima, Helmut. "Die Union der Siebenbürger Rumänen und der Wiener Staatsrat im theresianischen Zeitalter." *Südost-Forschungen* VI (1941), Heft 1/2: 249-56.

Klopp, Onno. *Corrispondenza Epistolare tra Leopoldo I. Imperatore ed il P. Marco D'Aviano Capuccino*. Graz: Libreria 'Styria', 1888.

Korolevskij, Cirillo. "L'Uniatisme." *Irénikon* II, nrs. 5-6. Amay sur Meuse: J. Duculot, 1927.

Krones, Franz von. *Ungarn unter Maria Theresia und Joseph II, 1740-1790., Geschichtliche Studien im Bereiche des innern Staatslebens*. Graz: Leuschner & Lubensky,
1871.

____. "Zur Geschichte der Jesuitenordens in Ungarn seit dem Linzer Frieden bis zum Ergebnisse der ungarischen Magnatenverschwörung 1645-1671." *Archiv für österreiichische Geschichte*. 79 (1893): 277-354.

____. "Zur Geschichte Ungarns (1671-1683). Mit besonderer Rücksicht auf die Thätigkeit und die Geschicke [sic] des Jesuitenordens." *Archiv für österreichische Geschichte* 80 (1894): 351-457.

____. "Zur Geschichte Ungarns im Zeitalter Franz Rákókczi's II. Historische Studie nach gedruckten und ungedruckten Quellen," Erste Abteilung. *Archiv für österreichische Geschichte* 42 (1870): 251-361.

____. "Zur Geschichte Ungarns im Zeitalter Franz Rákóczi's II," Zweite Abteilung. *Archiv für österreichische Geschichte*, 43 (1870): 1-102.

Kyriakos, A. Diomedes. *Geschichte der Orientalischen Kirchen von 1453-1898*. Leipzig: A. Deichert, 1902.

Lacko, Michael. *Synodous episcoporum ritus byzantini catholicorum ex antinqua Hungaria Vindobonae a. 1773 celebrata*. Roma: Pontificium Institutum Orientalium Studiorum, 1975.

Lamalle, Edmond, S.J. "Les catalogues des provinces et des domicles de la Compagnie de Jésus. Note de bibliographie et de statistique." *Archivum Hisitoricum Societatis Iesus* XIII (1944), Fasc. I-II: 77-101.

Lăpĕdatu, Alex. *Doi cărturari braşoveni din sec. XVIII şi Câteva documente îpotriva Unirii*. Bucureşti: Tipografia Carţilor Bisericeşti, 1915.

Lăpědatu, Alex. *Istoriografia Română Ardeleană; in Legătură cu Desfăşurarea Vieţii Politice a Neamului Românesc de peste Carpaţi*. Discursuri de Recepţiune, Academia Română. Bucureşti: Cultura Naţională, 1923.

____. "Pater Ianoş." *Prinos lui D. A. Sturdza*. Bucureşti: Inst. de Arte Grafice "Carol Göbl," 1903, pp. 303-10.

Laurianu, A. Treb. *Magazinu Istoricu pentru Dacia*, III. Bucureşti: Tipariul Collegiului National, 1846.

Libloy, Friederich, Schuler von. *Kurzer Ueberblick der Literaturgeschichte Siebenbürgens, von der ältesten Zeit bis zu Ende des voringen Jahrhunderts*. Hermannstadt: Georg v. Closius, 1857.

____. *Materialen zur siebenbürgischen Rechtsgeschichte*, I (1862), II-IV (1861). Hermannstadt: Th. Steinhaussen.

____. *Siebenbürgische Rechsgeschichte*, I-III. Hermannstadt: Buchdruckerei der v. Closius'schen Erbin, 1868.

Lupaş, I. "Contribuţiuni documentare la istoria satelor transilvane." *Studii, conferenţe şi comunicări istorice* IV (1943): 173-317.

____. "Desbinarea bisericească a Românilor ardeleni, în lumina documentelor din I-a jumătate a veacului al XVIII-lea." *Studii, conferinţe şi comunicări istorice* I (1927): 231-67.

____. "Doi precursori ai lui Horia în audienţă la Curtea împărăească din Viena." *Studii Istorice* V (1945-6): 97-128.

____. *Istoria bisericească a Românilor ardeleni*. Sibiu: Editura şi tiparul tipografiei arhidiecezane, 1918.

____. "O încercare de reunire a bisericilor române din Transilvania la 1798." *Studii, conferinţe şi comunicări* I (1928): 389-405.

____. "Sfârşitul suzeranităţii otomane şi începutul regimului habsburgic în Transilvania." *Analele Academiei Române, Memoriile Secţiunii Istorice*, Seria III. XXV (1943): 805-34.

____. *Ursprung und Entwicklung der bedeutendsten konfessionellen Minderheiten in Rumänien*. Jena & Leipzig: Wilhelm Gronau, 1936.

Lupşa, Şt. "Biserica ardeleană în anii 1764-1774." *Anuarul Academia Teologică "Andreiana" Ortodoxă Română din Sibiu* XXIII (1946-1947), V: 22-52.

____. *Biserica ardeleană şi "unirea" în anii 1697-1701*. Bucureşti: Editura Institutului Biblic şi de Misiune al Bisericii Ortodoxe Române, 1948.

____. *Istoria Bisericească a Românilor Bihoreni*. Oradea: Monografia-Almanah a Bihorului, 1935.

____. "Ştirii şi documente despre Biserica ortodoxă română din Ardeal după 1761, culese din arhiva Consiliului de stat şi a cabinetului imperial din Viena." *Omagiu Înalt Prea Sfinţiei Sale Dr. Nicolae Bălan Mitropolitul Ardealului*. Sibiu: Tiparul Tipografiei Arhidiecezane, 1940, pp. 524-29.

Mailáth, Johann Grafen. *Geschichte der Magyaren*, I-V (1825-1831). Wien: F. Tendler.

Mailáth, Johann Grafen. *Geschichte des österreichischen Kaiserstaates*, I-V (1834-1850). Hamburg: Friedrich Perthes.

____. *Neuere Geschichte der Magyaren von Maria Theresia bis zum Ende der Revolution*, I-II. Regensburg: G. Joseph Manz, 1853.

Maior, Petru. *Istoria Besèricei Românilor*. Buda: n.p., 1813.

Maloney, George A. *A History of Orthodox Theology Since 1453*. Belmont: Nordland Publishing Co., 1976.

Manuila, Sabin and Mitu Georgescu. "Populaţia României," *Enciclopedia României*, I. Bucureşti: Imprimeria Naţionalâ, 1936, pp. 133-60.

Marczali, Henry. *Hungary in the Eighteenth Century*. Cambridge: Cambridge University Press, 1910.

Mârza, Iacob. "Interferente culturale între Transilvania şi Slovacia (mijocul secolului al XVIII-lea--primele decenii ale secolului al XIX-lea)." *Revista de Istorie*, Tom. 38 (1985), Nr. 3: 277-283.

____. *Şcoala şi naţiune*. Cluj-Napoca: Editura Dacia, 1987.

Mateiu, Ion. *Contribuţiuni la istoria dreptuluii bisericesc*, I. Bucureşti: Tipografia Cărţilor Bisericeşti, 1922.

____. *Preoţimea românească-ardeleană în veacul al XVII-lea*. Sibiu: Tiparul Tipografiei Arhidiecezane, 1911.

____. *Vacanţele Mitropoliei ortodoxe din Ardeal în veacul XVII-lea*. Cluj: Tipografia Dr. S. Bornemisa, 1922.

Maurer, Joseph. *Cardinal Leopold Graf Kollonitsch, Primas von Ungarn*. Innsbruck: Fel. Rauch, 1887.

Melchisedec, Episcopulŭ. *Biserica ortodoxă în luptă cu protestantismulŭ in specialŭ cu calvinismulŭ in veaculŭ XVII-lea*. Analele Academiei Romane, Memoriile Sectiunei Istorice, Seria II, Tom. XII. Bucuresţi: Carol Göbl, 1890.

Meteş, Ştefan. *Istoria Bisericii şi vieţii religioase a Românilor din Transilvania şi Ungaria*, I, Ediţia II. Sibiu: Editura Librăriei Arhidiecezane, 1935.

____. "La vie menée par les Roumains en Transylvanie du XVI-e au XVIII-e siècle." *La Transylvanie*. Bucureşti: Imprimeria Naţională, 1938, pp. 261-336.

____. *Mănăstirile româneşti din Transilvania şi Ungaria*. Sibiu: Tiparul Tipografiei Archidiecezane, 1936.

____. *Păstori ardeleni în principatele române*. Arad: Tiparul Tipografiei Diecezane, 1925.

____. *Relaţiile bisericii româneşti ortodoxe din Ardeal cu Principatele Romane în veacul al XVIII-lea*. Sibiu: Tiparul Tipografiei Arhidiecezane, 1928.

____. *Şerban-Vodă Cantacuzino şi biserica Românească din Ardeal*. Vălenii-de-Munte: Tipografia "Neamul Românesc," 1915.

____. "Viaţa bisericească a Românilor din Ţara Otltului, Note istorice." *Transilvania*, Anul 60 (1929), nrs. 1:17-32, 2:113-128, 3:193-208, 4-5:289-304, 6:449-464, 7-8:545-60, 9:689-704, 12:990-1003.

Micu, Emil. *Contribuţiuni la istoricul regimentului grăniceresc întâi valah*. Bucureşti: Imprimeria Naţională, 1943.

Micu, Samuil. *Scurtă cunoştinţă a istorii romînilor*. Ed. Cornel Cîmpeanu. Bucureşti: Editura Ştiinţifică, 1963.

Minogue, K.R. *Nationalism*. New York: Basic Books, 1967.

Miron, Greta Monica. "Silviu Dragomir – istoric al 'unirii' religioase." *Revista Istorică* III (1992), nr. 5-6: 599-604.

Mladin, N. "Lupta pentru unitatea bisericească." *Omagiu Înalt Prea Sfinţiei Sale Dr. Nicolae Bălan, Mitropolitul Ardealului, 1905-1955*. Sibiu: Tiparul Tipografiei Reintregirea, 1956.

Moga, Ioan. "Contributiuni privitoare la tipărirea cărţilor bisericeşti în veacul XVIII pentru Românii din Transilvania şi Ungaria." *Omagiu Înalt Prea Sfinţiei Sale Dr. Nicolae Bălan Mitropolitul Ardealului*. Sibiu: Tiparul Tipografiei Arhidiecezane, 1940.

Moldovanu, Joane M. *Acte sinodali ale baserecei romane de Alb'a Julia sî Fagarasiu*, I. Blasiu: S. Filtsch, 1869.

____. *Acte sinodali ale baserecei romane de Alb'a Julia şi Fagarasiu*, II. Blasiu: Tipografi'a Seminariale, 1872.

____. *Spicuire in istori'a baserecesca a Romaniloru*. Blasiu: W. Krafft, 1873.

Murăraşu, D. *Istoria Literaturii Române*, 2nd ed. Bucureşti: Editura "Cartea Roâanească," n.d.

Negulici, Dorina, "Familia Radu Tempea în cultură naţională." *Cimidava* II (1979-1980), Nr. 1: 363-373.

Nemec, Ludvik. "The Ruthenian Uniate Church in Its Historical Perspective." *Church History* 37 (1968), nr. 4: 365-88.

Netea, Vasile. *Dela Petru Maior la Octavian Goga*. Bucureşti: Cugetarea – Georgescu Delafras S.A., 1944.

Nilles, Nicolao. "Die Rumänen unter der Herrschaft der protestantischen Fürsten Siebenbürgens." *Zeitschrift für katholische Theologie* II (1880), 189-92.

____. "Inedita zur Geschichte der lateinischen Theologen des griechisch-katholischen Bischofs von Siebenbürgen." *Zeitschrift für katholische Theologie* IV (1880), 778-88.

____. *Symbolae ad illustrandam historiam ecclesiae orientalis in terris coronae S. Stephani*, I & II. Oeniponte: Typis et Sumptibus Feliciani Rauch, 1885.

____. "Ueber das Wirken der Jesuiten unter den katholischen Rumänen." *Zeitschrift für katholische Theologie* III (1879: 803-08.

____. "Ueber die Wiedervereinignung der Rumänen in Siebenbürgen mit der katholischen Kirche." *Zeitschrift für katholische Theologie* IV (1880), 373-84.

____ "Weitere Inedita zur Geschichte der kirchlichen Wiedervereinigung der Rumänen," *Zeitschrift für katholische Theologie*, IV (1880, 575-87.

Nistor, I. "Emigrările de peste munţi." *Analele Academiei Române. Memorile Secţiunii Istorice*, Serie II, XXXVII (1914-15), 815-65.

Obál, Béla. *Die Religionspolitik in Ungarn nach dem Westfälischen Frieden während der Regierung Leopold I.* Halle a. S.: Wischan & Burkhardt, 1910.

Pacăţian, Teodor V. "Contribuţiuni la istoria Românilor ardeleni în sec. XVIII." *Anuarul Institutului de Istorie Naţională* III (1924-5), 161-79.

Pâclişan, Zenove, "Biserica românească şi Calvinismul dela moartea lui Gavrilă Bethlen până la Unirea cu Roma." *Cultura Creştină* II (1912), nr. 6/7: 167-78 & nr. 9: 259-66.

Pâclişanu, Zenovie. "Alegerea şi denumirea episcopului unit Ioan Patachi." *Cultura Creştină* VI (1916), nr. 2: 37-43 & nr. 3: 68-75.

____. "Contribuţii istorice privitoare la situaţia materială a preoţimii române din Ardeal şi Ungaria." *Cultura Creştină* VI (1916), nr. 5: 135-40 & nr. 6:164-71.

____. "Contribuţiuni la biografia episcopului I. Patachi." *Cultura Creştină* XVII (1937), nr. 2/3: 129-37.

____. "Corespondenţa din exil a episcopului I. Incoenţiu Micu Klein." *Cultura Creştină* VI (1917), nr. 13: 394-400.

____. *Corespondenţa din exil a episcopului Ionchentie Micu Klein, 1746-1768.* Bucureşti: Cultura Naţională, 1924.

____. "Din istoria bisericească a Maramurăşului." *Cultura Creştină* III (1913), nr. 8: 229-34, nr. 9: 261-67, nr. 10: 295-300, & nr. 11: 326-8.

____. "Din istoria bisericească a Românilor ardeleni. 'Teologul' vlădicilor uniţi." *Memoriile Sectiunii Istorice.* Academia Romana, Seria III, I (1923): 149-92.

____. "În jurul 'Diplomei a doua Leopoldine'." *Cultura Creştină* XVIII (1938), nr. 8/9: 464-72.

____. "Discuţii Mărunte," *Cultura Creştină*, XIX (1939), nr. 1/2:43-55.

____. "O statistică a Românilor ardeleni dela începtual veacului al XVIII-lea." *Societatea de Mâine* IV (1927), nr. 13/14: 183.

____. "Statistique des Roumains de Transylvanie au XVIII-e siècle." *Revue de Transylvanie* I (1934), 2: 203-13.

Păcurariu, Mircea. *Istoria Bisericii Ortodoxe Române*, vols. 2 & 3. Bucureşti: Editura Institutului Biblic şi Misiune al Bisericii Ortodoxe Române, 1981.

____. *Istoria Bisericii Ortodoxe Române, Manual pentru Seminariile Teologice.* Sibiu: Tipografia Eparhială, 1972.

Pădureanu, L. *Ce a fost unirea Roma în biserica românească din Ardeal.* Bucureşti: Tipografia Dacia Triană, 1948.

Pall, Francisc. *Ein siebenbürgischer Bischof im Romischen Exil: Inochentie Micu-Klein (1745-1768).* (Köln: Böhlau Verlag, 1991).

Papiu Ilarianu, A. *Istori'a Romaniloru din Daci'a Superiore*, I. Vienna: C. Gerold şi Fiiu, 1851.

Pascu, Ştefan. "Les régiments frontaliers de Transylvanie." *Memoriile secţiei de ştiinţe istorice*, Seria IV, IV (1979): 69-79.

Patacsi, Gabriel S.J. "Die unionsfeindlichen Bewegnungen der orthodoxen Romämen Siebenbürgens in den Jahren 1726-1729." *Orientalia Christiana Periodica* XXVI (1920), 2: 351-400.

Patek, Franz. "Die Jesuiten in Ungarn." *Ungarische Rundschau für historische und soziale Wissenschaften* IV (1915), Heft 1:143-48.

Perbal, A. "Projets, Fondation et Débuts de la Sacrée Congrégation de la Propandande." *Histoire Universelle des Missions Catholiques*, II. Ed. S. Delacroix. Paris: Librairie Grund, 1957, pp. 109-131.

Pieper, Anton, "Römische Archive." *Römische Quartelscrift für Christliche Altertumskunde und für Kirchen-geschichte* I (1887), 80-99.

Piru, Al. *Literatura Romînă Premodernă*. Bucureşti: Editura pentru Literatură, 1964.

Platon, Gh. "Transilvania şi conştiinţa naţională a românilor în secolul al XVIII-lea." *Memoriile Secţiei de Ştiinţe Istorice*, Seria IV, IX (1984): 61-69.

Pleşia, Dan Gr. "La noblesse roumaine de Transylvanie. Structure et évolution." *Revue Roumaine d'Histoire* XXVI (1987), No. 3: 187-215.

Polgár, Ladislaus. *Bibliografia de Historia Societatis Iesu in Regnis olim Corona Hungarica Unitis (1560-1773)*. Roma: Institutum Historium S.J., 1957.

Polgár, László, S.J. *Bibliography of the History of the Society of Jesus*. Rome: Jesuit Historical Institute, 1967.

Pop, Alexandru. *Desbindarea în Biserica Românilor din Ardél şi Ungaria, 1697-1701*. Bucureşti: Wiegand, C. Savocu & C-nie, 1892.

Pop, Ştefan. "Din istoria bisericească a Bihorului. Ultimii arhidaconi-vicari ai episcopului latin." *Cultura Creştină* III (1913), nr. 12: 363-69.

____. "In jurul hirotonirii a doua alui Atanasie Anghel." *Cultura Creştină* III (1913), 15:458-67.

Pope'a, Nicolau. *Vechi'a metropolia ortodosa romana a Transilvaniei, suprimerea şi restaurarea ei*. Sabiniu: S. Filtsch, 1870.

Popescu, Prof. Teodor M. "Uniaţia în lumina adevărului istoric. Cauzele ei sociale şi politice." *Biserica Ortodoxă Romană* CIX (1991), nr. 1-3: 43-62.

Popovici, D. *La Littérature Roumaine à l'Epoque des Lumières*. Sibiu: Centrul de Studii şi Cercetări privitoare la Transilvania, 1945.

Popoviciu, George. *Uniunea românilor din Transilvania cu biserica romano-catolică sub împĕratul Leopold I*. Logoj: Tipariul Tipografiei Diec. din Caransebeş, 1901.

Predescu, Lucian. *Enciclopedia Cugetarea*. Bucureşti: Georgescu Delafras, 1940.

Prodan, D. "La lutte de Inochentie Micu pour le relèvement politique des Roumains de Transylvanie." *Revue Roumaine D'Hisitoire* IV (1965), nr. 3: 477-96.

____. *Problema iobăgiei în Transilvania 1700-1848*. Bucureşti: Editura Ştiinţifică şi Enciclopedică, 1989.

____. *Supplex Libellus Valachorum*. Cluj: Editura Universităţii "Victor Babeş," 1948.

Protase, Maria. "Le 'Procanon' de Petru Maior, Replique sud-est européenne des Attaques Antipapales du XVIIIe siècle." *Enlightenment and Romanian Society*. Ed. Pompiliu Teodor. Cluj-Napoca: Editura Dacia, 1980, pp. 245-59.

Puşcariu, Ilarion. *Documente pentru limbă şi istoriă*, I. Sibiu: Tiparul Tipografiei Archidiecesane, 1889.

Radu, Jacob. *Foştii elevi romani-uniţi ai şcoalelor din Roma*. Beiuş: Tiparul Tipografiei "Ateneul," 1929.

Radu, Jacob. *Istoria diecezei române-unite a Orăzii-Mari*. Oradea: Tipografia "Ateneul" Societate Anonimă, 1930.

____. *Istoria vicariatului greco-catholic al Haţegului*. Lugoj: Tipografia "Gutenberg," 1913.

____. "Manuscriptele din Biblioteca Episcopiei Unite din Oradea-Mare." *Memoriile Secţiunii Istorice*, Seria III, I (1923), 263-310.

Révész, Imre. "Esquisse de l'histoire de le politique religieuse hongroise entre 1705 et 1860." *Studia Historica*, nr. 26. Budapest: Academiae Scientiarum Hungaricae, 1960.

____. "La Réforme et les Roumains de Transylvanie." *Archivum Europae Centro-Orientalis* III (1937), Fasc. 4:279-316.

Rimely, Carolus. *Historia Collegii Pazmaniani*. Vienna: Typis et Sumptibus Congregationis Mechitharisticae, 1865.

Schaguna, Andreas Freiherrn von. *Geschichte der griechisch-orientalischen Kirche in Oesterreich*. Hermannstadt: Josef Drotleff, 1862.

Schmidt, Wilhelm. "Die Jesuiten in Karlsburg von Jahre 1713, bis zur endlichen Aufhebung des Ordens derselben im Jahre 1772." *Archiv des Vereines für siebenbürgische Landeskunde* VII (1866), 41-50.

Schwicker, J. H. *Geschichte der Österreichischen Militärgrenze*. Wien u. Teschen: Karl Prochasta, 1883.

____. *Politische Geschichte der Serben in Ungarn*. Budapest: Ludwig Aigner, 1880.

Şincai, Gheorghie. *Chronica Românilor*, III, 2nd ed. Bucureşti: Tipografia Academiei Române, 1886.

Sîrbu, Corneliu. "Disputa teologică Filioque în actualitate." *Orthodoxia, Revista Patriarhiei Române* XXVIII (1976), nr. 2: 424-26.

Şotropa, Valeriu. *Districtul grănicerescc năsăudean şi locul său în lupta pentru progress social şi libertate naţională românilor din Transilvania*. Cluj-Napoca: Editura Dacia, 1975.

Spácil, T., S.J. "Universitas Tyrnaviensis in Slovachia et catholici ritus orientalis." *Orientalia Christiana Periodica* III (1937), nr. 1/2: 275-78.

Spielman, John P. *Leopold I of Austria*. New Brunswick: Rutgers University Press, 1977.

Stăniloae, Dumitru. "Ortodoxia românească şi patria." *Ortodoxia, Revista Patriarhiei Române* XXXII (1980), Nr. 4: 579-81.

____. "Universalitate şi etnicitatea Bisericii în concepţia ortodoxă." *Ortodoxia, Revista Patriarhiei Române* XXIX (1977), Nr. 2:143-52.

Steinhuber, Cardinal Andreas, S.J. *Geschichte des Collegium Germanicum Hungaricum in Rom*, I & II. Freiburg im Breisgau: Herdei'sche Verlagshandlung, 1895.

Stoica, Emilian. "Informatii noua privitoare la 'protectorii Unirii' din Transilvania." *Revista Istorica* XIX (1933), nr. 4/6:155-58.

Streit, Rob., O.M.I. *Bibliotheca Missionum*. I: *Grundlegender und Allgemeiner Teil*. Münster i. W.: Verlag der Aschendorffschen Buchhandlung, 1916

Suciu, Coriolan. *Dicţionar Istoric al Localităţilor din Transilvania*, I (1967) & II (1968). Bucureşti: Editura Academiei Republicii Socialiste România.

Surdu, Bujor. "Liniile dezvoltării social-economice a Transilvaniei în secolul al XVIII-lea pînă la răscoala lui Horea." *Anuarul Institutului de Istorie din Cluj* III (1960), pp. 103-70.

Szász, Carolus. *Sylloge tractatum aliorumque actorum publicorum historiam et argumenta b. diplomatis Leopoldini*. Claudiopoli: Typis Collegii Ev. Reformatorum, 1833.

Szent-Ivani, Martinus. *Opusculorum Polemicorum*, I (1718) & II (1730), 2nd ed. Tyrnaviae: Academicae Tyrnaviensis Typographiae.

Szent-Ivany, Martinus, S.J. *De Ortu, Progressu, ac Diminutione Schismatis Graeci*. Tyrnavia: Typis Academicis, 1703.

Szentivany, Martinus, S.J. *Dissertatio Paralipomenonica rerum Memorabilium Hungariae*. Tyrnaviae: Typis Academ., 1699.

Szentiványi, Roberto. *Catalogus Concinnus Librorum Manuscriptorum Bibliothecae Batthyanyanae Albae in Transsilvania*. Szeged: Editio Auctoris, 1947.

Szilágyi, Sándor. *Monumenta Comitialia Regni Transylvaniae*. XXI. Budapest: A. M. Tud. Akadémia Könyvkiadó-Hivatala, 1898.

Szilas, Laszlo, S.J. "Quellen der ungarischen Kirchgeschichte aus ehemaligen Jesuitenarchiv." *Ungarn-Jahrbuch*, 1972: 172-89.

Tapié, Victor-L. *The Rise and Fall of the Habsburg Monarchy*. New York: Praeger Publishers, 1971.

Tăutu, Aloisie, et al. *Biserica Română Unita. Două sute cinci zeci de ani de istorie*. Madrid: Rivadeneyra, 1952.

Tempea, Radu. *Istoria sfintei besereci a Şcheilor Braşovului*. Ed. Octavian Şchiau and Livia Bot. Cluj: Editura pentru Literatură, 1969.

Teodor, Pompilu. *Interferenţe iluministe europene*. Cluj-Napoca: Editura Dacia, 1984.

____. "Romanian Political Enlightenment." *Enlightenment and Romanian Society*. Ed. Pompiliu Teodor. Cluj-Napoca: Editura Dacia, 1980, pp. 117-42.

Teutsch, Fr. *Die Kirchlichen Verhaltnisse Siebenbürgens*. Halle a.S.: Eugen Strien, 1906.

Togan, Nicolau. *Românii din Transilvania la 1733. Conscripţia Episcopului Ioan In. Klein de Sadu*. Sibiu: Tipariul Tipografiei Archidiecesane, 1898.

Tóth, Zoltán. *Az erdélyi román nacionalizmus elsö százada, 1697-1792*. Budapest: Athenaeum Rt., 1946.

Trausch, Josephus. *Chronicon Fuchsio-Lupino-Oltardinum*, II. Coronae: Johannes Gött, 1848.

Trede, Th. "Die Propaganda fide in Rom." *Deutsche Zeit=und Streit=Fragen*. XIII (1884), Heft 201 321-52.

Turczynski, Emanuel. *Konfession und Nation, Zur Frühgeschichte der serbischen und rumänischen Nationsbildung*. Düsseldorf: Pädagogischer Verlag Schwann, 1976.

Turczynski, Emanuel. "Nationalism and Religion in Eastern Europe." *East European Quarterly* V (1972), nr. 4: 468-486.

____. "The National Movement in the Greek Orthodox Church in the Habsburg Monarchy." *Austrian History Yearbook* III, Pt. 3 (1967): 83-128.

Ursu, I. "Un manifest românesc tiparit cu litere latine al Impăratului Leopold I din anul 1701." *Analele Academiei Române, Memoriile Secţiunii Istorice*, Seria II, XXIV (1911-12): 1049-63.

Vasiliu, Cezar. "Relaţiile dintre Biserica Romano-Catolică şi Biserica Ortodoxă de la anunţarea Conciliului Vatican II (ianuarie 1959) pînă in decembrie 1970." *Ortodoxia Revista Patriarhiei Române* XXVIII (1976), nr. 1:51-235.

Vasiliu, Virginia. "Constantino Brâncoveanu e il Cattolicismo, Alcune notizie nuove intorno alla sua politica religioasa." *Ephemeris Dacoromana* III (1925):110-28.

Vaughan Williams, Ralph. *National Music.* London Oxford University Press, 1934.

Vêntu, George C. *Unirea Românilor din Transilvania cu biserica romano-catolică.* Bucureşti: Tipografia "Cărţilor Bisericeşti," 1889.

Vering, Friedrich H. *Lehrbuch des katholischen, orientalischen und protestantischen Kirchenrechts.* XIX. Freiburg im Breisgau: Herder'sche Verlagshandlung, 1881.

Voicu, Constantin. *Biserica strămoşească din Transilvania în lupta pentru unitatea spirituală şi naţională a poporului român.* Sibiu: Tiparul Tipografiei Eparhiale, 1989.

Voileanu, Mateiu. *Să se facă lumină, Biserica românilor din Ardeal în veacul al XVIII-lea.* Sibiu: Tiparul Tipografiei Arhidiecezane, 1926.

Vornicescu, Nestor. "Pentru refacerea unităţii Bisericii străbune. Alba Julia, 27 februarie 1939." *Biserica Ortodoxă Română* CVII (1990), Nr. 7-10: 143-174.

Vries, Wilhelm de, S.J. *Der christliche Osten in Geschichte und Gegenwart.* Würzburg: Augustinus Verlag, 1951.

____. *Rom und die Patriarchate des Ostens.* Freiburg/München: Verlag Karl Alber, 1963.

Wagner, Walter. "Die Bestände des Archivio della Nunciatura Vienna bis 1792." *Römasche Hisitorische Mitteilungen*, Heft 2 (1957/8): 82-203.

Wessely, Kurt. "A doua Diplomă Leoplodină." *Memoriile Secţiunii Istorice*, Seria III, XX (1938): 271-88.

Zach, Krista. *Orthodoxe Kirche und rumänisches Volkbewusstsein im 15. bis 18. Jahrhundert.* Wiesbaden: Otto Harrassowitz, 1977.

Zernov, Nicolas. *Eastern Christendom, A Study of the Origin and Development of the Eastern Orthodox Church.* London: Weidenfeld & Nicolson, 1961.

Zieglauer, Ferdinand von. *Die politische Reformbewegung in Siebenbürgen in der Zeit Joseph's II und Leopold II.* Wien: Wilhelm Braumüller, 1881.

____. *Harteneck, Graf der sächsischen Nation, und die siebenbürgischen Parteikämpfe seiner Zeit, 1691-1703.* Hermannstadt: Th. Steinhaussen, 1869.

Zschokke, Hermann. *Die Theologischen Studien und Anstalten der Katholischen Kirche in Österreich.* Wien und Leipzig: Wilhelm Braumüller, 1894.